the
top
100
CANADIAN
albums

the
top
100
CANADIAN
albums

Bob
Mersereau

GOOSE LANE

Printed in Canada.
10 9 8 7 6 5 4 3 2 1

Library and Archives Canada Cataloguing in Publication

Mersereau, Bob, 1960-
    The top 100 Canadian albums / Bob Mersereau. — 2nd ed.
Includes index.
ISBN 978-0-86492-520-6

1. Popular music — Canada — Discography. 2. Popular music — Canada — History and criticism. I. Title. II. Title: Top one hundred Canadian albums.
ML3484.M574 2008   781.64'0971   C2008-904551-3

Written by Bob Mersereau
Produced by Susanne Alexander and Goose Lane Editions
Susanne Alexander: vocals, tambourine
Julie Scriver: art direction, pianos/synthesizers, vocals
Kent Fackenthall: cover and book design, drums
Kathleen Doucette: logistics, banjo, pedal steel
Viola Spencer: booking & financial management, guitar, harmonica
Colleen Kitts: tour management & publicity, guitar, background vocals
Angela Williams: artist relations & legal management, bass, background vocals
Luke Gallagher: shipping and receiving, percussion, cowbell, triangle
Edited and mixed by Barry Norris
Proofread and engineered by Lisa Alward
Album photography by Roger Smith
Road crew, merchandising and vinyl management: Lloyd Hanson, Eric Hill, Kirk Lahey, Stephen May, Bob Mersereau, Ed Mullaly, Barry Norris, and Marc Perry
Guitarist artwork on the cover by Michael Newell, who appears courtesy of iStockphoto.com

Goose Lane Editions would like to thank all the artists, labels, and management that provided artwork (and music) for this project. Rock on.

Goose Lane Editions acknowledges the financial support of the Canada Council for the Arts, the Government of Canada through the Book Publishing Industry Development Program (BPIDP), and the New Brunswick Department of Wellness, Culture, and Sport for its publishing activities.

Recorded and mixed during the summer of 2007. Remastered from the original recordings in 2008 at
    Goose Lane Editions
    Suite 330, 500 Beaverbrook Court
    Fredericton, New Brunswick
    CANADA E3B 5X4
    www.gooselane.com

Now I'm going back to Canada
On a journey thru the past
— Neil Young

I drew a map of Canada, Oh Canada
And your face sketched on it twice.
— Joni Mitchell

The girls are out to Bingo and the boys are gettin' stinko,
And we think no more of Inco on a Sudbury Saturday night.
— Stompin' Tom Connors

Introduction

Bob Mersereau
Fredericton, 2008

Welcome to the new edition of *The Top 100 Canadian Albums*. The hardcover edition, published in October 2007, met with great success in its first year. It became a national bestseller, garnered lots of press coverage, including full-page articles in almost every major Canadian newspaper, was featured on dozens of radio and television shows, and even wound up as the basis of a joke on *This Hour Has 22 Minutes*, surely a cultural touchstone. Debates raged on talk shows, in print, and on the Internet, with discussion groups voicing arguments about which albums were and weren't on the list. Negative or positive, the goal of the book was achieved: to engage Canadians in discussions about our popular music and to point out the quality of albums our artists have produced.

When the first edition was released, I embarked on a series of trips that took me across the country. This was the highlight for me — a chance to talk to music fans in person or on radio call-in shows about their favourite Canadian music. The enthusiasm they had for their beloved albums was thrilling. There were many great moments. One was heading out into unfamiliar Hamilton at 3 a.m. with Garth Hudson and his wife Maud in a successful search for a barbecue joint. The young kids in the restaurant didn't know what to make of this old fellow with the wild hair and the Los Lobos tour jacket. When the waiter asked me who he was, I told him to Google his name on his laptop. All of a sudden, the kids were clamouring to take cell-phone photos. That same weekend, I got to serve as Daniel Lanois's personal MC for three different shows, present the first double bill of local legends Teenage Head and Simply Saucer in thirty years, banter with Tom Wilson of Blackie and The Rodeo Kings, and present Garth Hudson with The Band's Lifetime Achievement Award. In Calgary at a book launch, in the middle of a question-and-answer session, I heard someone at the back of the bookstore yell, "Lies! It's all lies." I looked up to see the beaming face of Kelly Jay of Crowbar. All I could answer in return was, "Ladies and gentlemen, here's the man who wrote 'Oh What A Feeling'."

In Vancouver, I went to the beloved Commodore Ballroom to see Wintersleep, a group I'd just interviewed a week before in Fredericton at the East

Coast Music Awards. In Winnipeg, I played music trivia with some major fans, including the dean of Manitoba music history, author John Einarson. It's a good thing he was up to date on his MacLean & MacLean trivia. In Toronto, waiting to appear on *Canada AM*, I met British novelist Ian Rankin. As any fan knows, Rankin loves music and uses references frequently in his books. It turns out he has a special fondness for Canadian music, and fans mix CDs here and mail them to him. I was thrilled as he flipped through the book and knew all about Broken Social Scene, The Tragically Hip, The Weakerthans, and others I would have thought were under the radar in his country.

In Halifax, we launched the book with a party as part of the annual Halifax Pop Explosion, a festival I've attended several times. It was a thrill to have a band from *The Top 100*, Eric's Trip, perform a set from their *Love, Tara* album, which shows up at # 39 in the list. I've covered the group many times over the years, whether together or in their solo careers, and consider them all friends.

The best event of all involved no rock stars or media and happened in the smallest place I visited. I was asked to speak at the library in tiny Amherst, Nova Scotia, a place I know well. It was the last night of the book tour. I was flying into nearby Moncton that day already, so it was convenient. To my delight, I arrived to find the place decorated from the front door to the stage with ribbons and paper that matched the red-and-black colour scheme of the book, plus a wall full of vintage Canadian vinyl, much-loved and much-played pieces from someone's precious collection. There were hits from the book and obscure pressings that immediately caught my collector's eye. There was a bowl of punch, cake, and homemade squares. Everyone listened to every word and then started in with question after question: "Do you remember so-and-so? Whatever happened to them? Do you know that Feist was born around here?" There were young people and old people, and they all loved music. It was the perfect discussion of Canadian music.

What's changed for this edition is the addition of more interviews. Some artists were unavailable when I wrote the first edition, and I'm pleased to add more interviews now. The inclusion of their own reflections on the work they've created is, in my opinion, the best way to gain more appreciation for each album. We've also lost two of the artists who appear in the book. The great songwriter Willie P. Bennett passed on after the publication of the hardcover edition — it turns out the interview I did with him while he was recovering from an initial heart attack was one of the last he gave. The world also lost the man who was arguably the last of the classic jazz greats, Oscar Peterson. Oscar truly belongs in the list that includes Ella, Frank, Louis, Dizzy, Bird, and Miles. His passing marks the loss of the last connection to that golden era.

It's too early to do another complete poll and compile a new ranking of *The Top 100 Canadian Albums*. Perhaps a few more years should pass to let opinions change and the importance of certain albums settle in. Yet, since the initial voting took place, many of the artists here — among them Arcade Fire, Feist, Joni Mitchell, Joel Plaskett, Neil Young, Alanis Morissette, Rush, Bryan Adams, Blue Rodeo, Sloan, Daniel Lanois, k.d. lang, Ron Sexsmith, Hayden, The Weakerthans, The Constantines, Rufus Wainwright, The Sadies, and Sam Roberts — have released albums that rate among their best. Cowboy Junkies even re-recorded their *Trinity Session* disc, featured here. Improbably, Teenage Head and Eric's Trip reunited, to acclaim. Amazingly, Simply Saucer not only reformed but recorded their

Standing, left to right: Neil Young, Jeff Weaver (CBC Radio, Victoria), Frank Sampedro (Crazy Horse, guitar), Bob Mersereau (author), Ralph Molina (Crazy Horse, drums). Seated: Billy Talbot (Crazy Horse, bass). The author meets Neil Young & Crazy Horse backstage at Harbour Station, Saint John, NB, in 1996. Also in the photo is Jeff Weaver, the first juror to vote in the survey. Coincidentally, he voted for Young's *Harvest*, the eventual winner of the poll.

first true album and are now enjoying a level of fame and success they never approached in their initial 1970s incarnation. At the time of writing, Sarah McLachlan and Robbie Robertson have recorded songs for upcoming projects, and Leonard Cohen took the stage for his first tour in fifteen years with a magical opening night in my hometown of Fredericton.

So, while much has changed, the reasons for creating this book remain the same. It is, above all, a celebration. It's been compiled and written to honour one of the most exciting art forms of our time, the popular music album. Most Canadians read books, many enjoy films, and smaller numbers appreciate everything from fine art to dance to poetry, but virtually all of us listen to music, on disc, downloaded, live, or on radio. Yet, even though the majority of Canadian

popular music since the 1950s has been made into record, CD, and digital albums, I was shocked to discover that never before had there been a book devoted to ranking, and honouring, the best albums produced by the country's artists. You can certainly find out what are considered to be the best US or British albums of all time. There are books that look at albums from all over, and Canada is always well represented. But many great Canadian albums go unheralded beyond our borders, so I simply decided that it was high time to celebrate a major piece of Canadian culture.

In preparing the book, I asked many people what they thought of the idea of honouring our best albums this way. It was met with complete enthusiasm, especially from the musicians themselves.

Overwhelmingly, their first reaction was that it was about time. Next came the question, who should decide on the Top 100 albums? There are two obvious ways. One is to conduct a huge poll of anyone wishing to vote, perhaps on an Internet site or through ballots placed in music stores, much like baseball fans vote for the all-star teams. The problem with that is that it is open to repeat voting and tends to measure overall popularity rather than quality. Another method is to sequester the top critics, writers, and musicologists in the country. That would give you a very knowledgeable selection, but I felt it would leave out the important element of popularity. Critics and experts listen for different qualities in albums than the public. They want recordings that match their ideal of what makes a great one instead of what simply makes them feel really good. But there's a reason certain albums resonate with the public, even if critics dismiss them. This is the great divide between music experts and music fans. What I wanted to find was some sort of happy medium between critical choices and popular ones, between music nerds and people who just like to be entertained.

So, instead of using a small jury, I chose to compile a big one, with the idea that the more people were involved the more representative it would be of the entire country. You will already know many of the people in the jury. They are your local deejays and music reviewers. They are your favourite musicians, including Jim, Ed, and Tyler of Barenaked Ladies; Alan Doyle and Bob Hallett of Great Big Sea; Neil Peart of Rush; Ryan Peake of Nickelback; Sass Jordan; Jill Barber; Ron Sexsmith; Corb Lund; George Pettit and Wade MacNeil of Alexisonfire; Sarah Slean; and many more. There are music company employees, broadcasters, managers, agents, bookers, retailers, roadies, instrument makers, festival operators and volunteers, theatre and club managers, collectors, and Web site managers.

Each juror was asked to provide a list of their Top Ten Canadian albums. They were allowed to use whatever criteria they felt best: their own favourites or the music they felt was the most important. They could choose music from any style they wanted, in any language, from any area of the country. It could be a greatest hits collection, a live album — everything counted. To be considered Canadian, however, a solo artist must have been born in Canada or have moved to Canada before they made the album in question. Bands had to have a majority of Canadian members when the album was made. This means The Band, four of whose five members were born here, was eligible, but not Crosby, Stills, Nash & Young, with only one Canadian. As for those who had been born in Canada but moved away, a book about great Canadian albums without Neil Young and Joni Mitchell would be unthinkable.

To ensure every style would be represented, I paid attention to the demographics of the voters, whom I believe are a good mix of ages, men and women, anglophones and francophones, widely multicultural, and people from big and small communities right across the country. There are college radio and young music fans and an equal number of older veterans. Close to six hundred people responded to my request to vote. Their top pick was awarded 10 points, the number-two choice 9 points, and so on.

The final list that makes up *The Top 100 Canadian Albums*, therefore, is a consensus. Jurors submitted wildly different lists, depending on what music they preferred, how old they were, and where they lived. But there was always that one album from each list that would come up in others. Heavy metal fans, for instance, often included Quebec's Voivod, as did many alternative music fans. The youngest jurors would recognize Neil Young, and some of the oldest would vote for Arcade Fire. A surprising number of people from Western Canada voted for East Coast artists Joel Plaskett, Eric's Trip, and Sloan. Language played little part in the selection of three Harmonium albums.

Once the votes were counted and the Top 100 compiled, my next step was to write the text. I contacted as many of the musicians responsible for the albums as I could. I was sure they had wonderful stories to tell, and I wanted readers to hear from first-hand sources about how these albums were created, which might get them interested in checking out music with which they were unfamiliar. The artists, too, might have new information to impart or fresh perspectives on their work after the passage of time.

In the introduction to the first edition, the last words I wrote were "let the arguments begin." They certainly did. Travelling the country on the promotional tour, I listened to countless complaints and passionate pleas for individual favourites. Where was Anne Murray? The New Pornographers? D.O.A.? Hank Snow? Many people thought I had excluded artists from the list myself or had a bias against their region. There were accusations that Western Canada, or Quebec, had been maligned. The language debate, always part of any national consensus, was raised. I wish now that I'd had room to present the Top 150 albums, or 200, or 500 — so many of the complaints could have been addressed. Where was David Wiffin's *Coast To Coast Fever*? Why, at # 102, of course. How about favourite francophone artists? You could find Beau Dommage's self-titled album at # 113, Malajube's *Trompe-l'oeil* at # 116, and Jean Leloup's *L'amour est sans pitié* at # 124, to name a few.

In many cases, for specific genres, regions, or individual artists, voters couldn't decide which album they liked the best. Vote splitting caused several albums to disappear below the magic Top 100 mark. Thirteen different Bruce Cockburn albums, for instance, received votes, which caused him to land only one in the Top 100. Regional voting was equally complicated. Often, voters in one province would include nothing from their area. This happened quite a few times, even in Quebec, where francophones often chose only albums by English-language artists. At the same time, there were many votes from across the country for francophone artists. Of course, it was impossible to know who was bilingual or what level of knowledge each voter had of music styles. Some people suggested that the poll should have been left to those critics with the best knowledge, but they turned out to be an unpredictable bunch at best. Even with an artist such as Neil Young, critics differed wildly, a few choosing *Harvest* as his best while others picked *Tonight's The Night*, *Everybody Knows This Is Nowhere*, *On The Beach*, or even *Time Fades Away*.

The point is, there's no perfect system. Opinions change, everyone uses their own criteria, and your own taste is as valid as the next person's. The list isn't even the most important part of the book. It's not about who's in here but that we have 100, 200, 500 albums to celebrate. Check them out and all the other discs people recommend passionately. It's wonderful to hear people talking about Canadian music at parties, on-line, and on phone-in shows, asking questions about artists they've never heard before. *The Top 100 Canadian Albums* has become one of the most talked-about books on the shelves, so let the arguments continue.

1 Harvest

Neil Young
Reprise, 1972

Out On The Weekend | Harvest | A Man Needs A Maid | Heart Of Gold |
Are You Ready For The Country | Old Man | There's A World | Alabama |
The Needle And The Damage Done | Words (Between The Lines Of Age)

Like so many of Young's albums, *Harvest* was born out of necessity. He'd written a bunch of new songs and needed to get them recorded right away. Young has trusted his instincts over his career, for better or worse, and prefers spontaneity when it comes to new work — he likes to record the moment. It doesn't mean he'll release everything right away; on the contrary, he hangs onto songs for years, decades. But when an album comes together in his head (and he seems to think in albums), it's time to record. For *Harvest*, he happened to be heading for Nashville.

The 2007 release, *Live At Massey Hall 1971*, reveals a lot about what led to *Harvest*. The Massey Hall tapes exist only because the concert had been recorded for a live album meant to follow up the commercial success of *After The Gold Rush*, from 1970. *Gold Rush* had been a largely acoustic album, and this time Young was going out on tour as a solo artist. He had to sit on a stool for each show, since chronic back pain had forced him into a restrictive brace. As he hit the road, his songwriting tap turned on, and several major new compositions emerged.

As he tells the Massey Hall audience, he had nothing else to do with them but play them live.

The Toronto concert is surprising for what it does and doesn't include. All the new material forced many of his best-known songs out of the set list, including almost all the *Gold Rush* tunes. Fans that night got to hear early versions of songs from the greatest Canadian album of all time. The tape reveals appreciative applause for "Old Man", greater interest in a medley of "A Man Needs A Maid" and "Heart Of Gold", and a great reaction to "The Needle And The Damage Done".

Young now had a choice to make. A proposed double album of the Massey Hall show would mean he'd have to use the new songs. Although he could still do studio versions for a later release, it would take away their thunder and perhaps undermine the public's interest in them. Young states that his producer at the time, Elliot Mazer, was in favour of the live album; Young himself has suggested he might have made a mistake not releasing it at the time. Instead, Young chose to release studio recordings of the new songs.

Off to Nashville to appear on the Johnny Cash TV show, he decided he'd try to get some recording done while in that venerable music city. Nashville was still pretty cool to rock stars, then — Dylan had done his greatest work there — and Neil Young certainly didn't have a problem with country music.

Some of the material needed a band, and Young cornered two of the best-known sidemen in the city, drummer Kenny Buttrey and bass player Tim Drummond. With country in the air, a steel guitar player was needed, and that was Ben Keith, a man who would fill that and other roles in Young's camp for many years. Also in the mix was Young's oddball partner, the famous LA producer Jack Nitzsche, who had been working with Young since the Buffalo Springfield days, was deputized into Crazy Horse, and was always a wild card in any of Neil's projects.

Young's the man. Every good band loves him, every music critic thinks he's God, and he's a hippie who never sold out.

— Andrew Lord, CHOM-FM

This small group weren't there to make a lot of noise. Young's back problems meant he was restricted mostly to acoustic guitar and harmonica. Keith was the perfect colourist. His ringing, haunting pedal steel is dominant on "Out On The Weekend", setting the tone for the album. It is countrified hippie music, warm and soothing. Young's harmonica becomes his solo instrument, replacing the electric leads he'd wailed on *Everybody Knows This Is Nowhere*. The combo really hit the mark on

"Heart Of Gold", which sees Young's harmonica and Keith's steel trading solo lines, both hitting inspired passages. Friends Linda Ronstadt and James Taylor, snatched away from the Cash show taping, sing harmonies. The instantly memorable opening guitar riff, strummed on acoustic, helped turn the song into a huge hit — a campfire classic, a song every guitar player learned.

If Young hadn't been suffering, the record could have been a lot louder. "Are You Ready For The Country" has all the parts needed for a raging stomper; instead, barroom piano and slide guitar provide the spark. On "Alabama", Young gets in some signature slicing electric guitar, but The Stray Gators are still in country mode, and the acoustic piano and slide guitar link the song back to the other tracks.

With the tour headed to Europe, Young and Nitzsche decided two of the new compositions could use a different feel than that provided by the Nashville players. Nitzsche, a master arranger, had contracted with and wrote scores for the London Symphony Orchestra to play on "A Man Needs A Maid" and "There's A World". The contrast between Young's weary vocal and searching lyrics and the beautiful score on "A Man Needs A Maid" is certainly one of the great moments of his career, and Nitzsche's work on this track rarely gets the recognition it deserves.

As he's done many times over the years, Young decided he simply couldn't improve on the concert version of one other song. "The Needle And The Damage Done" had become the centrepiece of the solo tour, its stark lyrics fitting the simple acoustic guitar backing. At a UCLA concert, he had played and sung it perfectly. At the end, instead of fading applause and a brief moment of silence before

the next track, the recording cuts harshly to the odd opening chord of "Words", one of the best moments on the album.

Famously, Neil Young turned his back on the notice *Harvest* brought him, recording instead a series of bleak and uncommercial records. While he didn't like the results of his popularity, he certainly appreciated the album, and the songs have come and gone in his set list since then. No matter what he does to confuse his audience, from the electronic experiment *Trans* to the wimpy rockabilly of *Everybody's Rockin'* to the two-decade tease of the promised Archives series, he can't alienate his fans for long. They've always been willing to come back whenever words like acoustic, country, or *Harvest* are mentioned. Eventually, even Young felt ready for the country again, and got the old gang back together for *Harvest Moon*. Of course, it proved to be his best seller in years.

2 Blue

Joni Mitchell
Reprise, 1970

All I Want | My Old Man | Little Green | Carey | Blue | California |
This Flight Tonight | River | A Case Of You | The Last Time I Saw Richard

Blue is a stunning collection anyway you approach it, whether it's an examination of the lyrics, the melodies, the vocal performance, or the emotional wallop. *Blue* also does something else: it heads for your heart and stays there your whole life. No one who has ever come under *Blue*'s spell leaves it behind.

I can remember the first time I heard *Blue*, where I was, whom I was with, and how it made me feel, and I remember it as one of the best moments of my life. I remember feeling special that I was the one who brought the album, and I remember the admiration of the other young people with me for my owning it. And I remember the woman who took it home and never returned it. I can't even blame her.

In the underappreciated Richard Curtis movie, *Love, Actually*, Emma Thompson's character states, "Joni Mitchell taught me what it meant to feel like a woman." But a lot of men of that generation and later have also learned from *Blue* what a woman feels. It was very scary knowledge, too, that someone feels such depth of emotion. And it was a huge lesson on the origin of great art, reminding us that painters and composers and writers often turn to these lows and highs for their inspiration. Do we all feel this deeply,

> Upon first listen many years ago, it seemed curious (or even paradoxical) to these young ears to have such an intimate personal album sound so comfortable and relaxed.
>
> — Ray Auffrey, Spin-it Records

or do we just lack the skill to translate it to an artistic medium? Can we just do it if we really try? For a great many singers and songwriters, this album is one of the most important influences on their career.

Released at the height of the singer-songwriter album days, *Blue* surpasses them all. The first word on the album is "I," and it shows up in nine of the ten songs. No doubt there are great truths here, although no real names appear. The details are obvious and well documented: Mitchell had split with Graham Nash and gone on a private tour of Europe that turned into one of self-discovery. You can follow her from Paris to Greece; you might even find out that "The Last Time I Saw Richard'" was about her first husband, Chuck Mitchell. These details, the little bits of gossip we all love to pass back and forth as if we're in some secret loop, don't matter a bit to the importance of the record. That stuff is tabloid front page compared to an essay inside a good newspaper.

This is not simply a break-up album — that's merely part of the journey. There are just as many feel-good songs here, including "All I Want", "My Old Man", and "Carey". This is an examination of what it's like for someone to be in love, to be alone, to want fun and warmth, to worry about counting on love and happiness and wanting to give it in return. That's what Emma Thompson's character was talking about; and her husband, who was having an affair at the time, just thought she liked Joni Mitchell albums.

Do yourself a favour sometime and play *Blue* just for the music. It's a wonderful example of less is more. No one can deny that the songs are powerful, yet there's no studio trickery or walls of amps or guitar effects. Mitchell produces herself and does most of the playing on piano, guitar, and dulcimer. Her composition, especially on "River", brilliantly sets the mood. The melody itself is not that sad, but the piano chords are. Listen to her voice as she tells us about making her baby cry. Words, piano, voice — just three elements, but all the amp'ed-up guitar heroes of the day couldn't match that power. Jimmy Page and Robert Plant knew it, writing Led Zeppelin's "Going To California" about a desire to be near Mitchell.

Each song has moments to treasure. Her higher-register singing on "The Last Time I Saw Richard" is beautiful and fragile, then she lowers as she toughens and talks of being alone to grow strong again. "This Flight Tonight", with its strange tuning and strong lower-note chords, survived perfectly as a hard-rock song covered by Nazareth. *Blue* could rock. "River" has settled into a new life as a perennial Christmas favourite, covered many times over by the likes of Sarah McLachlan, James Taylor, Aimee Mann, Linda Ronstadt, k.d. lang, and Holly Cole. As with those of so many Canadians, Mitchell's Christmas thoughts turn to past winters, the desire for a river to skate away on. On the songs that feature the dulcimer, there's a marvellous interaction with the acoustic guitars played by James Taylor or, on "Carey", Stephen Stills. It grabs you right off the bat on "All I Want", and its special association with this album has made it pointless for other musicians to borrow.

All these elements show that the importance placed on the confessional nature of the record over the years has been foolish and shallow. None of those gossipy details matters to the enjoyment, and the proof is in the one song whose lyrics don't include the word "I": "Little Green". Everyone who loves the album loves this track, as they do all the others. Yet, for years, no one picked up on the fact that it includes the most important story of Mitchell's life, fully detailed. Perhaps because she didn't say "I" or sing about a juicy break-up, people didn't look closer but just enjoyed the song. "Little Green" speaks of a child, of lies sent home, of papers signed, and of wishes for the child's happy ending. Only much later did the world hear the story of Mitchell's unwed pregnancy and the daughter given up for adoption. It was all in the song, but people were just too busy trying to figure out if "Carey" was some

famous rock star. She had confessed her biggest secret and it had gone unnoticed.

Yes, *Blue* is a confessional album, but it's so much more that such a label does a huge disservice. It's such a superficial way to approach the songs, each of which stands on its own merits. They are points to stop at along Mitchell's journey, and the details would certainly contribute to a fine autobiography if she ever chose to write the book. *Blue* is not that book, just the art her life inspired. Enjoy the album for that.

3 After The Gold Rush

Neil Young
Reprise, 1970

Tell Me Why | AfterThe Gold Rush | Only Love Can Break Your Heart | Southern Man |
Till The Morning Comes | Oh, Lonesome Me | Don't Let It Bring You Down | Birds |
When You Dance You Can Really Love | I Believe In You | Cripple Creek Ferry

Neil Young's third solo album arrived just in time to make him a major star. He was already getting lots of attention as the newest member of Crosby, Stills, Nash & Young; now *After The Gold Rush* introduced his softer, acoustic work that helped usher in the singer-songwriter movement. Yet it also includes some of his electric intensity, making it the best of both worlds for the many fans who admire both sides of this period.

On Young's previous album, *Everybody Knows This Is Nowhere*, his new backing band, Crazy Horse, had received credit on the cover, but not this time. Their omission probably had more to do with what the album was supposed to be: a soundtrack to a film. The jacket states "most of the songs were inspired by the Dean Stockwell-Herb Berman screenplay 'After The Goldrush'." Stockwell was a pal of Young's, but plans to shoot the science fiction script fell through. That didn't deter Young from making good use of the material he had on hand. Young's title song for the movie was typically cryptic, taking place in a dream where he time-travels from a medieval celebration to a modern war zone and finally to

a future with aliens. The environment has collapsed, and the aliens are saving Mother Nature, one of Young's recurring concerns throughout his long career.

"After The Gold Rush" joins two other songs in an acoustic trio that starts off the disc. They are among the most melodic of his career to this point. "Tell Me Why" is a lovely and simple guitar tune, strummed by Young and Danny Whitten of Crazy Horse and featuring a chorus of hippie angels on harmony. The vocal performance is obviously inspired by his CSN buddies, and Stills is one of the singers here, along with Whitten, Horse drummer Ralph Molina, and the newest member of the group, nineteen-year-old Nils Lofgren, a star-in-waiting being mentored by Young. "After The Gold Rush" is one of Young's best vocals — as he moves into his highest register, his fragile voice speaks for the scared everyman. There are those who hate Neil Young's voice, but most people appreciate the honesty and brave attempt. "Only Love Can Break Your Heart" is another acoustic singalong featuring the California choir. This is no simple song but a gem featuring some of Young's best lyrics. Along

with the pearl of wisdom in the title, he speaks to a great fear of loneliness, a theme later taken up in "A Man Needs A Maid".

The brevity of "Till The Morning Comes" points to its being part of the unused soundtrack. It's a lyric fragment but a lovely melody, with an uncredited horn part and more harmonies, this time led by Young with an impossibly high falsetto. He should have found another buyer when the first film went nowhere; you can picture Butch and Sundance riding off with this playing over the scene. "Cripple Creek Ferry" has more body, with an actual verse, but is still only a fragment. It has a compelling first verse, though, and you're drawn into the story immediately, introduced to the troubled ferry captain and the gambler on a losing streak. It's always felt like such a shame there wasn't more.

On an album filled with some of Young's best songwriting, he uncorks one his biggest surprises, a rare and excellent cover. "Oh, Lonesome Me" had been a big country hit for Don Gibson, but Young throws away Gibson's bouncy tempo and comes up with a new melody that fits the words even better. He sounds truly lonesome and blue. It's one of the best productions on the album, with all the players getting in on the heartbreak.

With "Southern Man", Young began a habit of sticking his nose in where many feel it doesn't belong. His limited exposure to the US South led him to write this stinging condemnation, famously challenged by Lynyrd Skynyrd's riposte, "Sweet Home Alabama". It's out of place on this album, yet it's one of Young's best rockers, with an inventive electric guitar solo and a solid chord structure pounded out on piano. It's also remarkably brief for this kind of Young song, given

As close as any one album comes to capturing Neil's full scope of talents. His songwriting is unusually disciplined and streamlined. Powerful and gentle, beautiful throughout.

— J.C. Douglas, Q104

the nine- and ten-minute epics of "Cowgirl In The Sand" and "Down By The River" — it actually seems to end prematurely at 5:41. The other hard-edged rocker here, "When You Dance You Can Really Love", is underrated, and reaches its full potential only in the 1979 version on *Live Rust*.

On the album's second side, there is more heart-ache and beauty. "Don't Let It Bring You Down" is a sorrowful tale of a blind man struck by a car one night, the red lights of the ambulance cutting through the darkness. "Birds" includes another stark and sad image, as love flies away. Once again, Young's plaintive voice makes the song special, a well of emotion he seems to have plumbed only for this album. Later songs, even "Heart Of Gold", don't express such sadness. He has never again seemed this fragile, even in his darkest period of *Tonight's The Night*. Tender is not a word generally associated with Neil Young, yet it describes a song like "I Believe In You". It's not so much in the words as in the performance.

After The Gold Rush has always seemed to end far too quickly — perhaps because of the two partial songs, but really because we simply don't want it to end. *Harvest* has "Heart Of Gold", which tips the balance in that album's favour as Young's best, but *After The Gold Rush* is a classic.

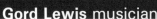

Top Ten Canadian Punk Albums

In the fifties, there were punks such as Gene Vincent; punks in the seventies featured Johnny Rotten; and punks in the nineties had Kurt Cobain. Punk fans argue among themselves over which is the true punk generation. Gord Lewis doesn't care, he likes them all. He knows a thing or two about punk rock, as the guitar player and founder of Teenage Head, the first punk band many Canadians saw in concert. With plenty of rockabilly and Glam rock influences, Teenage Head created its own, Hamiltonian version of punk, and Gord got to see and hear some pretty cool bands along the way. Here's his list of favourites:

1. The Doughboys
   Crush

2. The Killjoys
   Starry

3. The Forgotten Rebels
   Boys Will Be Boys

4. The Start
   Hey You!

5. The Demics
   Talk's Cheap

6. The Diodes
   The Diodes

7. The Villains
   Life Of Crime

8. Teenage Head
   Teenage Head

9. Headstones
   Picture Of Health

10. The Shakers
    In Time

4 Music From Big Pink

The Band
Capitol, 1968

Tears Of Rage | To Kingdom Come | In A Station | Caledonia Mission | The Weight | We Can Talk |
Long Black Veil | Chest Fever | Lonesome Suzie | This Wheel's On Fire | I Shall Be Released

> The greatest album ever made ever by anyone.
> — Colin Linden

Garth Hudson lives in Stone Ridge, New York, not far from a landmark in rock history, a once-pink house he once occupied: "It's in Saugerties, it'd be forty-five minutes through a couple of valleys." Hudson and his bandmates had followed their then-employer, Bob Dylan, to the area: "Albert Grossman, Bob's manager, had found property, a house in Bearsville, a beautiful place. This is near Woodstock. They found this little town charming. Bob had a look at it, and bought a house there. So we moved nearby, halfway between Woodstock and Saugerties. That was Big Pink."

The retreat had two purposes. Dylan wanted his group around to work on new material while he hid out after his motorcycle accident. That became the *Basement Tapes*, recorded in the basement of Big Pink. Meanwhile, the other players were creating a new music that would become their first album, *Music From Big Pink*.

Turning seventy in 2007, Garth Hudson is still much in demand as a performer, session man, and keyboard expert. Preparing for the interviews for this book, he got to thinking about what went into making

Music From Big Pink. Much has been written about the times in which this historic album was made: different opinions, conflicting stories, old wounds. Garth Hudson was there, and he wanted to point out some important elements and stories — things he felt had been forgotten or ignored — that made *Music From Big Pink* one of the greatest Canadian albums.

Hudson was part of Canada's very first wave of rock and roll: "I joined Bob Liley and his group The Capers [later Paul London and The Kapers], one of the first rock bands in London, Ontario, and we played various places, teen hops. Also, we'd heard of Ronnie [Hawkins], and we'd go in and watch him on Saturday afternoons at the Brass Rail in London. Liley and Conway Twitty and Ronnie — anybody that's interested in rock and roll in Canada would get the picture. All this is source material [for *Big Pink*], and it's very important. I went with The Capers to Detroit and Levon [Helm, Hawkins's drummer] came out to the Torch Bar in East Jefferson to see my group. So they asked me if I would consider playing in the group. I didn't join for some time, but I finally did join up with Levon and Ronnie. Levon, of course, was the leader [of The Hawks] then, and still is. He did the hiring and firing. Levon and Ronnie were the two originals."

Also in the band were Richard Manuel and Rick Danko, from southern Ontario, plus young Toronto guitar player Robbie Robertson, who all went on to form The Band. Together, they played the raucous rockabilly of the day, but fuelled it with blues, more r'n'b than the standard early rockers. They became a crack unit, but chafed under Hawkins's tough rules and schedules. "We were working seven nights a week," remembers Hudson. "The decision was that we would leave." The group became known as Levon and The Hawks and covered the club circuit through Ontario and Quebec, down to New Jersey and New York. Eventually, they got the job backing Dylan, barely survived the commotion of the electric tours that saw the group booed every night, and wound up at Big Pink.

It was actually the three rural Ontario guys — Hudson, Danko and Manuel — who lived at Big Pink. They would get together to play, and songs started arriving. Some were written first with Dylan, including Richard Manuel's "Tears Of Rage", and Rick Danko's "This Wheel's On Fire". When Dylan left, the group began working on their own material. Hudson describes it as a long process of sharing and talking, something they'd been doing since he'd joined them in 1961: "Each person contributed to the vignettes. Everyone was a storyteller, and from these stories and our feelings about family and the rural life where we were brought up, this kind of heart was carried on. And being closer to a small town and rural community [Saugerties] only reinforced a lot of the thinking about the vignettes and the scenarios that went into the poetry."

Music From Big Pink has rightly been hailed as a great return to roots music, an album that turned its back on the modern trends of psychedelia and studio experimentation and embraced old-time values of songwriting, ensemble instrumentation, and performing. The album is also often described as a new reflection of rural America, even though the group were four-fifths Canadian. Certainly, there are Southern references in "The Weight" — names and places Helms threw into the songwriting pot. The group also had a deep love of the r'n'b and rock and roll they'd heard booming across the border on US radio stations. Hudson, however, says look past the lyrics and into the music, and you'll find Canada, too. Always considered the musical professor of the group, he points to direct references in the songs that relate to music they'd learned in Canada: "We're gathering and exhibiting, sampling from rhythm and blues from the get-go. This all went into making the music. If you listen to the introduction of 'Chest Fever', do-do-diddle diddle-diddle loo, and then you hear a skip, wa-da-digadigadiga-da-da, that's a bagpipe lick."

Hudson also deconstructs the musical elements of "The Weight": "I remember when we went to record it, I played piano on it, and I remember trying to get this feeling, a bit of this Serbo-Croatian polka band feeling, oonk-ka, oonk-ka, oonk-ka, and it was tricky. I'd heard it done by some of the Delta blues guitar-harmonica players. That was the main problem for me, finding that rhythm. Strangely enough, I've never heard anybody really do it as well. I've never heard anybody else play that feeling and pull it off, really."

When they were crafting the songs, Hudson, Danko, and Manuel worked from a base of musical knowledge that only small-town Canadians of that era would have had: "Rick and Richard were born in '43, '44, 'round that time. So they heard Canadian radio. They listened to the CBC, as I did. All these little melodies and tunes and country stylings were part of our heritage. I can give you a list of about twenty names: we listened to Don Messer and His Islanders, and King Ganam, and Calvin Jackson, and The Happy Gang, and The Craigs, and Ed McCurdy. You must know about Ed McCurdy? Whew . . . it was a 6 pm show — that's where I heard 'Jack Was Every Inch A Sailor', songs like that. He's a folk singer, he's a real character. I would name him as one of the three or four basic Canadian folk heroes. And Quentin Maclean, Kate Stokes — that's where I first heard Hammond organ. This all went into *Big Pink*. All this stuff is more important than how we sat around and mulled it out. I just want people to know that I'm Canadian. The Don Wright Chorus — you can't leave that out. This all goes into the hopper, it's very important. This is what The Band is founded on."

Randy Bachman musician

A Dozen Favourite Canadian Guitarists

Hey, if Randy Bachman doesn't want to follow the rules and make it a Top Ten, who are we to refuse? He's responsible for five of the Top 100, with three Guess Who discs, one BTO, and as producer of Trooper's *Hot Shots*. Randy collects favourite guitar players like he collects vintage guitars, a priceless collection numbering in the hundreds. Here are his picks.

"Listed in no particular order, because each in their own way is a great player and has added to the richness of Canadian music. They have rocked the world: Lenny Breau, Liona Boyd, Neil Young, Alex Lifeson, Domenic Troiano, Kim Mitchell, Rik Emmett, Jeff Healey, Colin James, Brian Smith, Paul Dean, Keith Scott."

JEFF HEALEY   COLIN JAMES   BRIAN SMITH   LIONA BOYD   ALEX LIFESON

5 Fully Completely

The Tragically Hip
MCA, 1992

Courage (For Hugh MacLennan) | Looking For A Place To Happen | At The Hundredth Meridian | Pigeon Camera | Lionized | Locked In The Trunk Of A Car | We'll Go Too | Fully Completely | Fifty-Mission Cap | Wheat Kings | The Wherewithall | Eldorado

Fully Completely was the third full-length album by the Kingston, Ontario, band. Quickly becoming the biggest group in the country, they had done it on their own terms, making no concessions to style, trends, charts, or music company demands. The members had been friends from the start and were determined to stay that way. "We all knew each other in high school, and played in different bands," says guitar player Rob Baker. "We decided to stop competing and throw our minimal talents together. The very first gig was November of 1985." The lineup, which has not changed since, consisted of Baker and vocalist Gord Downie, Gord Sinclair on bass, drummer Johnny Fay, and Paul Langlois on guitar. After a first, self-titled shorter album ("the baby record," Baker calls it), The Tragically Hip had grown in stature with each new album, *Up To Here* and *Road Apples*.

Fully Completely is packed with Canadian classics. "Courage (For Hugh MacLennan)", "At The Hundredth Meridian", "Fifty-Mission Cap", and "Wheat Kings" share something in common: they're full of solid, unmistakable references to Canada. The group's lyrics

had been that way from the start, rolling out topical songs and history lessons, bringing up Jacques Cartier, painter Tom Thomson, and old Maple Leafs. Only in Canada would this be considered risky, says Baker: "I'm not exactly sure where it comes from except that we always wanted to be honest in our songwriting.

> Can't get much more Canadian than The Hip, and this was their best release in my opinion.
>
> — Paul Borchert, *Mote Magazine*

When we started out, there were a lot of Canadian bands that were trying to look and sound like American bands, and dropping American place names and things as if that would somehow ingratiate themselves into the American market. We found that kind of repulsive. And we just reacted by, well, you write what you know, you write about who you are and where you're from. And there are so many great untold stories in this country,

I think we always had the freedom. I think the day that we shot down the guy from BMG who wanted us to be a country band and wanted to bring in the songwriters, and we said, you know what? We'd rather not make records than make a record like that.

— Rob Baker

or stories that don't get the same kind of airplay that so many American stories would get. America's very good about tending to their mythology. They do the weeding and they take good care of that garden. Canadians tend to let it get a little grown over."

Nobody twisted lyricist Gord Downie's arm to include Canadiana, but his lyrics don't sound forced, either. It often just happened because Downie and the group members were interested in Canadian culture. Hockey, for instance: "Fifty-Mission Cap" tells the tale of Bill Barilko, the Leafs' Stanley Cup hero who disappeared in a plane accident after scoring the Cup winner. Baker reports that Downie was doing a typically Canadian thing at just the right moment: "Gord Sinclair had a little bass riff which turned into the verse figure for 'Fifty-Mission Cap', and we just started playing it over and over, trying to lock into a groove, find a feeling for it. While we were doing that, Gord Downie was standing with his snippets of lyrics and workbooks on the music stand. He was opening some packs of hockey cards and eating the gum and checking out who he'd got. And in one of the packs was the Bill Barilko card, the famous shot of him scoring the goal, and he flipped it over and basically started reading the back of the card, but singing it. He enhanced it, and changed it a little bit, but certainly

more than the germ of the lyric is right there on the back of the hockey card."

It's a small country by the way. The man who wrote that hockey card, #340 of the Pro Set 1991-92 Series One edition, is James Duplacey, one of this book's jurors, music collector, historian, author of dozens of books on hockey — and my roommate and Best Man at my wedding.

It's a small country by the way. For *Up To Here*, The Hip wrote "38 Years Old", about a prison break in the seventies from Millhaven Penitentiary. One of Canada's most famous prisoners heard that song while he was fighting to clear his name. Baker says it led to another song on *Fully Completely*: "We were contacted by David Milgaard, who was in prison at the time for a crime he didn't commit. He was thirty-eight at the time, and wondered if the song had been written about him; he had been very moved by it. The song hadn't been written about him, but it got Gord thinking about what it would feel like to be in prison for saying you did something that you didn't do. He just wrote a 'what if' kind of song, and that's 'Wheat Kings'. I wouldn't say it's a song about Milgaard, but in some ways it was inspired by Milgaard's situation."

When the dust settled on *Fully Completely*, this most Canadian of albums had become a huge seller, certified for a diamond award (ten times platinum) for one million copies sold in Canada alone. Normally, this level of success earns a band a lot of freedom on the business side of their affairs, but Baker says they had fought and won that freedom years before, refusing to work with companies that wanted to mould them: "I think we always had the freedom. I think the day that we shot down the guy from BMG who wanted us to be a country band and wanted to bring in the songwriters, and we said, you know what? We'd rather not make records than make a record like that. And we walked away from the meeting thinking we'd probably never make another record, and we were okay with that. I think we had the freedom from day one."

Baker says the biggest change was on the road: "The breakthrough with *Fully Completely* was we went from a club act to an arena act." The Hip used their clout to do what they'd always dreamed of doing: set up their own rock festival. For three years, Another Roadside Attraction toured the country, and the group members got to pick their favourite bands to play. Baker enthuses, "We got to be deejay for the day. That's the impulse that leads a lot of people to become musicians anyway. You feel that your taste is better than other people's. Maybe that's what the name of the band means. Gord Sinclair and I and Gord Downie and Johnny were the guys that would go to the high school party with a stack of records under our arms and commandeer the stereo. Then you get into a band and cover tunes that no one else covers, and you think this is a great song that these people should hear. And maybe our taste is so good that they won't get it. Maybe we're 'tragically hip'."

The Tragically Hip (left to right): Johnny Fay (drums), Paul Langlois (rhythm guitar), Rob Baker (guitar), Gord Downie (vocals, acoustic guitar), and Gord Sinclair (bass)

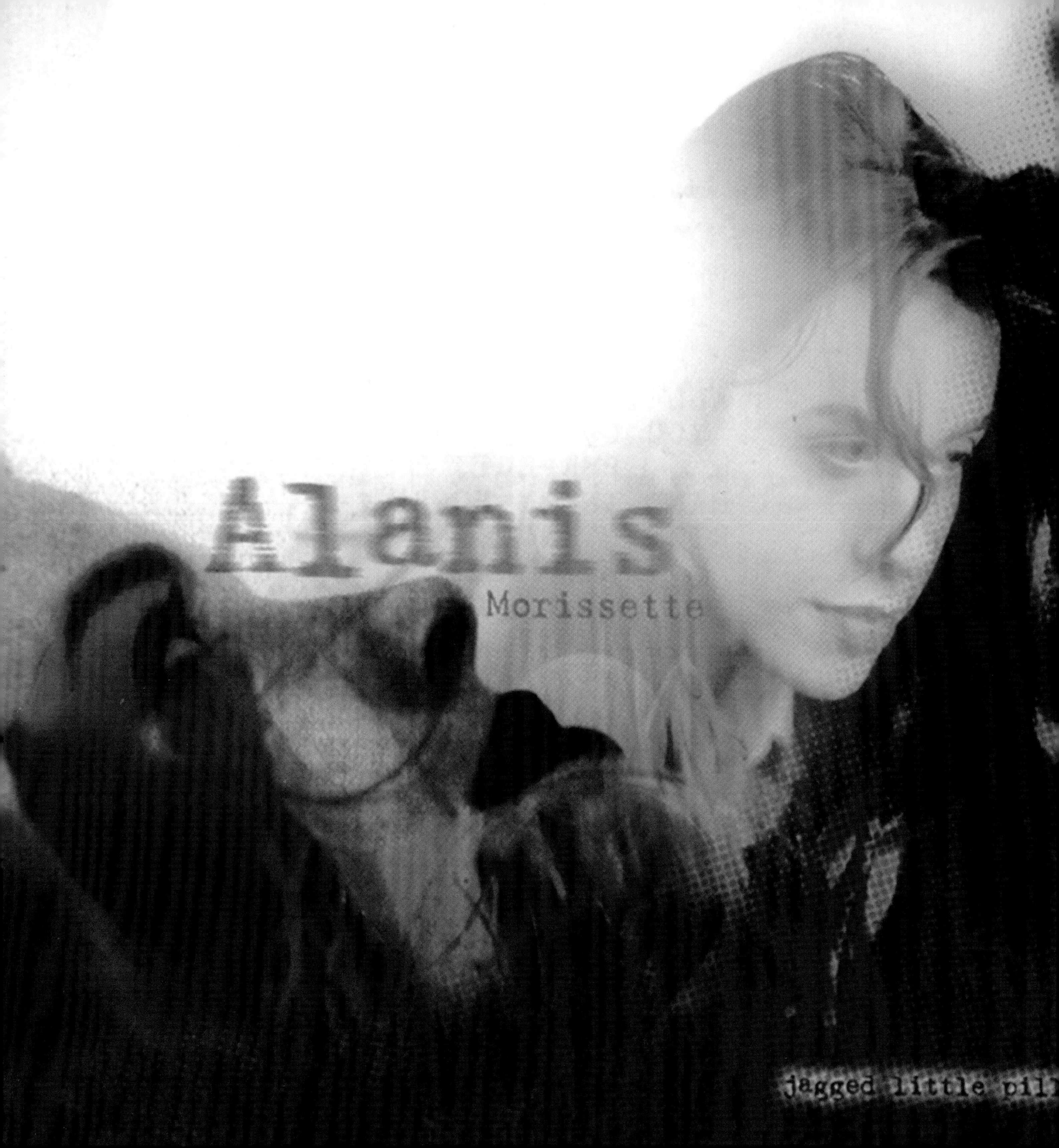
Alanis
Morissette
jagged little pill

6 Jagged Little Pill

Alanis Morissette

Maverick, 1995

All I Really Want | You Oughta Know | Perfect | Hand In My Pocket | Right Through You | Forgiven | You Learn | Head Over Feet | Mary Jane | Ironic | Not The Doctor | Wake Up

> Who thought this teen pop singer would come out in the nineties with a rough album?
>
> — Marie Lefebvre, Rock Détente

Canadian music reviewers don't like hype. It makes them suspicious, it gets their backs up, and they usually react with a review that is negative, rather than excited. I'm hyped so seldom, in fact, that a tiny taste of it surprised me back in 1995. It came in the form of a phone call from my friendly local Warner rep alerting me to a new disc I'd be receiving, from Alanis Morissette. The rep assured me it was going to be huge, really huge — like, the biggest thing in years. Wait a second, I said, Alanis . . . not THE Alanis, the kid who sang dance music, Canada's answer to Debbie Gibson? He sheepishly admitted it was indeed the same, but she'd grown up, moved to the States, and completely changed her music. It wasn't dance pop anymore; it was tough-edged rock music, alternative, but like nothing ever before. Right, I said, okay, I'll check it out. That was the biggest hype I'd ever received from this veteran music employee, and knowing him as someone whose taste ran to jazz and classical, I didn't believe a word of it. I simply thought head office had told him to place the calls.

When the album arrived, I was prepared: no one was going to hype me. In fact, I think I'd already written my review. I listened to the CD to make sure, and I sniffed. I hated her sneer, I hated that tone in her voice. I found it fake. I thought she was trying way too hard to be angry, and that the swear words had been dropped in for shock value. I listened just once, and filed my so-clever one-line review: Come back, Tiffany, all is forgiven.

The public immediately accepted my dismissal, by buying only twenty-eight million copies. In Canada alone, two million were sold, making it the first double diamond recipient of the CD era. It became the greatest-selling debut album and the greatest-selling female album ever. Alanis has never thanked me for what happened to her in 1995.

Other reviewers loved it, but it really didn't matter. That hadn't been a hype phone call, but a friend passing on a fact. Everyone (well, almost) who'd heard the album knew it was going to explode. This was the sound of something really important happening. It was an artistic, emotional, and individual outpouring that struck a chord hooked up to a wall of sound.

The album said a lot to a lot of people. It said a woman could rock with the best. It said you shouldn't be a jerk to someone. It showed many young women it was possible to stand up for oneself. Perhaps it made a lot of men pause to think. With its frank talk and explicit lyrics, it said there were no boundaries for women in expression. It proved truth always strikes home with people. It showed Americans that Canadian artists weren't just acoustic-based folk singers — not that there's anything wrong with that. It defined young female empowerment a year before The Spice Girls arrived with a cartoon version of it in *Girl Power*.

Morissette showed Canadians you shouldn't judge someone by their past. And it showed reviewers (well, one) that sometimes you don't know a damn thing about what you're hearing.

Much of the art and power is in Morissette's raw openness, her public exposure: the ultimate self-portrait of a songwriter. Much has been made of the objects of her wrath, but the lyrics are a one-sided conversation. We learn lots about her, but only bits and pieces of what fuelled the album. Morissette has often stated that expressing her rage in songs such as "You Oughta Know" was healthy. This is pretty sound psychological advice, and Morissette obviously had lots of issues in her young life by this time. The manipulative and shallow lover she describes here joins pressures heaped on her as a child star, a notoriously unhealthy profession. She's spoken of how her Catholic upbringing encouraged her not to express such emotion, so the cleansing in these songs must be seen as liberating just in their creation. To have them broadcast and speculated on with such intensity might have created another set of problems, but she seems to have adjusted to fame with dignity intact.

The hits meant that some of the album's more positive messages were overlooked. The title, for example, comes from the song "You Learn", which is about taking strength from the worst things life throws at you. She recommends getting hurt in romance — every bad thing can teach you an important life lesson. The medicine hurts going down but heals you quickly. It's a great title and a great metaphor, and it said a whole lot more than the sexual references dotted through the disc. In "Ironic", she says life can work out even when you think everything is going wrong. The song is a winner thanks to its soft verse-raunchy chorus format, and the words are fun to follow. "Hand In My Pocket" is downright happy, as Morissette announces that everything's "fine, fine, fine."

Morissette had moved to Los Angeles to find someone to help build her new career. She was determined to continue recording, which gives you a good indication of her internal strength. The spark she needed was meeting Glen Ballard, who earned a lot of the credit for the hit sound — indeed, his participation actually became one of the straws detractors clutched as they tried to knock the album off its perch. Songwriter-producer Ballard was part of the establishment, working with such acts as Wilson Phillips, Michael Jackson, and Aerosmith. That was why, so the theory went, the album was not "alternative" — his involvement meant it couldn't be a groundbreaking or, ultimately, landmark recording. In the next breath, they would give Ballard's responsibility for making it so good as a reason Alanis still couldn't be the real thing. In fact, the contradictory arguments — was Ballard's presence poison or gold? — cancel each other out; his chief role is typical of many producers who work closely with an artist. All the words are hers, although Morissette credits Ballard with encouraging her lyrical liberation. Ballard was simply the right person for the job, and he did it brilliantly.

How confident Morissette had become is evident in "Right Through You". Someone who'd wronged her, who couldn't even say her name correctly, gets to hear her last laugh, loud and clear, payback for the brush-off. She actually predicts she'll become "Miss Thing" and "a zillionaire," and he won't be in the credits. Within months, she would be just that. No one, including that man, would be mispronouncing her name. In Canada, she'd still be Alanis, but now the name would be said with respect.

Ra McGuire musician

Top Ten Canadian Anthems

A rock anthem is a song everyone knows by heart. They're played at hockey games to get the crowd going, and advertisers offer huge amounts of cash to license them for car and beer commercials. Sing one line and the song will stay in your head all day. They are now clichés but only because some Canadian songwriters thought of the words in the first place. Our judge for this Top Ten list, Ra McGuire, is quite familiar with this phenomenon, having written a couple of them himself for his band Trooper.

"Here's my (and probably everyone else's) version of the Top Ten Canadian anthems. I'm a little self-conscious about the two Trooper songs — but I've been told many times that both songs were eminently qualified!"

1. Steppenwolf
   "Born To Be Wild"

2. Neil Young
   "Rockin' In The Free World"

3. Alanis Morissette
   "You Oughta Know"

4. Kim Mitchell
   "I Am A Wild Party"

5. The Tragically Hip
   "New Orleans Is Sinking"

6. Tom Cochrane
   "Life Is A Highway"

7. Bachman-Turner Overdrive
   "Takin' Care Of Business"

8. Parachute Club
   "Rise Up"

9. Trooper
   "Here For A Good Time"

10. Trooper
   "Raise A Little Hell"

KIM MITCHELL

BTO

THE TRAGICALLY HIP

THE BAND

7 The Band

The Band
Capitol, 1969

Across The Great Divide | Rag Mama Rag | The Night They Drove Old Dixie Down | When You Awake |
Up On Cripple Creek | Whispering Pines | Jemima Surrender | Rockin' Chair | Look Out Cleveland |
Jawbone | The Unfaithful Servant | King Harvest (Has Surely Come)

Which album is better, *Music From Big Pink* or *The Band*? It's a great debate, but The Band themselves were quite satisfied with the critical and popular reaction to their groundbreaking first album. Garth Hudson, though, had been concerned at first: "It seemed all right. I think my concern was, would it sell records? I thought that it was a little bit, well, 'arty' is one word. I didn't know just how it would be evaluated. But with folk people and serious music listeners, through the years, we've received many compliments."

So it would be business as usual as the group reconvened to record album number two. There were some changes, though. For one, they had to wait to satisfy the demands for live performances, as Rick Danko had been hurt in a car accident. They eventually got some gigs under their belts, however, and the return to their first home, the concert stage, made The Band that much better. Hudson seems to lean toward this album as the better of the two: "Of course, everybody was becoming more proficient, and we had played live, performed some of these things live by then.

The whole experience was more evenly tempered and well rounded."

Much of the group's first album had been created by swapping stories and trying out parts. Hudson says that, although this continued, their situations had changed a bit since the success of *Big Pink*: "The stories went on — perhaps rather than in a Cadillac pulling a trailer through the hills of Illinois, the stories were being told by the pool."

The group had decided to record in Los Angeles and, renting Sammy Davis Jr.'s property, they turned the pool house into a studio. Despite this most Hollywood of settings, The Band once again created an album that focuses on heritage sounds and words, real instruments, and musical teamwork. "This always went on, it was a continuous thing," says Hudson of the group's writing methods. "And also we listened to certain music. This went on, the gathering and the sampling; songs and melodies went way back."

There was one other person involved, producer John Simon. As he had done on the first album, Simon provided his musical skills on keyboard and horns, and is actually credited on *The Band* as an equal of the other performers. It's a position Hudson says he deserves: "I thought that John Simon did an excellent job in contributing to the sounds and also the musicality and the blending and the arrangements. I think his part has been perhaps underplayed. It was really an inspiring thing for everyone to have him, an excellent keyboard player, there. He was very good in scheduling, and patient, too. He played euphonium, a baritone horn, and trombone a little bit as well."

They could play and they could sing like no others. The Band boasted three distinct and terrific singers. They divvied up the lead vocals, but when they came together for collective vocals and harmonies, the magic exploded. Garth Hudson can analyze any kind of music down to its roots but struggles to add anything to the obvious evidence that exists on record, saying that all the old clichés about their voices are just words that can't possibly do the music justice: "To me, their voices were different, the characters. They blended together well. I suppose I could write something poetic, not

> It's my favourite Band album today.
> Last week it was *Music From Big Pink*,
> and next week it might be *Stage Fright*.
> — Bill Hayes, Q107

hackneyed and so on. I've heard this kind of cohesion described in many ways before. Homogenous is one — like in a sax section, the baritone sax has a homogenous quality, it blends well with the tenors." Just go the three-minute mark of "The Night They Drove Old Dixie Down", as the final chorus begins,

and hear the sound Hudson's referring to, as the three singers blend like a horn section.

Even when the lyrics don't directly reflect past events, the group use instruments that evoke old-time music. "Sometimes, in order to add colour, character, to the words, we would use a mandolin or a pump organ sound," confirms Hudson. "The Lowrey [organ] that I used had a reedier sound and a slow attack, which you found with the accordion tab, the stop. It sounded like a harmonium, melodion, pump organ, and that would hopefully take you back a bit." So did the choice of particular words; "Up On Cripple Creek" is full of them, with Levon Helm singing about nags, taking a pull, and Spike Jones — yet nothing in the lyrics suggests it couldn't be a modern love song. Throughout, Hudson imitates a Jew's harp on his clavinet, further cementing the old-timey feel.

Robbie Robertson gets most of the songwriting credits, but an important ingredient in the album are the songs of Richard Manuel. Teaming with Robertson, he contributes two dreamy and tender numbers, "When You Awake" and "Whispering Pines". Again taking a look backward, the songs are set in the past tense. But it's the evocative instrumentation and vocals that fool you into thinking these songs are from another era. In "When You Awake", the singer's car freezes up overnight — a very Canadian experience, it should be noted. "Whispering Pines" is a tearjerker: our narrator, sad and alone in his room, with just the stars and the trees for company, his true love lost. As veteran barroom performers, the group knew how to mix things up to appeal to the whole crowd. "I think Richard wrote more heartfelt songs for the ladies, as it were," explains Hudson.

Garth Hudson believes that all these old feelings don't really have much to do with Americana. He can

The Band (left to right): Robbie Robertson (guitar) and Levon Helm (drums).

rattle off jigs and reels and long-forgotten performers he listened to religiously back in Ontario. Speaking of religion, he can even point to the parts that came directly from his youth, playing organ in the Anglican Church: "Four-part voice reading, melodic tendencies are there, too. I played the service, you know."

All this old-time music was mined for the sound that makes *The Band* (and *Big Pink*) so different from the rock and pop of the day. Both albums continue to be among the most influential in what's now known as roots music. Hudson knows where he got ideas. He knows what he shared with his bandmates to make up the songs. Now seventy, and with Danko and Manuel in the grave, Hudson wants to make sure people know

this music came from Canada: "It's important because . . . I am from there, and I remember more about it than most of the people that would be reading this. And so did Rick and Richard. And all this went into the formation of the band. This was The Band."

8 Funeral

Arcade Fire
Merge, 2004

Neighborhood #1 (Tunnels) | Neighborhood #2 (Laika) | Une année sans lumière |
Neighborhood #3 (Power Out) | Neighborhood #4 (7 Kettles) | Crown Of Love | Wake Up |
Haiti | Rebellion (Lies) | In The Backseat

An organ starts, a piano joins, a cello, some distorted but soft guitar, another piano joins, and we're just seconds into the first track of Arcade Fire's first album, *Funeral*. Already it was plain something fresh and exciting was happening with this Montreal collective. The lyrics to "Neighborhood #1" are just as interesting, starting in the middle of a sentence. They describe something only a Canadian-based band could consider: the possibility of a snowfall so great it buries the neighbourhood above the second floor, and the kids dig tunnels between their houses. A xylophone joins in later, an even more distorted guitar, still muted, though, and the snow has never left, the kids have grown to adults, still living outside.

That's quite an opening, with worlds and instruments to discover. *Funeral* continues with such discoveries on each track. It became the album of 2004 for alternative fans in Canada, and soon built a similar following in the US. The following year, prominent magazines and influential critics in England named it THE album of the year. The band shared the stage with an impressed David Bowie at his invitation. A new sound was born.

> Not only carved a new path, but reinvented music as we know it.
>
> — Scott Chasty, Rock 94

Arcade Fire were born in Montreal, even though some of the members weren't. Will Butler, a Texan, plays several instruments — well, they all do, really. He describes the journeys they took to get together: "Well, Régine was born and raised in Montreal (the South Shore of Montreal, but it's all in that same sort of area, you know). Win [brother Win Butler] came to Montreal for school, essentially, and because he'd heard that Montreal was a grand place. Richard and Tim and Sarah were in Montreal because it was a land of opportunity. A nice place to live, even for anglophones like us. Jeremy lived in Ottawa, because that's where he's from, but he's from Montreal now. I followed Win after I finished school."

Butler gives a lot of the credit for the creation of the album to the city: "I genuinely think being in a cold climate makes you go inside and be creative all winter.

Arcade Fire (left to right): Tim Kingsbury (in back) (guitar, bass), Jeremy Gara (drums, guitar), Sarah Neufeld (violin, strings), Richard Reed Perry (in back) (guitar, bass, keyboards, percussion), Régine Chassagne (keyboards, accordion, percussion, drums, lead vocals), Win Butler (guitar, bass, keyboards, lead vocals), Will Butler (guitar, keyboards, bass, percussion).

Otherwise you go crazy. People don't go crazy in nice climates. Well, they do, but in a different way. That's for different bands to figure out. Also, Montreal is a cheap place to live, so you could play music and not

have too many money-making distractions in front of you. Not a lot of deadly choices to be made."

As the group started making music, they found that the more involved it got, the better it felt. And the more instruments they added, the better the songs became. Will Butler can't even describe the evolution that led to *Funeral*: "I actually don't know. That's just sort of how the music happened. The sound was maybe determined by the number of people in the band, and the number of people was determined by the number of grand people we knew who we wanted to make music with."

Six members signed their names in the liner notes of the album, and a further nine added strings, horns, a harp, and more drums. As with Broken Social Scene in Toronto, Arcade Fire gathered as large a support group as possible, making the band lineup hard to follow. Violin player and arranger Sarah Neufeld became a full-time member, Owen "Final Fantasy" Pallett did full string duty on *Funeral*, and Arlen Thompson of Wolf Parade joined the parade of players.

For many listeners, hearing strings and horns combined with energetic, pulsing guitar rock was a glorious discovery. Will Butler points out that it's not rare, it just depends on the decade: "Strings have been part of the equation since the dawn of music. Through the forties, sixties, eighties (well, synthetically), and today — the nineties, maybe not so much. A lot of songs sound good with strings and horns. If they didn't sound good, hopefully they wouldn't be there." That's downplaying the vision, though. These songs could have been bare-bones guitar tunes and the band could have been a quartet; it probably would have sounded pretty good, too — maybe a bit like early Talking Heads. Adding everything — the horns, the keyboards, the percussion, the sampled and synthesized sounds, the effects, and especially the strings — allows for intricate composition within the structure of the songs. It creates dramatic tension and wonderful dynamics. There are layers of activity at different volumes. A lot of songs do sound good with strings and horns, but not many of them sound this remarkable.

Arcade Fire were just a little band from an often-ignored city on the worldwide rock map. Well, it used to be ignored. Now, new bands, anglophone or francophone or bilingual, are taken a lot more seriously outside the country. The band set out to create music that would challenge themselves and their friends, and ended up making one of the most influential albums in Canadian music and becoming the most-talked-about band of the new millennium. Says Butler, "It's all been hilarious and surprising and wonderful. I don't want to say it was all dumb luck that people like this album so much, but we're certainly lucky. There are a lot of good albums that people don't praise. There are a lot of bad albums that people praise. We happened to make a good album that people have praised. It's all very mysterious. I'm very glad that people like what we do. I mean, I'd still be doing it if they didn't, but it makes life a lot easier. We made an album that we're very proud of — everything that results from that is a surprise and a bonus."

Andy Curran musician

Top Ten Canadian Hard-Rock/ Metal Albums

With his band Coney Hatch or on his solo work, Andy Curran knows how to pump up the volume to eleven. Four out of five doctors warn that just reading this list could result in permanent hearing loss.

"On behalf of the legions of Canadian heavy rock fans, I submit my Top Ten favourite hard-rock/metal albums of all time."

1. Rush
   2112

2. Sons Of Freedom
   Gump

3. Goddo
   Who Cares

4. Bachman-Turner Overdrive
   Not Fragile

5. Max Webster
   High Class In Borrowed Shoes

6. Pat Travers
   Makin' Magic

7. Neil Young
   Rust Never Sleeps

8. Frank Marino
   Juggernaut

9. Streetheart
   Meanwhile Back In Paris

10. Priestess
    Hello Master

9 Moving Pictures

Rush
Anthem, 1981

Tom Sawyer | Red Barchetta | YYZ | Limelight | The Camera Eye | Witch Hunt | Vital Signs

Record label execs and fans never know what to expect from Rush. The band never stand still, always learning, developing, adding instruments, changing their sound from album to album. There's no other band like them, and it's impossible to label their music over the scope of their career. Are they a power trio? Is it hard rock? Progressive rock? Synth rock? Every time Rush have been pigeonholed or written off, they've emerged with something new and fresh, thrilling old fans and making new ones.

The end of the 1970s found Rush going through another change. The group had become known for big ideas and long songs on the hit albums *2112* and *A Farewell To Kings*, but they were ready to think past side-long songs and sci-fi lyrics. Drummer Neil Peart has been the group's chief lyricist since he joined Rush for their second album: "I was experimenting with giant epics and myth building through [the mid-seventies], and then [the 1980 album] *Permanent Waves* was the turning point. It was our response to New Wave music. It suddenly got much more punchy and direct and simplified, and we went, yeah. When those bands came along — Talking Heads and The Police and Ultravox, Elvis Costello, and Joe Jackson, all these undeniable great talents — I was a music fan, and went, 'I like this, and more, I want

> Not only does this album blast Rush to international notoriety but it does this with a recipe most unlikely to make them a household name. Imagine a band today presenting *Moving Pictures* to a record label exec.
>
> — Gordie Johnson

this to become part of our music.' So we started with *Permanent Waves* to pare things down, and then by *Moving Pictures* we really drew all the threads together, we had a sense of our kind of concision. Which, in the case of 'Tom Sawyer', was between four and five minutes long, a big, long complex time-signature instrumental in the middle, drum solos — it's our version of conciseness in that I suppose it's four and a half minutes of bombast instead of twelve."

Guitarist Alex Lifeson and bass player/singer Geddy Lee were in equal step with the move to newfound tightness and simplicity. Peart remembers it as one of the group's most creative periods: "We were in such a great place at the time. We did all the songwriting at Ronnie Hawkins's farm near Peterborough, Ontario. And it was in the summertime, and we were all in a great space and experimenting more. The unity of the music on *Moving Pictures* really stands out in my mind, despite the big variety of music. 'YYZ', the instrumental, and then the moody 'The Camera Eye', the long piece on side two. Then 'Vital Signs', unabashedly New Wave, driven by the sequenced keyboards of the New Romantic bands of the time, like Ultravox, and the guitar chops right out of The Police, and yet I was playing drums from King Crimson and mixing in reggae."

The biggest surprise was that the airwaves now embraced Rush, bringing them, and Peart, to a brand-new, much bigger audience: "With 'Limelight' and 'Red Barchetta' being on the radio, I remember travelling around at that time and hearing these songs, and that was certainly the height of our popularity. Suddenly our concert attendances doubled that year, we were, like, the 'in band' of the year with that album. These are not radio songs, but they were that year."

The success of *Moving Pictures* was the big payoff for years of hard work and ups and downs. Rush routinely ignored advice to write radio-friendly songs, to stick to what was safe. Instead, they did exactly what they wanted with each album, feeling that musical integrity and growth were more important in the end. Still, Peart is amazed that sticking to ideals actually worked: "We got away with it. A lot of times, I can only think, how did we get away with it? How accidental so much of our progress was. Had Mercury in 1976 been a well-organized, modern multinational company, we would have been dumped. Had radio in 1980 suddenly not been friendly to complicated guitar rock music, we wouldn't have gone on the radio. It's astonishing. Certainly, we have gone through different albums since then that have been more or less successful, but the concerts remain a constant. People that didn't like our last album will still come to the show. That's an important thing — we really built our reputation the hard way, but it's the enduring way, too. We couldn't know we were doing the right thing. We tried to do the right thing but you never know. There were those pieces of luck of the most bizarre kind that allowed us to sneak through. I have no doubt that we got away with our kind of stubbornness, too. I see a lot of bands cave in to what the record company tells them to do, and it doesn't seem to work very well, that method."

Rush are in a position few bands from the seventies enjoy. They are revered for this and other albums, classic rock radio loves them, and their old records continue to sell well. They're still a viable recording and touring act, with each new disc, including 2007's *Snakes And Arrows*, promoted as an important release, not some vanity project of a band past their prime. Neil Peart recognizes the band's good fortune: "I'm grateful because I don't like touring very much, and we're about to launch a major tour. I just had a reality check when I was looking at the *LA Weekly*, and they had a full-page ad for our shows coming up there, American Express, advance tickets, blah blah blah. And then way in the back there are bands like Asia, Toto, and they're playing at these little clubs in the valley that I've never even heard of. At least I'm pretty

Rush (left to right): Neil Peart (drums), Geddy Lee (bass, keyboards, vocals), Alex Lifeson (guitar)

glad I have the choice to go out and do a major rock tour and travel in a comfortable bus and ride my motorcycle every day and make the best of it."

Peart still likes to mix in old fan favourites, even though they've had plenty of hit albums: "Nothing like *Moving Pictures*, though. We were a cultural phenomenon to young people in the US and Canada. And I know by listening to classic rock stations in Los Angeles, where I live, the songs you're most likely to hear are 'Tom Sawyer' and 'Limelight'. Those are

definitely the mainstays [of live shows] because they are for the audience. That's the kind of good resonance of popularity, I guess. You have that enduring soundtrack of somebody's life. I have to say it's an important thing to me that twenty-five years later I still enjoy playing it. 'Tom Sawyer' is still one of the hardest songs in the world for me to play. If I can play it right night after night, that's perfectly okay. You can never get bored with that kind of material."

AMERICAN WOMAN · THE GUESS WHO

10 American Woman

The Guess Who
RCA, 1970

American Woman | No Time | Talisman | No Sugar Tonight/New Mother Nature | 969 (The Oldest Man) | When Friends Fall Out | 8:15 | Proper Stranger | Humpty's Blues/American Woman (Epilogue)

Happy accidents had followed The Guess Who their entire career. A smart record company person had released their 1965 single "Shakin' All Over" without the group's name on it, to tease people into thinking this was the newest hot British Invasion band. Instead, he put "Guess Who?" on the label, giving them a new name and their first hit. A TV producer let them play an original song, "These Eyes", on a national broadcast, which led to fame and fortune in the US and Canada. And, in 1969, Randy Bachman broke a string at just the right moment: "We got a gig in Canada, in Kitchener-Waterloo, at a curling rink. Typical Canadian dance: throw some plywood sheets down on the ice, book a band, and have a dance. In the middle of a set, I broke a guitar string. We took a break while I changed the string. When tuning up with the new string, I started to play that opening riff. The rest of the band eventually came on stage and we jammed the riff. Burton made up the lyrics on the spot. The song was born. A short while later, we recorded it and it became the number one single in 1970." Such was the birth of "American Woman".

After toying with all types of music on their first two albums, The Guess Who now had a distinctive rock and roll sound, powered by Bachman's signature Les Paul guitar riffs. They'd fought against being labelled a ballad group after being persuaded that the soft "These Eyes" and "Laughing" should be their first hits. Now they could release the rock they'd wanted to perform the past two years. "American Woman"

> The Guess Who's music should last forever. Arguably the best Canadian band of all time.
>
> — Ian Scott, music writer

had done it, and it was a complete surprise to the band and Bachman: "We had no idea what we had created. But we did know that we had found our sound, our place in the musical template of the time. The rest just sometimes happens, and you're so glad to feel it evolving and finally seeing the dream come true."

"American Woman" captured the top of the charts, and catapulted The Guess Who into rock royalty's

The Guess Who (left to right, standing): Burton Cummings (vocals, piano), Randy Bachman (guitar, vocals). (left to right, seated): Jim Kale (bass, vocals), Garry Peterson (drums, vocals).

highest circles. For years, they had idolized, memorized, and copied The Beatles; now, they'd knocked "Let It Be" off number one and overtaken the world's biggest band. "That year, we sold more records, albums and singles, than anybody," says Cummings. "I've heard that many, many times, so I'm starting to believe it's true. But I don't know how you'd actually authenticate that."

One song does not a classic album make, but *American Woman* is full of hits and other great tracks. Side one alone is among the greatest in rock history, with three bona fide classics in the title cut, "No Time", and "No Sugar Tonight/New Mother Nature". The last one was another happy accident involving the Bachman-Cummings writing team. Bachman remembers, "I had written 'No Sugar Tonight' but it was an incomplete song and needed a bridge or middle eight [bars]. Burton had written 'New Mother Nature', which needed the same. At the time The Beatles had two songs in one with 'A Day In The Life'. Since both our songs were in the same key, we tried to put them together. They not only worked back to back but they also worked overlapping them one over the other at the end."

Cummings says, "For some strange reason they were both in F-sharp, which is a brutal key on piano — it's all black notes, it's very difficult. We just squashed the two together and it worked. We were pretty good at putting pieces together. We joke about it on stage, when we do 'These Eyes'. He [Bachman] says one of my great talents is writing half a song, and Burton is great at writing half a song." However, radio doesn't like two songs in one, so for the hit single of "No Sugar Tonight", the "New Mother Nature" part was edited out, "which broke my heart at the time," says Cummings.

"No Time" was the second released version of the song, having first appeared on *Canned Wheat*. But Cummings says the band were horrified with the album's sound: "We had re-done 'No Time' because the one on *Canned Wheat* was far too long and it wasn't sonically as good. We were forced to do it in the old, ancient RCA Studios where Bing Crosby had recorded, and it was just antiquated. It was one of those corporate things contractually we had to do."

It had been a long road to the top for Randy Bachman. He'd joined Chad Allan and The Silvertones in 1961 and worked non-stop to do the impossible: take a regional Canadian band to the top. His drive, integrity, and business skills had made him the leader of the group, and with the help of some timely accidents and worthy advice, he reached his goal and celebrated — by leaving. "I'd been with The Guess Who since the early sixties. We grew together and then we grew apart. At the time I had a serious gall bladder problem, which was the most painful experience of my life. I needed medical attention and time off. We had hit number one and the band had to keep going."

There were other issues, too. Says Cummings, "Things weren't going great, Randy was very religious at that time. He had joined the Mormon Church and he had some kids and he wasn't partying, you know, and [bassist Jim] Kale and I were partying — we were into the rock and roll pretty heavy. And [drummer Garry] Peterson was somewhere in between. It worked for a while, but then Randy — he had health problems and issues with our lifestyle. It just came to an end in 1970. It was bizarre, of all the times, when we were on top of the world."

That left Randy Bachman back at the start again, while his old band kept going: "Yes, I felt I missed out on a lot of the glory and money from many years of hard work. But had I not left at that time, there would have been no chapter two of my rock story and no Bachman-Turner Overdrive. In a way, it was branching out or franchising the Canadian rock sound without realizing it. It seemed, and was, insane at the time but now it seems cool. Only because BTO worked. If it hadn't, who knows where I'd be today. It took four or five years of hard work but I did finally reach number one [on the] album and singles charts with BTO." Without its leader, some felt The Guess Who would soon fail. Burton Cummings, however, was not one of them.

George Canyon's Top Ten Canadian Albums

Hey, don't let that cowboy hat fool you. Canada's favourite country idol has a yen for rock and roll, too. The pride of Pictou County, Nova Scotia, he shows a soft spot for some Maritimers here, but he's also caught on to Western vibe, too, now that he's ranching it in Alberta. He doesn't just like country, he likes THE country.

1. Bryan Adams
   Reckless: "Timeless. I have it permanently on my iPod. Some of Jim Vallance's and Bryan Adams's best songs are on this album."

2. Stan Rogers
   Home In Halifax: "This album helped shape me as a writer — I go back to it all the time."

3. Nickelback
   Silver Side Up: "Solid album, great to work out to."

4. Dave Gunning
   Two Bit World: "One of the best storytellers Canada has, and he can sing, to boot!"

5. John Allan Cameron
   Free Born Man: "This one needs no explanation."

6. Ian Tyson
   Cowboyography: "A classic Canadian cowboy album."

7. Ron Hynes
   Cryer's Paradise: "Ron is one of the best songwriters in the world."

8. Blue Rodeo
   Five Days In July: "I've been a fan of Blue Rodeo's for years, plus Jim Cuddy is a hockey buddy of mine."

9. Michael Bublé
   Michael Bublé: "Love it! You can hear Connick and Darin in there."

10. The Cruzeros
    El Nino: "Barry and Curtis are always true to their music."

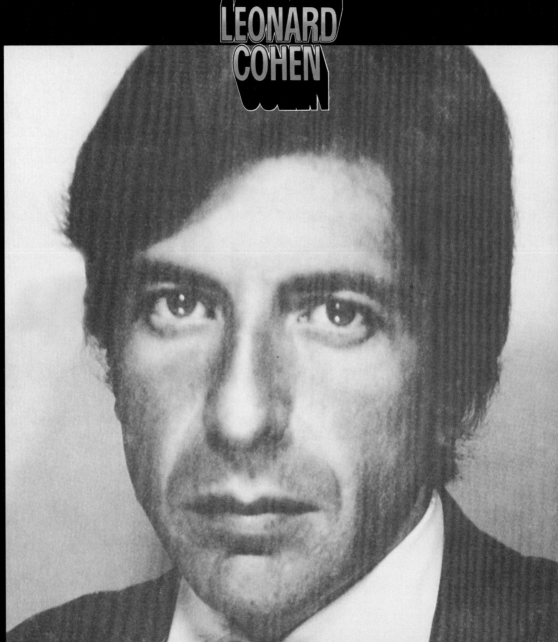

11 Songs Of Leonard Cohen

Leonard Cohen
Columbia, 1967

Suzanne | Master Song | Winter Lady | The Stranger Song | Sisters Of Mercy | So Long, Marianne | Hey, That's No Way To Say Goodbye | Stories Of The Street | Teachers | One Of Us Cannot Be Wrong

Leonard Cohen was a famous Canadian poet and novelist in the 1960s. In literature, he was a star. Now he was going to do something radical with his writing — he was going to become a pop star.

It was a basic need. "Financial," he confirms. In the 1960s, he wasn't making money: "No, I wasn't, not as a writer, not at all. I published my first book of poetry, *Let Us Compare Mythologies* [1956], and it sold a few hundred copies. Then I published *The Spice-Box Of Earth*, and that didn't sell at all. [The 1966 novel] *Beautiful Losers*, it was panned. It sold maybe three thousand copies worldwide."

Cohen didn't have a professional career on which to fall back. All he'd done before was play in a little country and western combo in Montreal called The Buckskin Boys. "When I discovered I couldn't make a living as a writer, I naturally returned to the other thing I could do."

Cohen had missed the whole folk boom: "I didn't know too much about it. I was living in Greece and listening to the Armed Forces radio, which was mostly country music, which I always loved. So when I came back to Canada, I figured I'd try to go down to Nashville — I was going through New York, and that's where I came across the so-called folk song renaissance. I bumped into Judy Collins and I found out what was going on. So I thought I'd try my hand at it. I played her a couple of songs that I had. She didn't like them very much. She said, if you have any other songs, give me a call. So I went back to Montreal and started writing, and I wrote 'Suzanne'. I played it for a couple of friends, and they said it sounds like everything else. I phoned Judy Collins up and I played it for her over the phone, and she liked it and eventually recorded it."

More singers would cover his material, with praise for "Sisters Of Mercy", "So Long, Marianne", and "Suzanne". Cohen had achieved his goal: "It was very positive. I don't want to keep harping on this, but that was foremost on my mind, to survive, and if the album did well, I could make a living from it."

It's now been forty years since Cohen recorded this album, and the songs have not just lasted but grown in reputation: "I think they stand up pretty well. People are still singing them, they're doing cover versions. As I've often said, if I knew where those songs come from, I'd go there more often."

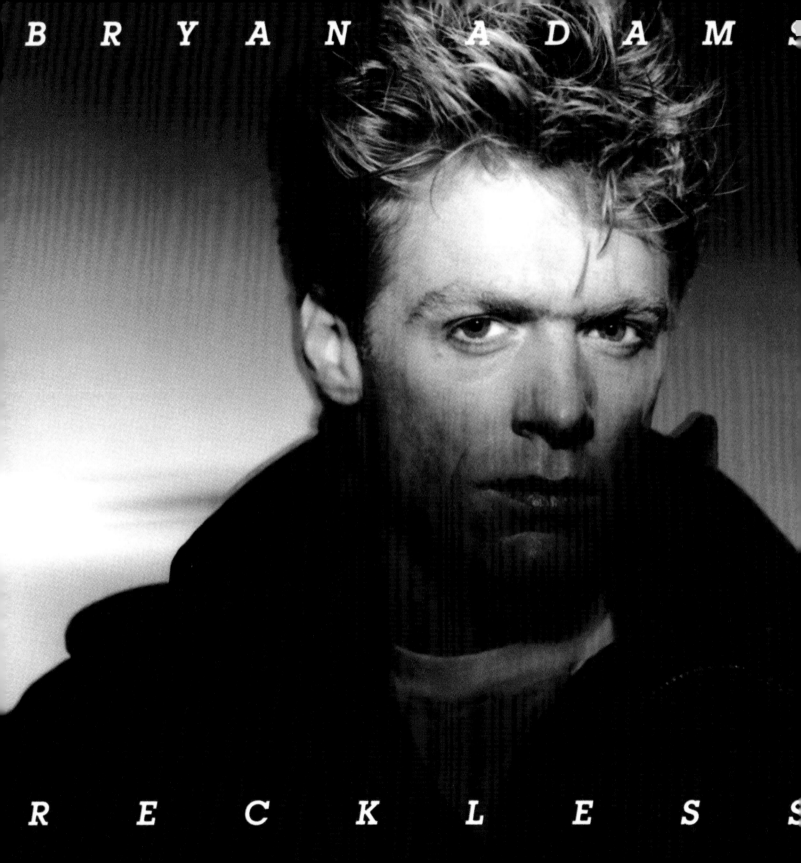

12 Reckless

Bryan Adams
A&M, 1984

One Night Love Affair | She's Only Happy When She's Dancin' | Run To You | Heaven |
Somebody | Summer Of '69 | Kids Wanna Rock | It's Only Love | Long Gone | Ain't Gonna Cry

It was a glorious time for the music industry. Multi-platinum artists were exploding, with Michael Jackson's year-old *Thriller* the biggest-selling album in history, Prince's *Purple Rain* a surprising and massive hit maker, and Bruce Springsteen topping charts with *Born In The USA*. Each of these big sellers had something in common: they boasted several huge singles — seven in Springsteen's case — that kept the albums on the charts for months, even years. At the end of 1984, a Canadian artist fully aware of the power of singles was ready to join this multi-platinum, world-conquering club.

Bryan Adams's writing partner since the start of his solo career had been Jim Vallance. The two were inseparable: there aren't many examples of co-writers receiving nearly equal billing with the boss. Adams and Vallance were the Elton John and Bernie Taupin of the eighties. Vallance says they certainly knew the goal they

Big sound! Great hooks! Identifiable lyrics! Who can't relate to the anthemic "Summer Of '69" in some way? It made you want to go get your first guitar.

— JD Moffat, Bayshore Broadcasting

were aiming for: "In the eighties there were only two ways to measure a song's success: sales and airplay. If you weren't selling records or you weren't on the radio, then you hadn't arrived."

Adams and Vallance wanted radio hits, and nothing else would do. "When we were writing," Vallance says, "Bryan and I tried to picture what might work on the radio, and then we'd fill in the gaps. We always tried to write something that sounded like it belonged on the radio or on a record. If you're writing for radio, you're trying to write anthems. That's what "hit" songs are — anthems. Just because you try doesn't mean you're going to succeed, but that's often what we were trying to achieve, quite unashamedly."

Of the ten songs on *Reckless*, six became hits. The darker "Run To You" was first, cementing Adams's leather-jacket-rock image. "Somebody" was a singalong, filled with memorable hooks. Then came "Heaven", the number one hit love ballad. It was the next single, though, that put them over the top and that remains Jim Vallance's favourite: "Our early writing was formative, and our later material was overwrought. Right in the middle, I think that's where we peaked as a songwriting team. 'Summer Of '69', that was Bryan and me at our best. I think the songs were simple and anthemic." Although it's not even their biggest hit, as a piece of pop perfection nothing else has topped the "Summer Of '69", from the summer of '85.

FIVE DAYS IN JULY

13 Five Days In July

Blue Rodeo
Warner, 1993

Five Days In May | Hasn't Hit Me Yet | Bad Timing | Cynthia | Photograph | What Is This Love | English Bay | Head Over Heels | Till I Gain Control Again | Dark Angel | Know Where You Go/Tell Me Your Dream

Blue Rodeo (left to right): Jim Cuddy (guitar,vocals), Bazil Donovan (bass), Glenn Milchem (drums), Greg Keelor (guitar,vocals), Kim Deschamps (pedal steel guitar), James Gray (keyboards)

It really was created in five days in July. Blue Rodeo packed up their gear, moved out to Greg Keelor's farm, and made the album of their career. "We just set up in the living room of my house, moved all the furniture out on the lawn, and five days is what it took," says songwriter and vocalist Keelor, sharing these duties with long-time friend Jim Cuddy.

The idea of moving out of the studio had its roots way back after Blue Rodeo's first album, 1987's *Outskirts*, when the experience hadn't gone to Keelor's satisfaction: "We were disillusioned with the process of making *Outskirts*. We were happy with the success, but we didn't love the sound of it — it was a little too eighties. It wasn't exactly how we heard the band."

Keelor got some important advice from famed producer Daniel Lanois: "I was telling him we didn't like the process, we didn't like the studio,

the engineers were bugging us. He said 'you don't have to do that, you can just go anywhere and get gear there'. That was a revelation, we hadn't thought of that."

The album featured Blue Rodeo's latest lineup shuffle. Mainstay Bazil Donovan still held down bass, but now the group included Kim Deschamps on pedal steel, James Gray on keyboards, and Glenn Milchem on drums. "It was a crazy time. We did a tour of Australia that winter and spring. The band, for lack of a better thing to do, would sit around and play music all the time. We had all these new songs, there were new members, and the pot was really great in Australia. *Five Days* is a very pot record. We would just get stoned and play and play and play and play. When we got back to Canada, we knew all these songs inside and out. We knew them inside and out and stoned."

The vibe at the farmhouse hits

at the core of the Cuddy-Keelor partnership. It goes back to the reason Greg Keelor wanted to write songs in the first place, and to do it with Cuddy: "I was greatly inspired by Jim and his friends. We were all out in Lake Louise one summer, and everyone would sit around and play guitars and get high and sing. It just seemed like the greatest thing in the world to me, so I wanted to be part of that. [*Five Days*] is the most acoustic record we have, and it's a good group of songs. Every song holds up on its own. They're all fun songs to play, fun songs to sing."

14 Twice Removed

Sloan
Geffen, 1994

Penpals | I Hate My Generation | People Of The Sky | Coax Me | Bells On | Loosens | Worried Now | Shame Shame | Deeper Than Beauty | Snowsuit Sound | Before I Do | I Can Feel It

Sloan (left to right): Chris Murphy, Jay Ferguson, Andrew Scott, Patrick Pentland

Sloan started in Halifax in the heyday of Grunge. The band's first album, *Smeared,* sold well enough that Geffen Records offered big money for another. Everyone expected another noisy album. The band, however, had already cooled on that. "We were really conscious of being of the time, and I think we wanted to go from being on the caboose of the Grunge scene," says bass player Chris Murphy. "We thought it was over, and we wanted to get off the train before it crashed."

The album headed in a new direction. Big production numbers, such as guitarist Jay Ferguson's "Snowsuit Sound", reference sixties' tracks. Patrick Pentland contributes the gentle "I Can Feel It". Drummer Andrew Scott's "People Of The Sky", has ba-ba-ba-da-ba backing vocals and big bright guitars.

So what happened between *Smeared* and *Twice Removed*? "Part of it is money," Murphy believes. "Twelve

hundred dollars versus a hundred and twenty thousand. And the music we were listening to at the time, [John Lennon's] *Plastic Ono Band*, and the Lindsay Buckingham era of Fleetwood Mac. We just thought that was cool. It really wasn't in vogue at the time. Everyone was going, was this record made in 1980 or 1990 or 1965? We really felt *Smeared* was made in 1991 and there was no getting around it."

Now it was time to present it to Geffen. Murphy acknowledges, "I was terrified. I was having a bird. When [Geffen] heard it, they were like, 'oh man, this is a totally different band, you're making it really tough for us to market you.' I never thought of anybody being the bad guy or the man or the corporate anything. We just made it really difficult for them to do their job. They definitely said, 'we're not going to promote this, you should do some re-recording.' I was the biggest chicken. I probably would have

said, ya, I'll do whatever you want. We're happy just to be here, I just couldn't believe we were on Geffen. But, as a band, we just stuck to our guns. And then Geffen really stuck to their word and didn't promote it."

Things went better in Canada. College stations and the alternative press embraced the album, and MuchMusic took a liking to the band, especially the openness and humour Murphy and Ferguson offered in interviews. Rather than underground, Sloan and *Twice Removed* were given underdog status.

One other little detail complicated matters. "I think it also got a lot of accolades because right around that time we broke the band up. So I think a lot of people liked it almost as an 'Aw, what a drag they broke up, and this record is so good'."

15 Up To Here

The Tragically Hip
MCA, 1989

Blow At High Dough | I'll Believe In You (Or I'll Be Leaving You
Tonight) | New Orleans Is Sinking | 38 Years Old | She Didn't Know |
Boots Or Hearts | Everytime You Go | When The Weight Comes Down |
Trickle Down | Another Midnight | Opiated

ADMIT ONE WITH THIS INVITATION
ROCK 'N' ROLL THAT
SHOOTS FROM THE HIP.
THE TRAGICALLY HIP
LIVE IN CONCERT

DATE: _____
TIME: _____
VENUE: *MISTY MOON*

EXPERIENCE ROCK 'N' ROLL
THE WAY IT'S SUPPOSED TO BE
AS **THE TRAGICALLY HIP** SHOWCASE
THEIR DYNAMIC MCA RECORDING
up to here

With a massive fan following and a penchant for writing songs with historical or geographical Canadian references, The Tragically Hip made it cool again for rock bands to be Canadian. How ironic, then, that Canada's favourite band couldn't work out a record deal with a Canadian company but signed instead with a big US label. "We'd been demo'ing for Capitol Records," says guitar player Rob Baker. "We thought we'd been demo'd to death. By this point, this had been going on for the better part of a year. I think they were thinking we needed a songwriter, a guaranteed Top Forty hitmaker, and we weren't ever going to bow to that."

Luckily, a rep from MCA Records in Los Angeles heard them at the Horseshoe in Toronto and offered them a deal on the spot. "Our A&R guy, Bruce Dickenson, had a very sympathetic approach," says Baker. "This guy said, 'you're going to develop as a band, develop your own sound, and three, four, five albums in, you'll achieve critical mass.' He was very protective of us. I don't think those guys exist anymore."

Some musicians can't remember how they wrote particular songs, or even what album they're on. Rob Baker, however, can remember the exact moment of creation for most of *Up To Here*: "My parents had gone away for a week, probably to a judges' convention or something, and we set up in their living room. We got 'Blow At High Dough', it was one that just poured out. I think it was done, lyrics and all, in about ten or fifteen minutes. 'Boots Or Hearts' came out of the same session."

Another jam provided the first big hit of The Hip's career, "New Orleans Is Sinking": "We were jamming to [the sixties' hit] 'Shakin' All Over'," remembers Baker. "We would take a song and twist it around, we'd do that as a regular course, just stretch things out, play with the riff, elongate it, shorten it, flip it backwards. Suddenly, Paul just started playing the lower line and I started doing the fiddly guitar bit up above it. We thought, that's good, that's a keeper."

Rock fans will remember that "Shakin' All Over" had once inspired The Guess Who, whose 1965 cover was their first hit. The Guess Who were the first Canadian rock group to stay home and make it big, to write about Canadian places, to fly the flag proudly. Such displays had been out of favour for a long time, but The Tragically Hip were going to do it again.

STEREO

6349

NEIL YOUNG
WITH CRAZY HORSE
EVERYBODY KNOWS
THIS IS NOWHERE

16 Everybody Knows This Is Nowhere

Neil Young with Crazy Horse
Reprise, 1969

Cinnamon Girl | Everybody Knows This Is Nowhere | Round & Round (It Won't Be Long) | Down By The River |
The Losing End (When You're On) | Running Dry (Requiem For the Rockets) | Cowgirl In The Sand

> Young's breakthrough album; a sound and image that defined him for decades.
>
> — John Einarson, Neil Young biographer

Neil Young wanted to be in a band, but he wanted to be a leader too. After Buffalo Springfield's bust-up and his first solo album, Young went out and found a new band he could lead. He took the core of The Rockets and renamed them Crazy Horse.

This time, there was no disputing who was in charge. Young was already a recording artist, if not yet a star. He had lots of material, and would serve as singer and lead guitar player. The new Crazy Horse featured Danny Whitten on guitar, Billy Talbot on bass, and Ralph Molina on drums. They were not flashy players or particularly subtle. They played rock and roll, either fast or slow, and they played loud. That's all Young would need.

Free from competition within his own band, Young could now do all the electric guitar playing he wanted. His response was to turn up the volume and play a lot. *Everybody Knows This Is Nowhere* is dominated by two lengthy tracks: "Down By The River", at 9:13, ends side one, and "Cowgirl In The Sand", covering just over ten minutes, finishes side two.

Neil Young's guitar playing doesn't impress you with speed or the intricate lines that show an advanced musical ear. What Young does give you is feeling: raw emotion, mixed with volume. If he plays a chord, he will crunch it. If he reaches up the frets for a high note, it will shriek. If it shrieks well, he'll keep doing it. The songs might have only three chords and his solos only three notes, but he makes the best of them. Those notes never knew they had it in them.

Listen to the riff in "Cinnamon Girl": it's probably his most memorable electric opening and one of his most popular songs. There's so much electricity pouring through the strings it sounds like he's playing a hydro poll. The guitar is the star here.

The impact of this album would be enormous for Young. The trio of big songs ("Cinnamon", "Cowgirl", and "River") formed the core of his electric set for years. When he returned to this music, he'd invariably try to conjure up that kind of writing. You can hear it in "Cortez The Killer", "Like A Hurricane", "Rockin' In The Free World". With his plaid shirts and stringy hair, Young set the standard for the noisy slacker groups that became known as Grunge bands. A tour and album in the nineties with Pearl Jam saw Young fulfill his destiny and become known as the Godfather of Grunge. It started here.

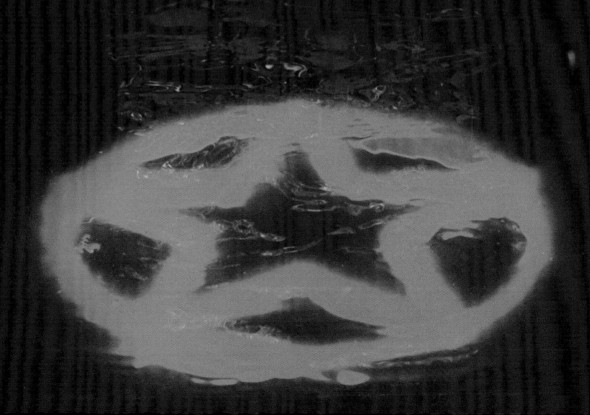

17 2112

Rush
Mercury, 1976

2112 | A Passage To Bangkok | The Twilight Zone | Lessons | Tears | Something For Nothing

I wore out the grooves on my vinyl copy of *2112*, falling asleep with my headphones on as a teenager. I played bass along to that album a thousand times in my bedroom. I had great parents!

— Andy Curran

There was a time when Rush were unpopular. Sighs Neil Peart, "*2112* was coming out of the darkest possible period of our career. We were touring small clubs and doing meagre opening shots, and even at the time we called it among the band and crew the 'Down the Tubes' tour. That summer of '75 we were unable to pay the crew salaries and our salaries. That winter of '75-'76, when we were just starting to work on *2112*, I remember I didn't have a car running. I was sleeping on a friend's coach when we were recording it. I was thinking about a return to the farm-equipment business with my dad to be a likely reality."

Things were so bad the group were officially considered a lost cause by their own record label: "We were with Mercury Records then, and they completely wrote us off of their next year's financial predictions. We did not even appear. We were truly written off."

"We were getting a lot of pressure from the business side to be more commercial and write some singles, and 'if things don't turn around, we're going to have to talk about material' and all of that. I was always a big contrarian, and grew up in all the beautiful purity and experimentation of the music of the sixties. I still hold that to be the highest ideal, music for music's sake, and I still don't brook any interference with it. We turned all of that rebellion and anger and frustration into the music, it seems. *2112* speaks not only literally a story of the individual against a faceless mask but it's also what we were facing. We were so tired of this interference that we thought, okay, we're going to stand up for what we believe in and fall trying. So I really believe all of that communicates itself through the music."

Instead of co-operating with a three-minute single, Peart wrote "a side-long opening piece and a couple of other weird songs." The A-side was the epic cut "2112". Peart was and is an extremely well read man, and the author of several books. "As I was putting together the futuristic dystopia and the individual rediscovering music in the machine age, I eventually went, hey, wait a minute, this is awfully like Ayn Rand's *Anthem*. So, realizing that was the case, I went, okay, I'll just give credit to it. But I had no intention of adapting that story directly. The story was born out of a different inspiration, but obviously subconsciously [it was *Anthem*]."

Rush gave Mercury Records exactly what they wanted, a huge hit album, by completely ignoring what Mercury told them to do. Corporations would no longer question Rush's music and motives. They'd learn those were among the few things they could count on for their financial predictions.

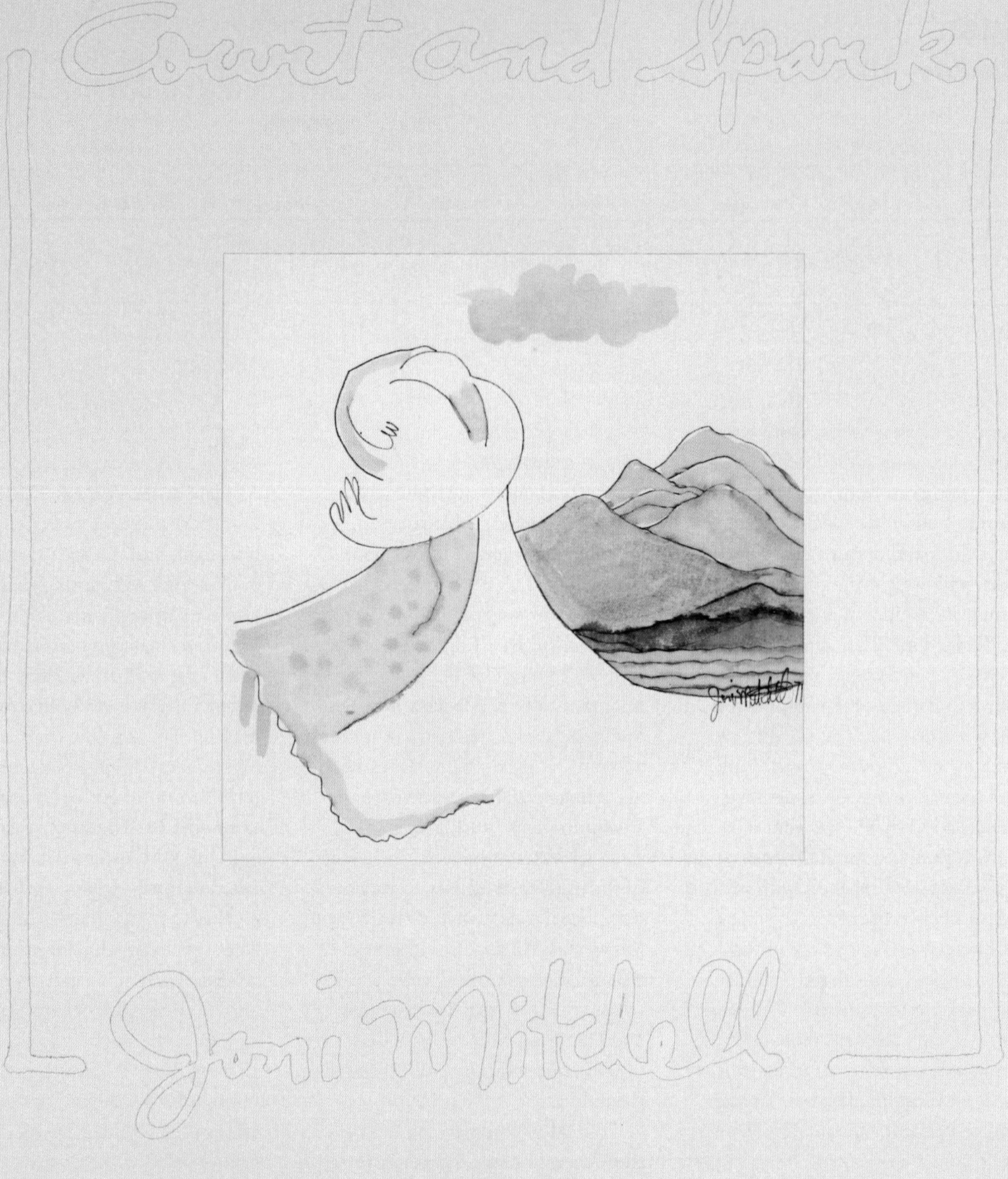
Court and Spark
Joni Mitchell

18 Court And Spark

Joni Mitchell

Asylum, 1974

Court And Spark | Help Me | Free Man In Paris | People's Parties | Same Situation | Car On A Hill | Down To You | Just Like This Train | Raised On Robbery | Trouble Child | Twisted

Court And Spark was a landmark album. "Help Me", "Free Man In Paris", and "Raised On Robbery" proved conclusively that this woman can rock with the best of them.

— John Biggs, CHAM

Blue made Joni Mitchell one of the biggest stars of the confessional singer-songwriter era. But *Court And Spark* saw her jump headfirst into a full band sound, and the public leapt with her. Mitchell hooked up with session group The LA Express, who played a lighter style of jazz-fusion, and they were an inspired choice: Mitchell's non-standard guitar tunings created music much more complicated than basic three-chord rock, so it would take sympathetic players used to experimentation to deliver her music.

"Help Me", which introduced her new sound to the airwaves, was an immediate smash and her first (and only) Top Ten hit. It teases by starting with her acoustic, but quickly the smooth band joins in. Her vocals soar over several notes right off the bat, on top of a bed of electric piano. Larry Carlton adds tasty lead guitar lines that are definitely jazz licks, and a subtle horn section punches home the

end of the chorus and then drives the bridge. It was a triumphant production, sophisticated yet catchy.

Then came another hit, and by now it was obvious the singer-songwriter days were done. Written from the viewpoint of a friend — the story goes it's her manager, David Geffen — "Free Man In Paris" captures the friend's feelings of release from all his headaches so well that one line has been widely quoted since to characterize the music industry and the star-maker machinery that Geffen helped create. Another intricate production, Mitchell's acoustic is doubled by Tom Scott's beautifully arranged and played reeds, on a sound possibly invented here. Instead of going to verse two after the chorus, the norm for a pop or folk song, they leave a full section where the guitars can hold a little duel. Here, Carlton is joined

by none other than José Feliciano. Only Steely Dan were doing anything similar.

Now she was finally ready to let loose, with both rock and roll and humour. "Raised On Robbery" cooks along, a great sixties'-style rocker some hot band, maybe Ronnie Hawkins and The Hawks, could've dreamed up. In fact, Robbie Robertson himself provides the ripping guitar, playing it as he did back in the day. Scott blasts a r'n'b sax solo, and Mitchell has a great time with the tall tale of a couple of barflies.

Court And Spark closes on an even bigger piece of fun. Displaying some serious vocal chops on a cover of the Lambert, Hendricks, and Ross tune "Twisted", Mitchell introduces a whole new generation to jazz vocal stylings. Everybody loved the new jazzy Joni.

19 Whale Music

Rheostatics
Sire, 1992

Self Serve Gas Station | California Dreamline | Rain, Rain, Rain | Queer | King Of The Past | RDA (Rock Death America) | The Headless One | Legal Age Life At Variety Store | What's Going On Around Here? | Shaved Head | Palomar | Guns | Sickening Song | Soul Glue | Beerbash | Who? | Dope Fiends And Boozehounds

Rheostatics (left to right): Tim Vesely (bass), Dave Bidini (guitar), Michael Phillip-Wojewoda (drums, producer *Whale Music*), Martin Tielli (guitar)

When Rheostatics played their retirement show on March 30, 2007, at Toronto's Massey Hall, the set list included many of the songs on what's regarded as the group's masterpiece, *Whale Music*. For good reason, according to guitar player and songwriter Dave Bidini: "It's hard to go wrong with really any song on that record. We all have a lot invested in them, we're all pretty committed, and we know they're all good, I suppose."

The title was borrowed from a book by Paul Quarrington. The album doesn't follow the text but the spirit does, says Bidini: "We named that album at the last moment. I'd read the book, loved it. I guess the character in the book, Desmond, had these ideas, huge musical ideas that can't possibly be realized. We kind of considered what we'd done on our record similar to the delusions of grandeur, I suppose. It was a great Canadian book that might have been a little overlooked, although I suppose it did win the Governor General's Award. So we asked Paul if we could use it."

It's easy to see why the book struck home with Bidini: "Desmond was in the studio in the late hours, concocting strange musical creations, and a lot of *Whale Music* was recorded the same way, with really no sleep, just around the clock. Lots of songs, big songs, lots of added stuff, lots of strings, keyboards, the kitchen sink, really."

Instead of a collection of individual songs, Bidini says there is an underlying theme to the track sequencing: "We thought it would be good to glue them together in terms of segues, so the album would have a fairly strong flow right from the top. All the songs were these little mini-journeys of themselves anyways, so we thought we could combine them into a greater journey. It really was easy in terms of sewing it all together with one continuing song, one continuous journey, stopping off at the least little places along the way."

As they headed to new projects in 2007, the group decided they needed

> I was torn between this and *Melville*, but these guys had to be on the list somewhere.
>
> — John Wiles, CKBW

a good last-night blast. Out came the *Whale Music* songs and many others that were simply fun to play. Bidini says it felt right, "instead of just being another gig. Not a lot of bands have last performances. We thought it was another way of doing it our own way, a statement, I suppose. I think everybody would love to be able to plan and attend their own funeral."

DANIEL

LANOIS

ACADIE

20 Acadie

Daniel Lanois
Opal, 1989

Still Water | The Maker | O Marie | Jolie Louise |
Fisherman's Daughter | White Mustang II | Under A
Stormy Sky | Where The Hawkwind Kills | Silium's
Hill | Ice | St. Ann's Gold | Amazing Grace

"Daniel, before you go on, Bob's going to introduce you," said the organizer at the 2007 Hamilton Music Awards. "What, Dylan's here?" answered Daniel Lanois, perhaps not joking. Alas, his friend Dylan was not in the house; the Bob in question was just me, in my role as MC that night. Lanois was back in his hometown to unveil his documentary, *This Is What Is*, a remarkable film about the creative process featuring Garth Hudson of The Band, Brian Eno, and U2.

Lanois has worked with some of the best musical minds in the world, including Dylan, Emmylou Harris, Willie Nelson, Peter Gabriel, Robbie Robertson, and even Raffi. That was when he started out producing, first in the studio he set up in his mother's basement along with his brother Bob and then at their Grant Avenue Studios. That work caught the ear of Eno, who was developing his trademark ambient sound, and chose Daniel as his partner.

In 1984, the team masterminded U2's *The Unforgettable Fire*, cementing Lanois's reputation.

Lanois had another project percolating: his own album. "I waited for the right kind of invitation," he says. "Eno's wife, Anthea Norman Taylor, presented me with an invitation and an opportunity to make *Acadie* the way I wanted to make it. At that time, I felt a poetic freedom within, and as the stars all seemed to align, I took it as a sign my stories were ripe and ready for harvest. I trusted my association with Eno and Anthea, it seemed natural, it seemed like the opposite end of the spectrum from force-fed record company manoeuvring."

Even though this was his debut album, he'd picked up valuable pointers from the world's best. "I learned about timing and confidence. Live life long enough to tell a story." Lanois had stories the pop world hadn't heard before. Born in Quebec and raised in Hamilton, he filled *Acadie* with Canadian stories, sung in both French and English, with themes of heritage, nature, and family. "What lives in your backyard might be most interesting once you leave it," he says, by then equally at home in New Orleans or Ireland. "My storytelling songs were about real experience. My experience was from two different languages. I also felt that this mixture was a fresh angle at songwriting."

His album stands equal to the work of the international stars he's worked with. "Nineteen years later, I can stand outside myself and feel the commitment in *Acadie*," he says. "A naive feeling running in tandem with commitment should override the sell-by date."

21 Day For Night

The Tragically Hip
MCA, 1994

Grace, Too | Daredevil | Greasy Jungle | Yawning Or Snarling | Fire In The Hole | So Hard Done By | Nautical Disaster | Thugs | Inevitability Of Death | Scared | An Inch An Hour | Emergency | Titanic Terrarium | Impossibilium

The Tragically Hip (left to right): Rob Baker (guitar), Gord Downie (vocals), Paul Langlois (guitar), Johnny Fay (drums), and Gord Sinclair (bass)

> After an EP and three spectacular albums, The Hip hit their high water mark. Hypnotic throughout, it was a showcase for a band in full control of their awesome power.
>
> — Ronan O'Leary, writer

Ever wondered why there are no individual writing credits on The Tragically Hip's albums? It's well known that Gord Downie writes the words, but you'll find only a simple mention that all songs are written by The Tragically Hip.

It goes back to a decision the band made at the start. Rob Baker: "We had a little meeting, and, in the interest of band longevity, we decided to go with a band songwriting credit. We envisioned trouble if one guy wrote a single and had a little pop hit and got all the royalties. It's a big problem when one guy writes all the songs and takes all the credit, and he doesn't need to tour to make a living and the others do. We were all students of rock, and we saw what happened when one guy has all the credit. So we formed a songwriting collective — I think it's one of the wisest things we ever did. We're all still here [all these] years later."

Hard feelings could still result if one member did much more than his share of the work. So, for *Day For Night*, the group decided to eliminate that possibility as well: "You'd have an hour-long jam, and when you were done you'd listen for a little bit that sounded like it was something. You'd say, here's three or four minutes where we really lock in on a good riff, let's work on it. They truly were written by the five or us. Gord would be coming up with the threads of words, lyrics, melody, and trying to expand that as we went along."

Coming off the huge reception for *Fully Completely*, the band were ready to stretch. They turned to a fellow Canadian, Daniel Lanois, who had a studio in New Orleans. But there was one problem. "We were

in the French Quarter and they had neighbours, and you couldn't wind out late at night," says Baker. Instead of abandoning nighttime recording, the group came up with a solution that created a different feel for the whole album: when it got dark, they switched their entire instrument setup, day for night. "With the day setup, we'd rock. At night, we'd work on more acoustic things. We had a different drum setup. And we'd play primarily acoustic guitars. We'd explore something different, some quieter songs."

Despite these changes, the band were as popular as ever. On the 2005 hits collection *Yer Favourites*, fans voted in "Grace, Too", "Scared", "Nautical Disaster", and "So Hard Done By" — all songs written by The Tragically Hip, of course.

NEIL YOUNG & CRAZY HORSE

RUST NEVER SLEEPS

22 Rust Never Sleeps

Neil Young & Crazy Horse
Reprise, 1979

My My, Hey Hey (Out Of The Blue) | Thrasher | Ride My Llama | Pocahontas | Sail Away | Powderfinger | Welfare Mothers | Sedan Delivery | Hey Hey, My My (Into The Black)

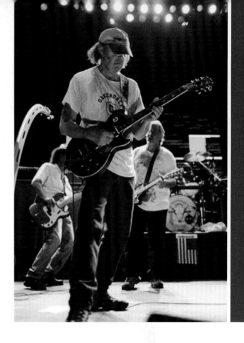

By 1978, Neil Young knew the sixties' dinosaurs were past their time. Punk rock and New Wave had captured the praise once heaped on folk rock and electric blues stars.

While involved in another of his rambling film projects, *Human Highway*, Young had become aware of the group Devo, who wore odd costumes and performed their punk-technology style with herky-jerky motions. Young put them in the movie and joined them in the filming of his new song, "Hey Hey, My My". As they sang "rock and roll can never die," the feeling was the opposite. Young was about to prove it wasn't dead, but it was certainly in convulsions. Young took all these new influences and created a fresh road show for 1978. If the punks could play loud, he would play louder.

Rust Never Sleeps is mostly a live album, recorded during the 1978 tour. Young has always manipulated tapes at will, considering this to be a legitimate part of the art creation. In this case, he strips the live audience from the tracks and adds overdubs to improve the basic tracks. What is there is raw and loud and distorted. *Rust*'s electric assault is some of the most incendiary music of Young's career. The guitar raunch of "Hey Hey, My My" is simply the nastiest thing committed to tape before hard-core punk. It holds Young's big message for the album. He puts the Sex Pistols' sneering Johnny Rotten side by side with the recently deceased Elvis, and announces it's better for artists to burn out than to fade away. Most people took the meaning far too literally, questioning why Young would applaud the early death of sad cases such as Sid Vicious. It's more likely just a shocking way to state his long-held belief that it's better to reach out and potentially fail than to play it safe.

The big noise and the shock attacks continue on other songs. The Civil War story in "Powderfinger" ends with the narrator's getting his face blown off. "Welfare Mothers" is trailer-park punk. The other side is slightly more controlled and conventional, starting with the acoustic "My My, Hey Hey". This time, the theme is posed as a question: is it better to burn out or fade away? "Thrasher", where he sings of boredom and leaving dead weight behind, can be read as a goodbye note to his California music pals.

Rolling Stone named *Rust Never Sleeps* the album of the year, as did many other critics' polls. It received a platinum sales award in the US, Young's first since *Harvest*. Instead of playing it safe, Neil Young had once again confounded everyone and come up with a great album, both artistically and commercially.

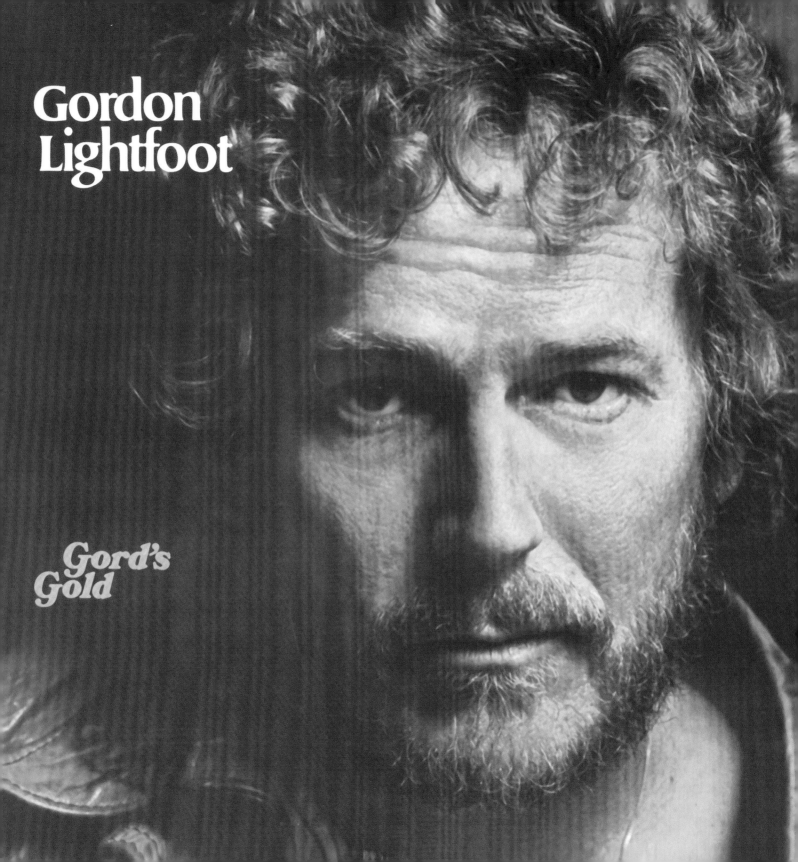

23 Gord's Gold

Gordon Lightfoot
Reprise, 1975

I'm Not Sayin'/Ribbon Of Darkness | Song For A Winter's Night | Canadian Railroad Trilogy | Softly | For Lovin' Me/Did She Mention My Name | Affair On 8th Avenue | Steel Rail Blues | Wherefore And Why | Bitter Green | Early Morning Rain | Minstrel Of The Dawn | Sundown | Beautiful | Summer Side Of Life | Rainy Day People | Cotton Jenny | Don Quixote | Circle Of Steel | Old Dan's Records | If You Could Read My Mind | Cold On The Shoulder | Carefree Highway

I was listening to *Gordie's Gold* in a bar in New York with my headphones on. It just sang so deeply to me. I remember deciding that I wanted to move back to Canada.

— Greg Keelor, Blue Rodeo

May 11, 2007, and Gordon Lightfoot walks on stage at the Moncton Coliseum: "Sorry, I'm four and a half years late." Lightfoot had cancelled this show because he was in hospital for internal bleeding. He nearly died. "We felt sorry when we missed those dates back in 2002," he tells the crowd. "It does my heart good, I'm really glad we came." Lightfoot plays a full two-set, two-hour show, many of the songs from *Gord's Gold*.

This collection is far from the usual Greatest Hits. Lightfoot was, as he recalls, "having a bit of a dry spell," and hit on the idea of re-recording some of his early songs from the sixties. His current label didn't own the rights to the old songs, so re-recording them would be a way to get versions for it to sell. These aren't simply copycats, though. Lightfoot adds an orchestra and does medleys he'd been doing in concert — not the cherished originals, but a new appreciation of the songs. Lightfoot can't even pick a favourite version, and has no problems today with the re-recordings: "It wouldn't matter — no, I like the orchestra."

The second album in this two-LP set contains regular versions of all the hits from the early seventies. This is Lightfoot at his peak of popularity.

But something was wrong, and he knew it. He says he had a serious illness back then, too: "I probably could've achieved more had it not been for alcohol. But at the same time, alcohol was the fuel that was driving my engine. I [quit drinking] in 1982, at the same time as a relationship came apart. It was being on my own and being alone that allowed me to do it. With some professional help. I'm actually quite lucky that I'm sitting here talking to you right now. I probably could have put myself away right there. It took a toll."

Gordon Lightfoot doesn't make any secret of his drinking problem, just as everyone knows about his 2002 illness. He felt lucky to be in Moncton that night, having battled through two life- and career-threatening illnesses. The audience felt lucky to have been there, too.

Top Ten Canadian Roots Albums

Colin Linden is one of the best roots performers and producers the country has ever produced. He started his musical apprenticeship by meeting and befriending blues legend Howlin' Wolf in a Toronto bar-restaurant before he was a teen. He's had a long, successful solo career, written the tune "Remedy" for The Band, and is one third of the national supergroup Blackie and The Rodeo Kings.

1. The Band
   Music From Big Pink
   "The definitive first album by the greatest group of all time (my opinion, folks). Everything I love about folk music, blues, rock and roll, and country music are all here in a synthesis that exceeds the sum of all its parts in all ways. The playing, singing, writing, recording, and arranging are done with such care, yet such abandon. The greatest album ever made ever by anyone."

2. Neil Young
   After The Gold Rush
   "So many of Neil Young's albums are masterworks, but I chose this one because it's burning over with promise, freedom, and amazing songs."

3. The Band
   The Band
   "I was only going to choose my favourite album by any given artist for this list, but The Band were so all-encompassing in roots music that I couldn't omit this classic. The songs on this record are heartbreakingly beautiful — and totally timeless."

4. Bruce Cockburn
   Nothing But A Burning Light
   "An unmitigated work of brilliance by the most consistently great singer-songwriter-guitarist in his country and likely anyone else's. This collaboration with the great T Bone Burnett brings Bruce face to face with a group of his peers and stretches him to mighty heights, and highlights his blues, folk, and country roots."

5. Junkhouse
   Strays
   "The poet laureate of Hamilton, Ontario, Tom Wilson's first blast at a major label record and mainstream radio elevates

Steeltown mythology to a level comparable only with David Lynch's *Twin Peaks* or Alan Lomax's Angola Penitentiary recordings."

6. Jesse Winchester
Jesse Winchester
"Tennessee's loss was Quebec's gain. Jesse Winchester's soulful and tender vision of life brought out the best in the people who listened. He brought the spirit of new discovery to Canada at a time when we all were trying to figure out who we were."

7. Great Speckled Bird
Great Speckled Bird
"Maybe the first genuine 'country-rock' record, Ian and Sylvia Tyson at one of their most exciting and edgy creative peaks. One of the truly great bands, featuring the incomparable Amos Garrett on mind-bending, string-bending guitar with a sound so unique you could recognize it across a hockey stadium."

8. Daniel Lanois
Acadie
"Genius producer-singer-guitarist-songwriter Daniel Lanois's debut album is that of an artist who kept behind the scenes for so long that when he chose to open his mouth, he really, really knew what to say."

9. Willie P. Bennett
Hobo's Taunt
"My hero, and Canada's greatest unsung singer-songwriter, Willie made this album with the cream of the crop of Ontario musicians, including Ken and Chris Whiteley and David Essig (who produced). This record was recorded by Dan Lanois at the legendary Grant Avenue Studio in Hamilton in 1976."

10. Blue Rodeo
Five Days In July
"This record shows that when you record in an unencumbered fashion, sometimes you get beautiful results. It doesn't hurt when you have two songwriters like Jim Cuddy and Greg Keelor, just hitting a new high in their work. Mixed by the truly masterful, enigmatic musician-engineer-producer John Whynot — himself a force to be reckoned with."

DANIEL

LANOIS

ACADIE

SARAH HARMER | YOU WERE HERE

24 You Were Here

Sarah Harmer
Universal, 2000

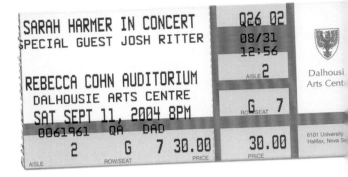

You Were Here has a lot to do with passages in Sarah Harmer's life. It marks her moving from the alternative band Weeping Tile to a solo career, the end of the professional and interpersonal relationships among the friends who made up the band. It also pays tribute to a close friend who passed away.

Weeping Tile came out of Kingston, Ontario, where Harmer was attending Queen's University. The band had great promise, a major label deal, but it just didn't happen for them. After they split at the end of 1998, Harmer, a fan of noisy guitar bands, found herself alone: "I'd written a few of the songs that ended up on *You Were Here*, but I'd never shown them to the band — they were more solitary. That was me stepping out on my own. I was liking the romance of the underdog. For the first time since I started writing songs in the early nineties, I was on my own, and I could do solo shows. With just an acoustic guitar it was freeing and exciting."

Harmer had a lot of new songs, but she also reached back for a very old one. "Basement Apt." would be her first solo hit: "Weeping Tile recorded that on our first EP, and I resurrected it. I kinda had the idea, because I thought it needed a second life. I wrote it feeling pretty dramatic, as you do in university, wondering if anybody was looking out for you. I can see that basement apartment at the end of a street in Kingston. There was a romanticized sense of deprivation, going to a poncy university but playing the part of a rough and tumble kid on the street."

The album's title track carried special meaning: "I wrote ['You Were Here'] with my friend Joe Chithalen in mind. He was Weeping Tile's first bass player. He died suddenly from a peanut allergy. He was such an important part of the Kingston scene, playing with so many bands. He was the first guy I played 'Basement Apt.' for, and I'm glad he's carried along in the name of that song, the name of the album."

Harmer realized her solo career wouldn't be a passing fancy: "I thought I had something when we went into the studio with that collection of songs. There's nothing like it when you get that feeling, it rarely happens. There was no one watching, Warner had dropped Weeping Tile and it was like I had my own little secret. I had this batch of songs and the feeling of excitement that there were no expectations. I really had this desire for something to happen. I wanted this to go somewhere."

Sarah McLachlan

fumblin
towards
ecstasy

25 Fumbling Towards Ecstasy

Sarah McLachlan
Nettwerk, 1993

Possession | Wait | Plenty | Good Enough | Mary | Elsewhere |
Circle | Ice | Hold On | Ice Cream | Fear | Fumbling Towards Ecstasy

> Great melodies, sensuous vocals,
> and a rich layered production;
> for me the choice of all her work,
> where everything comes together.
>
> — Todd Cornish, collector

Sarah McLachlan was a respected artist after her first two albums, 1988's *Touch* and 1991's *Solace*. She'd captured a strong alternative fan base, tapping into the modern electric and atmospheric sounds common around the Nettwerk world. She had something more, too: an ability to write direct, emotional ballads. That and an often angelic and always expressive voice made a potent combination, exploding with *Fumbling Towards Ecstasy*. With strong elements of pop and folk, a faraway feel, and enough modern touches to keep the alternative set happy, *Fumbling* put McLachlan in the national spotlight and launched her US career.

McLachlan has a knack for picking and sticking with good partnerships. Producer Pierre Marchand has worked with her on every album but her debut, and here the team reaches its heights. "Possession" is a powerful song, as heard in the heart-reaching piano and vocal version on the hidden track at the end of the disc. In the opening version, though, Marchand builds it into a solid rock song with layers of electric guitar, an airy organ, and heavenly harmonies from McLachlan. Heavy drums even make it a dance track.

"Good Enough" is another soft piano song that's given extra strength in the production, with the slow drumbeat pushed to the front, and fuzzy and spooky electric guitar lines moving in and out of the sadness. "Hold On" starts at a slow tempo but builds into something funky. McLachlan herself turns up the temperature with some of her most powerful vocals, soaring high and with rare volume. The organ and electric guitar are allowed to turn up a couple of notches, too.

McLachlan could have had a fine career in the New Age genre of Enya and Loreena McKennitt. "Fear" has that mix of traditional and modern, with multiple tracks of vocals behind a crystal-clear, heavily echoed main verse. The older sounds are featured when McLachlan reaches for the heavens in a sweeter voice than ever, with cello and fiddles combining with bodhran-type percussion. Mix in the keyboard effects, electronic pulse solos, and some console trickery, and you'd get an alternate-universe version of Celtic music.

Fumbling Towards Ecstasy is about choosing the right instruments and audio qualities to match the mood of the songs. There's careful control over everything, and all the music parts do the job of directing attention back to the words and vocals. Yet, we're never enveloped by too much sadness, though there is plenty of it in the lyrics. We understand that McLachlan is really singing about finding the strength to carry on, no matter what heartache comes.

THE TRAGICALLY HIP

ROAD APPLES

26 Road Apples

The Tragically Hip
MCA, 1991

Little Bones | Twist My Arm | Cordelia | The Luxury |
Born In The Water | Long Time Running | Bring It All Back |
Three Pistols | Fight | On The Verge | Fiddler's Green |
The Last Of The Unplucked Gems

By 1991, The Tragically Hip were established stars in Canada. They'd won a Juno award for Most Promising Group of the Year in 1990, and would win Entertainer Of The Year in '91. Yet they were a tough band to label. "We were too alternative for Top Forty and too regular for alternative," says guitar player Rob Baker. At first radio wouldn't play them, but listeners started demanding them. "It wasn't a case of us being forced on people over the radio, they forced radio to play us."

They'd enjoyed recording *Up To Here* in Memphis; now the group decided to check out another famous musical landmark, New Orleans. Only singer Gord Downie had been there before (see "New Orleans Is Sinking"), but the others were enthusiastic. Says Baker, "We really liked the idea, always have, of going someplace that we all wanna go, particularly if there's a musical connection. It's

not that you're looking for the spirit of the place to infiltrate the music. New Orleans was just a place we always wanted to go."

The city had an immediate effect on their lyrics. "Little Bones" describes their first night there: "We just toured around New Orleans and saw the sights and met some interesting and strange people. We just met some real characters the very first night, from a racist cab driver to trying to play pool and your hands are so sticky because it's so humid. So Gord said, better butter your cue finger up."

Downie's ability to capture the flavour of places is one of his strongest suits as a writer. Sometimes, just like Gord Lightfoot ("Carefree Highway"), all it takes is a road sign to spark his curiosity and imagination. Downie spied one in Trois-Pistoles, Quebec, and the song "Three Pistols" was born. But what tale goes with the name? In this case, it begins with the character

of Canadian painter Tom Thomson. "Everyone in Canada knows who Tom Thomson is," says Baker with a bit of exaggeration to make his point. "Yet there isn't the same kind of reverence paid. If you were an American painter who'd forged a new style and helped inform the national identity, the American mythology would be all over him, he'd be on coins, he'd be all over."

The more passionate The Hip became about their Canadian identity, the more Canadian audiences responded. They were something to cheer for, something that made people proud. The link forged then between the band and their Canadian fans remains strong. There's always excitement when The Tragically Hip come to town — it's just like fireworks on the first of July.

27 Gordon

Barenaked Ladies
Sire, 1992

Hello City | Enid | Grade 9 | Brian Wilson | Be My Yoko Ono | Wrap Your Arms Around Me | What A Good Boy | The King Of Bedside Manor | Box Set | I Love You | New Kid (On The Block) | Blame It On Me | The Flag | If I Had $1000000 | Crazy

Barenaked Ladies c. 2006 (left to right): Ed Robertson (vocals, guitar), Jim Creeggan (bass), Kevin Hearn (keyboards), Tyler Stewart (drums), Steven Page (vocals, guitar)

Barenaked Ladies started out as an indie band — independent, not signed to a major record company. They distributed their first release themselves, a cassette called *The Yellow Tape*. They were very different, and very funny. "If I Had $1000000" was everyone's lottery dream, the answer to the question, how would you spend it? Jokes about Kraft Dinner and K-Cars were corny but charming. "Be My Yoko Ono" lightly poked fun at the Beatle spouse. The pop culture references hit home with kids and adults alike.

Growing steadily in popularity, the group suddenly became front page news when a Toronto city official objected to a band with a name like theirs appearing at the New Year's Eve show at Nathan Phillips Square. Now everyone knew about Barenaked Ladies. Sales of the cassette reportedly topped one hundred thousand copies, the biggest-selling independent release ever in Canada.

The major labels took interest, and Barenaked Ladies signed with the US company Sire. Most musicians try to hide it if they are middle-class, suburban white kids, but these plainly typical Canadians had no choice but to admit it. Celebrating Scarborough was hardly hip, but it was something to which most young MuchMusic viewers could relate. Instead of trying to seem older and more mature, the group went for younger and goofier, making fun of their roots in the song "Grade 9". This was *Revenge Of The Nerds* on CD.

When Barenaked Ladies started, all the group could afford was a five-song cassette. People wanted it so badly, they bought it by the thousands, a business lesson that's stuck with the band. By 2004's *Barenaked For The Holidays*, they had gone indie again, believing record labels a thing of the past. Says drummer Tyler Stewart, "We figured that people are consuming these [songs] differently now. Albums are, I don't want to say they're dead, but a lot of people listen to music on MP3 or on their computer or satellite radio. It's much more of a random thing." The group recorded twenty-nine songs in 2006, but the old-fashioned album was not the priority. "Sometimes there's a little bit of confusion over what's out there," notes Stewart, "because we had a deluxe edition with all the songs, then we had the two CDs, we had a USB stick, the portable memory drive with all the songs, and then you could buy each song on-line. It's like, wow. Then there's a vinyl edition, too. Anyway you want it, that's the way you need it, to quote Journey."

Barenaked Ladies: once again, the best-known indie band in Canada.

BROKEN SOCIAL SCENE

YOU FORGOT IT IN PEOPLE

28 You Forgot It In People

Broken Social Scene
Arts & Crafts, 2002

Capture The Flag | KC Accidental | Stars And Songs | Almost Crimes | Looks Just Like The Sun | Pacific Theme | Anthems Of A Seventeen-Year-Old Girl | Cause = Time | Late Night Bedroom Rock For The Missionaries | Shampoo Suicide | Lover's Spit | I'm Still Your Fag | Pitter Patter Goes My Heart

Broken Social Scene (left to right, standing): Brendan Canning (vocals, bass), Evan Cranley (trombone), Kevin Drew (vocals, guitar), Amy Millan (vocals), Charles Spearin (guitar, trumpet), Justin Peroff (drums), Marty Kinack (sound designer), James Shaw (guitar). (Left to right, kneeling): Andrew Whiteman (guitar, vocals), Julian Brown (guitar), Jason Collett (guitar)

Kevin Drew and Brendan Canning had a problem. The new group they had formed in 2001 was too small. So they asked some friends in the alternative Toronto music scene to help them out. Canning says, "Kev and I spent a winter making music in his basement on a Tascam eight-track quarter-inch machine. It was done oh so quietly in the wee hours of the night. Those recordings would become our first album *Feel Good Lost*. After that, it was clear we had many friends who we wanted to make music with, and . . . voilà! Many shows were played, different line-ups occurred, loads of songs were written. The force was unstoppable."

Broken Social Scene exploded to eleven members. Most of them had other careers, including Feist, Emily Haines, and James Shaw of Metric, and Evan Cranley, who was in Stars. They could come when they could make it, tour if they were able. That made it fun, and the guest musicians kept

showing up. Says Canning, "It always seems amazing when it all comes together. You know, I can't believe we're in Mexico City together and our horn section is now a mariachi band that Charles and company [found]. Or, Jimmy, you're a diamond for hopping on that plane with twelve hours' notice because Bill just dislocated his shoulder after the Glasgow gig and we really need you. I don't expect anything, and I'm mostly delighted by it all."

This large, rotating group of players gave Drew and Canning the opportunity to create songs based around who was available. "There are many talented minds at work," according to Canning. "I'm not about to list off everyone who has ever been involved with this band, but there were, are, no weak links. In addition, [producer] Dave Newfeld played a big role in helping to shape our sounds.

He was able to wrangle some of the chaos that existed without suffocating what was essential to the sound of Broken Social Scene. The noise was beautiful, it just needed to be tempered . . . ever so slightly."

Canning says Broken Social Scene is all about being different from every other kind of group. "None of us wanted to be in some boring, fucking run-of-the-mill band that could be well placed in the alternative section of the record store or fit into the tiny confines of said radio station's format. What would be the point of that? So boring, so done, over and over and over." In music most times, less is more, but for Broken Social Scene, more is definitely more.

LEONARD COHEN

I'M YOUR MAN

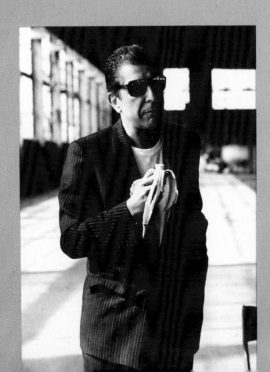

29 I'm Your Man

Leonard Cohen
Columbia, 1988

First We Take Manhattan | Ain't No Cure For Love | Everybody Knows |
I'm Your Man | Take This Waltz | Jazz Police | I Can't Forget | Tower Of Song

I'm Your Man produced half a dozen classics — you could almost call them standards, considering the abundance of cover versions drawn from this album — and that's no easy feat for an eight-song effort.

— Lorraine Carpenter,
Montreal Mirror

In 1984, Leonard Cohen tried to release the album *Various Positions*. But his record company, CBS, turned it down for US distribution, seeing little sales potential for it. Cohen had reached a commercial low point.

It might have made sense if he'd been at the tale end of his career, a faded star trying to hang on with lesser material. But *Various Positions* contains some of his finest work, including the romantic, European-styled "Dance Me To The End Of Love", "Heart With No Companion", and, above all, "Hallelujah". It's one of his best, a masterpiece that has only improved with age. Cohen now agrees it's a good one, but it almost disappeared back in 1984: "'Hallelujah'. That took twenty years to be a hit, and nobody mentioned it at the time. Except Dylan. Dylan started performing it."

It took another artist to bring Cohen's career back from the depths.

In 1987, his long-time backup singer Jennifer Warnes decided to pay tribute to her friend. On *Famous Blue Raincoat*, Warnes did several of Cohen's best-known songs and even a new one, the modern and edgy "First We Take Manhattan", that he gave her for the record. It was a surprise hit, sold well, and introduced Cohen to a new generation. It also had another effect: "That single-handedly resurrected my career. I liked that album a lot." Suddenly, Leonard Cohen was once more a hot name in music. "CBS started taking my calls again," he chuckles.

It was a new Cohen who roared back with *I'm Your Man*. He'd embraced a modern sound, producing himself, playing keyboards, and inventing a whole new persona — the cool elder statesman of pop. The lyrics were clear and hip, with Cohen half-speaking his vocals in a low register. The album was easy to love. On "Tower Of Song", he pokes fun at himself, with his greying hair and "golden voice." He'd never been more accessible.

For a time though, the album was set aside for a family crisis: "It was complicated. My son [Adam] had an auto accident while I was making the album. It was very serious, and I had to go to him. So I had to stop for a while, but he did recover, and that made me very happy, so then it was wonderful to finish the album."

It was good news all around, for his son and for his career. Of all things, a Leonard Cohen album that was warm and happy.

NEIL YOUNG
TONIGHT'S THE NIGHT

30 Tonight's The Night

Neil Young
Reprise, 1975

Tonight's The Night | Speakin' Out | World On A String | Borrowed Tune | Come On Baby Let's Go Downtown | Mellow My Mind | Roll Another Number (For The Road) | Albuquerque | New Mama | Lookout Joe | Tired Eyes | Tonight's The Night - Part II

> This is an album of songs that is so bleak and tattered, so lonely and haunting, that I feel strangely uplifted and cleansed after hearing it.
>
> — Jason MacIsaac, The Heavy Blinkers

Of all the bands Neil Young has led through his long career, he saves the top spot for 1969's Crazy Horse, featuring talented guitar player and songwriter Danny Whitten, whom Young grew to appreciate as his on-stage partner. The resulting album, *Everybody Knows This Is Nowhere* is one of his best.

In the next few years, Whitten developed a debilitating heroin habit. When Young was recruiting a band to tour after *Harvest*, Whitten could not perform even to that group's ragged standards. After being given his leave, Whitten begged Young for some cash, with which he bought the drugs that killed him. A favourite roadie, Bruce Berry, died of an overdose, too. The author of "The Needle And The Damage Done" couldn't even help those around him. In 1973, all this baggage went into the recording sessions for *Tonight's The Night*.

Young sounds shot, raspy, and tired. Behind the piano, he plucks rudimentary chords and adds some barrelhouse trills. Ben Keith matches him croak for croak on harmonies, almost in tune. Slower songs, such as "Speaking Out", plod along; rockers are bashed out with all the subtlety of the town's third-best garage band.

What, then, makes *Tonight's The Night* a classic? Don't question the deliberate sloppiness, embrace it. Appreciate the lyrics and stories, especially the chilling "Tired Eyes" and "Tonight's The Night". Once you get used to the execution, you will find some beautiful moments. On "Albuquerque", listen to Keith's moaning steel guitar, Nils Lofgren's tender piano, the dream-like gang vocals on the chorus. It allows you to ignore Young's quite obviously hitting the microphone twice with

his harp. It's a minor flaw in a brilliant performance, so why strike it from history? Nils Lofgren's guitar solo on "Speakin' Out" is one of the most inspiring blues licks you'll never hear mentioned, and much of Lofgren's and Keith's playing is impeccable. Such is *Tonight's The Night* — sometimes sloppy, sometimes gorgeous, ultimately a fitting tribute given the circumstances.

For once, even Neil Young sensed he'd gone too far. It went into the vault, to be released only two years later. In typically perverse disregard of his career, he cancelled the much more commercial *Homegrown*, with its echoes of *Harvest*, and gave people what they didn't want. Surprisingly, it didn't do too badly – eventually selling over seven hundred thousand copies. A one-line ad for this album might be: Neil Young — Feel Good Feeling Bad.

DECADE

Neil Young

31 Decade

Neil Young
Reprise, 1977

Down To The Wire | Burned | Mr. Soul | Broken Arrow | Expecting To Fly | Sugar Mountain | I Am A Child | The Loner | The Old Laughing Lady | Cinnamon Girl | Down By The River | Cowgirl In The Sand | I Believe In You | After The Gold Rush | Southern Man | Helpless | Ohio | Soldier | Old Man | A Man Needs A Maid | Harvest | Heart Of Gold | Star Of Bethlehem | The Needle And The Damage Done | Tonight's The Night (Part 1) | Tired Eyes | Walk On | For The Turnstiles | Winterlong | Deep Forbidden Lake | Like A Hurricane | Love Is A Rose | Cortez The Killer | Campaigner | Long May You Run

The emotional and musical range of *Decade* is what I find inspiring, from "Tonight's The Night" to (my favourite) "Winterlong" to "For The Turnstiles", by way of "Mr. Soul". And, like all great art, it's a very hard work to exhaust.

— André Alexis, CBC Toronto

Neil Young tells you more about the first ten years of his recording career here than anywhere else. He chose all the tracks, picking from his musical journeys with Buffalo Springfield, Crazy Horse, and CSNY, and each song's liner notes are scrawled in his own handwriting. With the generous group of previously unreleased tracks, *Decade* is a must-own collection.

The three-album set opens with an immediate highlight, a previously unreleased Buffalo Springfield cut, "Down To The Wire". It marked the start of a career pattern in which Young would record brilliant material only to shelve it, sometimes for years and

sometimes to this day. "Wire" was intended for the unfinished second Springfield album, *Stampede*.

"Star Of Bethlehem" was meant for the unreleased 1974 *Homegrown* album, pillaged for later projects. It's a gem from what would have been a return to Young's *Harvest* sound and, conceivably, the hit album everyone wanted from him. "Deep Forbidden Lake" also comes from these recordings; in the liner notes, Young calls it an end to his dark, mid-seventies' period of *Tonight's The Night* and *On The Beach*.

"Winterlong" is another song with a long history, going back to

his first days with Crazy Horse. "Love Is A Rose" is the cautionary tale of holding too tightly to love, in the style of a folksong that might have been brought by English settlers to Appalachia. Last of the new songs is "Campaigner", in which Richard Nixon appears as a mythic figure, and Young admits that even Tricky Dick had a soul.

With its multiple bonus tracks, *Decade* set the stage for the boxed sets of the CD era. It also alerted fans to the incredible wealth of material Young was holding back. He continued to tease fans with promises of a multi-volume archive series for two decades before uncorking 2006's *Live At The Fillmore East*.

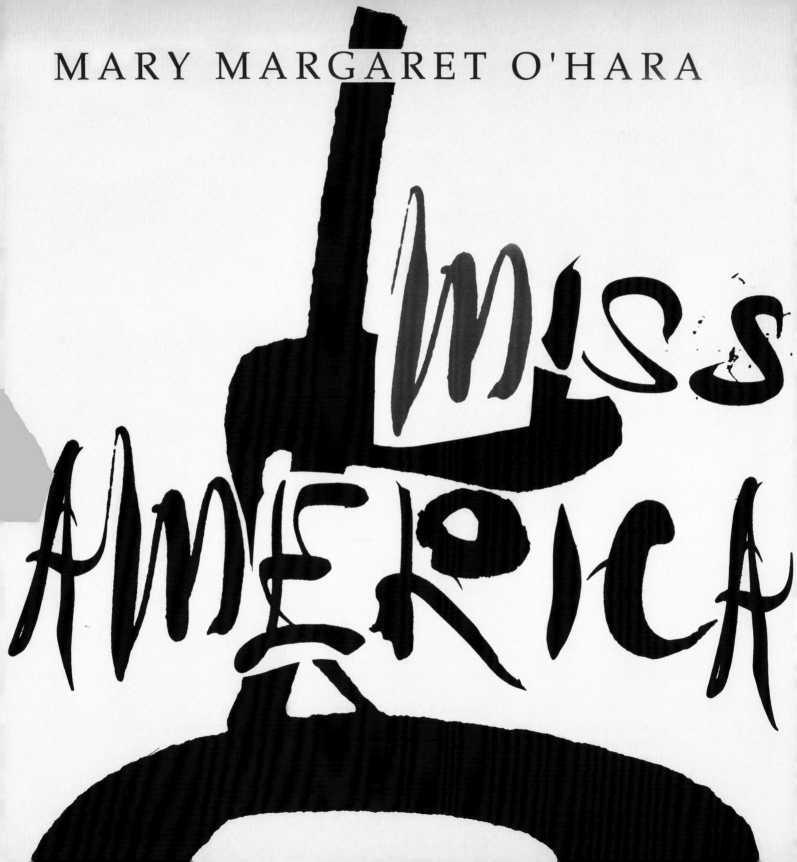

32 Miss America

Mary Margaret O'Hara
Virgin, 1988

To Cry About | Year In Song | Body's In Trouble | Dear Darling | Anew Day | When You Know Why You're Happy | My Friends Here | Help Me Lift You Up | Keeping You In Mind | Not Be Alright | You Will Be Loved Again

At Carleton University in Ottawa, we became friends. I knew she had genius in her then, but even I was astonished by this record, and still am.

— Mike Campbell, artist manager

Miss America still sounds as fresh and unique as it did in 1988. Nothing dates it, and nothing compares to it. No one has sung like this or composed like this. Writing and singing songs like these would be pointless and dull if you weren't Mary Margaret O'Hara.

No safe category describes what O'Hara tackles over the eleven songs here. Each is something new, and the usual conventions of a rock band backing a singer are missing. She's as individualistic a vocalist as Tom Waits or Capt. Beefheart, yet quite different from both. O'Hara goes with whatever is needed at the time, including leaps and moans, operatic highs and spoken-word lows, lovely inflection and garbled scat phrases, dissecting the words into nonsense syllables. Improvisation is at the core of several songs; others have carefully planned melodies. Confused? Good. If the album could be explained, it would have lost some of its magic since 1988.

When O'Hara calms down enough to stay on our planet for a time, the results are fantastic. "Anew Day" is joyous gospel; if there had been a big Southern choir behind her, it could have been about the Pentecost. On the page, it's an exciting poem; as a song, the musicians squeeze it into a form we can recognize, in which O'Hara proves she's a remarkable singer.

There are plenty of excellent singers around, though, and O'Hara has greater intentions. She's keen on deconstructing the usual forms and finding out where her voice can go. Instead of hitting notes with precise diction, she slurs around the consonants and the rhythm at the same time. If the music gets intense, she repeats passages and phrases and increases her own volume. She plays her voice like an avant-garde guitar soloist.

The album became a huge favourite in many critical circles in Canada, the US, and England. It made many Top Ten lists for the year. There was a tour, but many people found her on-stage behaviour bizarre. Then, nothing happened. O'Hara dropped out of the music world, concentrating on art instead. There have been occasional appearances, notably a 1991 Christmas four-song EP; guest vocal appearances for Morrissey, Bruce Cockburn, and others; a soundtrack album for the 2001 film *Apartment Hunting*, in which she also appeared; and various stage performances. She's released no true follow-up album, however, even though *Miss America* has never lost its status as one of the great cult albums of all time.

Sarah McLachlan — Surfacing

33 Surfacing

Sarah McLachlan
Nettwerk, 1997

Building A Mystery | I Love You | Sweet Surrender | Adia | Do What You
Have To Do | Witness | Angel | Black & White | Full Of Grace | Last Dance

With all due respect to *Fumbling Towards Ecstasy* and *Solace*, *Surfacing* is the pinnacle of Sarah's writing . . . so far, that is.

— Dave Wheeler,
Power 97

Surfacing is Sarah McLachlan's biggest-selling album, reaching diamond status in Canada, with a million copies sold, and topping eight million sales in the States. It produced five singles, including the smash "Building A Mystery". It's a wonderful example of playing to one's strengths. In McLachlan's case, that's to focus on her voice and highlight the emotion.

McLachlan works with a small team for this album: Pierre Marchand has produced every one of her albums except her debut; when drums are required, her husband, Ash Sood, is on call. There is some guest guitar, Barenaked Ladies' Jim Creeggan adds standup bass on four tracks, and that's about it. McLachlan wrote all the songs, with assistance from Marchand. The spotlight aims straight at McLachlan and her piano.

"Angel" is a highlight for many and explains the deep connection McLachlan has with her fans. The song is a hymn, but not religious — the angel here represents a universal longing for comfort, which McLachlan wishes for the restless person in her narrative. She doesn't want that person to have to work for this relief — merely to be pulled from the wreckage. It's empathy of the highest order, touching on the need to leave troubles behind to be at peace. Apart from Creeggan's gentle strokes on the bass, there are no other sounds but McLachlan's piano, voice, and a huge echo on her vocal microphone.

Not all the songs are quiet, and McLachlan can rock in her own way. "Black & White" has a steady beat from Sood and some funky bass. McLachlan gets a little louder, even throwing in some scat phrasing at the end. But no song gets to be that obvious here. Marchand puts layers of mist behind McLachlan, keyboard effects that surround the vocal track but never envelop it. They're building a mystery, don't forget.

Back to that hit: it features another solid groove, the lone guitar solo on the album, and the biggest sound on the disc. To put the focus back on McLachlan this time, Marchand builds layers of vocals, doubling the lead, letting her sing harmony lines throughout — a Wall Of Sarah that gives her much power.

In 1997, McLachlan launched one of the most successful female initiatives in pop music. The Lilith Fair tour, which ran for three years, took no political stance, though, not even on gender issues. It simply gave female performers a chance in a touring world then dominated by men. In 1997, with Alanis Morissette selling truckloads of *Jagged Little Pill*, Shania Twain's *Come On Over* heading to become the biggest-selling female album of all time, and McLachlan's double effort as multi-platinum artist and festival promoter, Canadian women were the most powerful recording artists of the day.

SLOAN
one chord to anothe

34 One Chord To Another

Sloan
murderecords, 1996

The Good In Everyone | Nothing Left To Make Me Want To Stay | Autobiography | Junior Panthers | G Turns To D | A Side Wins | Everything You've Done Wrong | Anyone Who's Anyone | The Lines You Amend | Take The Bench | Can't Face Up | 400 Metres

Sloan (left to right): Patrick Pentland, Jay Ferguson, Andrew scott, Chris Murphy

By 1995, Sloan were broken up. Locked in battle with their record label, US powerhouse Geffen, after altering their style for their 1994 album *Twice Removed*, they were no longer being promoted. To make matters worse, the once-close band of four Haligonians were fighting.

Chris Murphy had always had this vision of Sloan: "We split the money evenly, we all creatively contribute. We're a pretty true democracy. In the name of keeping the band together, I wanted everyone to sing songs and write songs and feel involved, and I didn't want anyone to quit, because it was the biggest opportunity of my life and I didn't want anyone to fuck it up."

Drummer Andrew Scott challenged that ideal. "We weren't getting along that well," says Murphy. "Andrew had just moved to Toronto, so I took that as a major fuck-you to me, you're fuckin' my chance of doing something, and I was mad at him."

It can happen only in the music industry: the band broke up but technically they couldn't say so. Murphy tries his best to explain: "If we said we broke up, then we were under a different set of rules. They [Geffen] would be able to hold us as artists and not pay us. We wanted them to let us out of the contract so that we weren't bound."

A final album was proposed, and Murphy recalls, "We said, well, we need some Andrew songs to make it a true Sloan record. I was still mad at him, and I thought that the songs I was going to get would be basically fuck-you songs. But he sent two songs and they were awesome, and I took it as a sign that he still wanted to be in the band. We tentatively talked about maybe doing a show, a couple of shows. We became a band again very gradually, because we were still licking our wounds a bit. We went back to Geffen to say, do you want to put this record out?" Geffen passed and let them out of their contract.

Chris Murphy thinks *One Chord To Another* is the group's best work: "It's my favourite partly because of the story. We were broken up, getting back together with Andrew. We did it my favourite way, on the cheap. I just think it sounds awesome, and it did really well, we sold eighty thousand copies in Canada, and that's as big as we've ever done. By then we had all had a hit single, so I had achieved my goal of making it a band with four heads, four faces, with irreplaceable people."

It should be noted that, shortly after, the other three members moved to Toronto.

LEONARD COHEN
SONGS OF LOVE AND HATE

35 Songs Of Love And Hate

Leonard Cohen
Columbia, 1971

Avalanche | Last Year's Man | Dress Rehearsal Rag | Diamonds In The Mine |
Love Calls You By Your Name | Famous Blue Raincoat | Sing Another Song, Boys |
Joan Of Arc

In 1971, Leonard Cohen released his third album in four years. He had taken on songwriting with the same level of professionalism and hard work he'd applied to his poetry and novels. It also helped that, this time, he was making a living at it: "That was always a part of it. By that time, things had smoothed out a bit on that level. I'd always just been interested in the activity [of writing], and that goes right up until right now. That became my work. I could envision blackened pages, I could write, that became my principal activity."

Cohen was also the composer, and equally passionate about his melodies. They are stirring, often with a European flavour. When asked about one of his best-known and -loved songs, "Famous Blue Raincoat", with its fascinating tale of a love triangle, Cohen's first thoughts are of the music: "The chord progressions are kind of nice. I remember singing it for my mother before it had words, at her house. She said, 'it has a kind of Spanish progression and I like it.' The story's good, it's an intriguing story. It's not quite clear what's happened. It's a mystery." So much for Cohen's just writing a poem and grafting it onto a tune.

Cohen isn't offering any more clues to the story of "Famous Blue Raincoat", though. What he wants is already there, in the form of a letter to a friend, signed by L. Cohen. Cohen's own blue raincoat was somewhat famous, but in this song it belongs to the other character. We're not told what, if anything, is fact.

Some parts he will explain, to give the listener a better understanding of the settings or feelings that led to the words. "Sing Another Song, Boys", with its pawnshop and Nazi dagger, goes back to Cohen's youth: "I was thinking of Craig Street in Montreal, stores that had daggers in the window. I used to hang around the pawn shops."

The album includes another major composition, "Joan Of Arc". Cohen, though, says he wasn't satisfied with the collection: "I wasn't really happy with that album. At that time I felt it wasn't quite what I was striving for. I felt I lost it, and I couldn't put my finger on it. I think was looking for something a little more like my first album, something where the songs were a little more amiable, more feelings, more love songs, where the songs were not so dark. I think probably that I wanted it, but that's not what came. You can't quarrel with it. It's not as though one has the luxury to spend them, to choose in what form they'll arrive."

Duophonic

Simply Saucer

Cyborgs Revisited

36 Cyborgs Revisited

Simply Saucer
Mole Sound, 1989

Instant Pleasure | Electro Rock | Nazi Apocalypse | Mole Machine | Bullet Proof
Nothing | Here Come The Cyborgs (Part 1) | Here Come The Cyborgs (Part 2) |
Dance The Mutation | Illegal Bodies

Simply Saucer (left to right): Kevin Christoff (bass),
Don Cramer (drums), Steve Park (guitar), Edgar
Breau (vocals, guitar)

How can a band that never released an album get to be in the Top 100 Canadian albums? It's one of the great comeback stories in all of rock and roll.

Simply Saucer came together in Hamilton in the early seventies. In 1974, they got booked into a new studio, called Master Sound, operated by brothers Bob and Daniel Lanois in their mother's basement. Edgar Breau, was the group's leader and guitar player: "It was very influenced by The Velvet Underground, the early Pink Floyd, and Hawkwind, that space-rock thing, long improvised music. We were into devices, effects pedals, tape loops, echo chambers, and the audio generators."

The band shopped the tape around and got all the usual rejection notices. They released one single, and by 1979, Breau decided that was enough, and the band split up. He sold all his gear, bought an acoustic guitar, and started

on a serious folk music career: "That kept me going for quite a while. I thought I'd put that all behind me. But [in 1987] I was playing at an open stage and I met this guy Bruce Mowat, who liked my stuff. He had written a history of Hamilton rock and had excluded Simply Saucer. I took umbrage at that, and he asked me if I had any tapes. I told him about this studio session with the Lanois Brothers."

"Nothing could've prepared me for what I heard," says Mowat. "*Cyborgs* was, and is, a bolt from the blue. Nobody, and I mean nobody, in this country was doing that mixture of Detroit street rock, German prog, and UK psychedelia at the time. It was too much." Mowat put out a limited edition of 920 vinyl copies. Says Breau, "We started getting great reviews right away. It got reviewed by *Cream*, *Spin*, and *New Musical Express*. It reared its

head again, and I had to deal with that, because I'd come to terms with its failing."

"Throughout most of the nineties, I just withdrew from the music scene. I just thought, I gotta kill this thing off because I didn't know how to deal with it. People kept saying to me they'd seen all kinds of stuff on the Internet on Simply Saucer." A re-release went ahead in 2003: "This time it really went over the top, the critical acclaim. That's when I really started thinking seriously — if we were to put the band together how would we do it? I didn't have an electric guitar, I hadn't played one in twenty years." On September 16, 2006, a regrouped Simply Saucer, with original bass player Kevin Christoff and Breau, took the stage in Toronto: "It was an awful lot of fun. I'd forgotten how much fun it was to play rock and roll."

Top Ten Funniest & Coolest Canadian Album Titles

Terry O'Reilly is one of the world's premiere advertising experts. He produces radio and TV spots with some of the biggest entertainment stars, including Keifer Sutherland and his dad Donald. Through his company Pirate Toronto, he's also produced weekly radio shows for CBC on the tricks of the advertising trade, *O'Reilly On Advertising* and *The Age Of Persuasion*. Terry knows that a great catchphrase can be the key to creating an instant impression, and that works for album titles, too. He's given us two lists of titles that help sell what's inside:

Ten Funniest Titles

1. Final Fantasy
   He Poos Clouds
   "Because, you know, who wouldn't if you could?"

2. The Lowest of the Low
   Shakespeare My Butt
   "You have to appreciate scorching honesty."

3. Art Bergmann
   What Fresh Hell Is This?
   "Bingo."

4. Sum 41
   Does This Look Infected?
   "Bango."

5. G7 Welcoming Committee Records
   Take Penicillin Now
   "Bongo."

6. Venetian Snares
   The Chocolate Wheelchair Album
   "An equal opportunity offender."

7. Me, Mom and Morgentaler
Clown Heaven And Hell
"A double whammy, band name and album title."

8. Canadian Compilation Album
More Of Our Stupid Noise
"Completely critic proof."

9. Fifth Column
36C
"I've never seen the cover, and I already like it."

10. Furnaceface
Just Buy It
"A special mention — simple, direct, and Nike-esque in its charm, minus the charm."

Ten Coolest Titles

1. Ian Tyson
Cowboyography
"There's a lot of living etched in Ian Tyson's face, and I love the imagery of the title."

2. The Guess Who
Wheatfield Soul
"Who ever thought you could make Winnipeg sound romantic?"

3. Sarah McLachlan
Fumbling Towards Ecstasy
"Kinda sexy, kinda hopeful."

4–5. Joni Mitchell
The Hissing Of Summer Lawns and *Turbulent Indigo*
"From a lady who knows how to name an album, both are just so vivid and unforgettable."

6. k.d. lang
Absolute Torch And Twang
"The perfect elixir of Ms. lang's style."

7. Neil Young
Rust Never Sleeps
"Just like Neil himself — he never stops moving. Still relevant after all these years — the ultimate achievement in rock."

8. The Band
Music From Big Pink
"Everything pink is new, isn't it? And this was about as fresh as it got."

9. Bruce Cockburn
Dancing In The Dragon's Jaw
"Always loved that title, an apt metaphor for life, n'est-ce pas?"

10. Hank Snow
Tracks And Trains
"Hank was cool, and this title says heartache and loneliness and longing and pain and distance and yearning and more."

k.d. lang

INGÉNUE

37 Ingénue

k.d. lang
Sire, 1992

Save Me | The Mind Of Love | Miss Chatelaine | Wash Me Clean | So It Shall Be | Still Thrives
This Love | Season Of Hollow Soul | Outside Myself | Tears Of Love's Recall | Constant Craving

One of the world's premiere torch singers. In fact, critics dusted off the term when this album appeared. As warm as a bath.

— Randy Renaud, CHOM-FM

k.d. lang had been a Canadian country star since 1984, when she released her first disc, *A Truly Western Experience*. Calling herself the reincarnation of Patsy Cline, her cat's-eye glasses, cropped hair, and Western gear made her fun and outrageous. By 1989's *Absolute Torch And Twang*, she was reaching a significant US audience.

Three years later, lang reappeared without a hint of country. She and her songwriter partner, on-stage fiddler, and now producer, Ben Mink, wrote a song-cycle of mature, adult vocal music, with elements of popular styles, some jazz flavours, and lots of small orchestral passages. lang wanted to sing of heartbreak and longing with a richer backing than the torch and twang of three years before, and Mink rose to the occasion. *Ingénue* is lush but not overly so. These aren't mini-symphonies, but they are sophisticated. There is room

for emotion, and these songs have plenty of it.

In interviews at the time, lang revealed that the songs detailed a failed relationship, a case of unrequited love on her part. She described writing them as painful, intense, but cathartic in the end. In what could have been pathetic and sad, lang instead holds her head up, making us feel for her and admire her strength. In "The Mind Of Love", we hear her scolding herself, asking, where is your head Kathryn? [k.d. stands for Kathryn Dawn]. Wisely, she adds the silly and sweet to the heartache: "Miss Chatelaine" is upbeat, and a great Canadian moment, as *Chatelaine* had once put her on the cover as Woman Of The Year.

As with Joni Mitchell's first foray into a new jazz-pop style, *Court And Spark*, lang's new album had

an ace up its sleeve: a hit single. Mitchell had "Help Me", lang had "Constant Craving". It is the most conventional song on the disc but a stellar production. Acoustic guitar is joined by accordion, and drums slap in when lang starts the verse. It's the first song from the new CD people heard, and it was an instant winner. lang never sounded better, and the multiple harmonies with Sue Leonard make the chorus special. As the closing track to the song-cycle, it also has an uplifting feel.

The album, in any case, is hardly a downer. If lang hadn't given the interviews, it's doubtful listeners would have picked out the story, even with small hints in the lyrics. The agony is muted, and it gave k.d. lang a completely new audience and a new career.

RHEOSTATICS

melville

38 Melville

Rheostatics
Intrepid, 1991

Record Body Count | Aliens (Christmas 1988) | Northern Wish | Saskatchewan | Horses | Christopher | Chanson Les Ruelles | Lying's Wrong | It | When Winter Comes | The Wreck Of The Edmund Fitzgerald | You Are Very Star

Rheostatics' first album, *Greatest Hits,* came out in 1987. Fans had to wait a long time for a follow-up. Group mainstay Dave Bidini says the band had to find itself: "We were exploring different directions, and we had to play out that period of exploration before we started to get to it. We knew [*Melville*] would be vastly different, much larger than our first record. We wanted to make a record that was big, because we thought the songs were big, a lot longer than any other songs we'd ever written, they had more parts."

That was the birth of the wonder-fully complex world of Rheostatics recordings. The band began a series of ambitious studio creations that saw genres collide inside a song, tales veer off in unexpected directions, all while keeping memorable hooks flying at you. "Listening back to the tapes, listening to how it was all coming together, was really exciting," Bidini recalls, "because we knew we had found our sound."

Then there were the words. Before it was cool, they were Canadian: "You gotta remember that in the late eighties for sure, Canadian bands were pissed on. People looked at you and thought you were somehow not ready for a serious career in music if you were too Canadian. It seemed absurd that you would be penalized or people would look down their noses at you if you were somehow singing about where you were from. I remember a band telling us we were never going to get anywhere if we kept writing about our lives in Canada. All we really had were our lives in Canada."

There's a French-language song, brazenly titled "Saskatchewan", and even a cover song from that prototypical Canadian songwriter, Gordon Lightfoot. Here's what they did to "The Wreck Of The Edmund Fitzgerald": "Really drag it through the muck, really get it dirty, spray it with mud and blood and fear and angst. It was essentially our punk rock version of that song, really trying to get it as frightful as possible. I think we all realized we could give a new look to this song, maybe reflect sonically some of the lyrics, more so than Gord's actual treatment, which was very clean and kind of jaunty, when in fact it's terrifying as hell, that song."

While the next album, *Whale Music,* is often singled out as the better of the two, this one is closer to Bidini's heart: "It's the birth of a sound for us, the birth of a sensibility. A lot of what we did on *Melville* we rounded into form on *Whale Music.* It was exciting on *Melville* because it was the first time that our aesthetic had been realized."

ERIC S TRIP

39 Love Tara

Eric's Trip
Sub Pop, 1993

Behind The Garage | Anytime You Want | Stove | Follow | Secret For Julie | Belly | Sunlight | June | To Know Them | Spring | Frame | May 11 | My Room | Blinded | Allergic To Love

Eric's Trip (left to right): Mark Gaudet (drums), Rick White (guitar, vocals), Julie Doiron (bass), Chris Thompson (guitar)

I've interviewed a lot of musicians, but this was the first time I'd been asked to meet a band at a member's parents' house. "It was my bedroom, and a rec room," confirms Rick White, Eric's Trip's guitarist, singer, and recording engineer. "A teenage boy takes over the rec room by a certain age."

Down in the rec room, I find White and bass player Julie Doiron. The then-couple are clearly comfortable there, with their instruments and a tape recorder. It certainly doesn't look like a recording studio, though. "We had a little quarter-inch eight-track," White remembers. "We recorded pretty much that whole record down there."

White was recording Eric's Trip in what was called "lo-fi": instead of spending thousands on professional sound, lo-fi musicians worked within the limitations to create their art. It wasn't simply a lack of funds, says White. "It was always important for us to be able to record ourselves. I

> The four-track recordings of Rick White made me realize you could do something interesting and emotional without a big studio.
>
> — Hayden

don't know how we ever got that theory at such a young age. We just didn't want to go into studios."

The do-it-yourself ideal extended to the packaging White put together: "We treated it more as an art project where we thought it was important to be us doing it. I still feel like that. I don't like it when other people make band's videos or produce their records. I get the feeling it's not them anymore."

Surprisingly, new label Sub Pop didn't want anything to change with the new deal: "Part of the attraction — we didn't realize at the time, I guess

— was that it was all homemade. Sub Pop sought that in us, and just wanted us to make the record we would've made and put out on cassette and they'd put it out [on CD]. Even when they dealt with my artwork. I'd send them my art and it was all taped together, collages. I had the intention of them taking the tape off to make it look better, but they left it on always, because they thought it was part of the art."

Sub Pop did everything to keep the group just the way they were: "They didn't give us new gear and stuff like some bands get when they sign, because they liked that our stuff would fall apart on stage. I didn't find this out until much later. It was a shtick we had that we didn't realize."

Despite a 1996 break-up, Eric's Trip members White, Doiron, guitarist Chris Thompson, and drummer Mark Gaudet have reunited several times, including for a 2007 tour.

ON THE BEACH

40 On The Beach

Neil Young

Reprise, 1974

Walk On | See The Sky About To Rain | Revolution Blues | For The Turnstiles | Vampire Blues | On The Beach | Motion Pictures | Ambulance Blues

It is the sound of a hard-won arrival from a darkness you were loath to leave. Best line: "I need a crowd of people but I can't face them day to day."

— Ken Beattie, Killbeat Publicity

The album starts with the sprightly "Walk On", the closest thing Neil Young had had to a hit since *Harvest*, two years before. The song's bright guitar hook, however, is not indicative of what follows. The lyrics are anything but happy: gossipers, supposed friends, are talking him down. He is confused and has no hope of changing the situation, so the best response is to walk on. It's as close to a positive statement as he makes on the album.

"Walk On" seemed Young's motto and *modus operandi* at the time — his reaction to the fame and demands thrust on him after *Harvest*'s huge success. This was Young's first subsequent studio album, and his wildly uneven film soundtrack *Journey Through The Past* and the poorly received live album *Time Fades Away* had pretty much assured that expectations would be low.

"For The Turnstiles" sums up Young's distaste for the commercial side of his career. He bemoans having to sing for the masses, urged on by the pimp at the door who wants his ten dollars a head. Young strangles the notes out of the banjo, aided only by running buddy Ben Keith on dobro. This is not entertainment but blues — and spooky blues at that.

You can make a pretty good case for describing *On The Beach* as the soundtrack to a horror film. At its core are three blues numbers, "Revolution Blues", "Vampire Blues", and "Ambulance Blues". You can be horrified by the sloppy performances or find them great examples of primitivism. Young's one-note solo at the end of "Vampire Blues" mocks his guitar-hero standing, serving to prove it's the feeling, not the proficiency, in the blues.

It isn't all messy , but it is all rough-hewn. "Ambulance Blues", clocking in at nearly nine minutes, contains some of the best acoustic guitar of Young's career. Musically, it is the performance of the album, and frames the most important lyrics. He warns you can get buried in the past by trying to keep a good thing alive, a remark often assumed to be directed at Crosby, Stills & Nash. Later, an unnamed friend tells him you're all just pissing in the wind. That's commonly believed to be Young's manager, Elliot Roberts, about the inactivity of CSNY. Young wouldn't be the one to fix things — remember that motto, "Walk On".

On The Beach sold poorly, and appeared on CD only in 2003. It remains obscure, yet ardent horror film fans always search out the rare gems.

41 Not Fragile

Bachman-Turner Overdrive
Mercury, 1974

Not Fragile | Rock Is My Life And This Is My Song | Roll On Down The Highway |
You Ain't Seen Nothing Yet | Free Wheelin' | Sledgehammer | Blue Moanin |
Second Hand | Givin' It All Away

BTO (left to right): Fred Turner (bass, vocals), Robbie
Bachman (drums, percussion), Randy Bachman (guitar,
vocals), Blair Thornton (guitar, background vocals)

Randy Bachman left The Guess Who at the height of the band's fame, with a number one single, "American Woman". And he was determined to pull it off again. He knew what that would mean: "The success of BTO was due to many, many years of hard work. Knocking on doors that no one would answer and financing it myself with my earnings from The Guess Who. It was a tough couple of years of rejections, but in the end it all seemed worth it, as I was able to forge a completely new style of heavier, more guitar-riffy music. You better believe I was proud when we made it."

Bachman was back in business: "I was a songwriter. Brave Belt and then Bachman-Turner Overdrive was to be the vehicle for my songs, but I was smart enough to know that I wasn't that great a writer. It was so hard to learn to write alone without Burton Cummings to bounce off of. But I did write some good songs on

my own. To balance out the sound of BTO and so we wouldn't be boring by me writing all the songs, I encouraged [Fred] Turner and the others to write alone and together. I chose the songs I felt best complemented each other and made a strong statement as an album."

> Soundtrack band to the seventies, back when you had your Canadian flag sewn on the back of your jean jacket.
>
> — Dave Schneider, KICX 106

Not Fragile was the album where it all came together, with Turner, brother Rob Bachman, and Blair Thornton all contributing songs. Still, it was one of Randy's, "You Ain't Seen Nothing Yet", that made this a number one album in North America: "I had a brother

[Gary] who stuttered. It was supposed to be a one-off song and kind of a joke. I was kind of embarrassed to put it on the album but did so at the urging of our record label VP, Charles Fach. It went to number one in about twenty countries and was BTO's only million-selling single."

If you want to know why Randy Bachman did all that work to come back to the top, he tells the whole story on another of his tracks, "Rock Is My Life And This Is My Song": "It was based on Garret Morris's bit on *Saturday Night Live* when he'd always say 'baseball been good to me — baseball is my life.' When I'd be in the trenches with BTO, driving hundreds of miles every night for ninety days at a time, people would ask me why I did it, and I facetiously would say 'Rock is my life and this is my song.' Rock's been good to me."

The Best of The Guess Who

VICTO

42 The Best Of The Guess Who

The Guess Who
RCA, 1971

These Eyes | Laughing | Undun | No Time | American Woman | No Sugar Tonight/New Mother Nature | Hand Me Down World | Bus Rider | Share The Land | Do You Miss Me Darlin' | Hang On To Your Life

The definitive collection of hits that broke down the barrier and made Canuck rock legit.

— Peter Sisk, The Good Brothers

"A lot of my friends thought it was too soon for a Best Of," says Burton Cummings. "But RCA were the ones really that said, 'look, you guys have an incredible string of monster hits here, we want to put out a Best Of,' and so who were we to argue? It sold a ton of records and even to this day it still sells a ton of CDs."

Cummings learned to write songs in Winnipeg with Randy Bachman. Remembers Bachman, "Burton and I got together every Saturday morning at his Granny Kirkpatrick's house on Bannerman Avenue in the North End of Winnipeg. I'd bring bits of songs or half songs and he'd pick out a part he liked and thought was strong. I'd do the same with his ideas, and we put the best ideas and parts together to make the songs. That was only one way we did it. Sometimes I'd do all the music and chords, and he'd do the lyrics or poetry. We wrote every which way we could."

The pair could even write under the gun. Says Cummings, "We had 'These Eyes' and it was a monster hit [in 1968], and it was a ballad. Don Burkheimer, the guy who signed us to RCA, took us to the Carnegie Deli in New York, just Randy and me, not the other two. He said, 'please give us one more ballad, something in the vein of 'These Eyes'.' Of course, we rebelled; we said, 'we're a rock and roll band, we don't want to have ballads, come on!' Well, he convinced us. Randy and I wrote 'Laughing' specifically as a follow-up to 'These Eyes'."

Best Of is split between the Bachman years and the new team of Cummings and Kurt Winter, drawing tracks from the 1970 *Share The Land* album. Winter was the surprise hit songwriter for the new Guess Who, and even Bachman was impressed:

"The Guess Who hits after I left continued the great tradition of great intros, great melodies, and hooks. Kurt Winter had a bagful of hooks that were mined for many years and produced many hit songs. I enjoy playing them."

Back together for the Bachman-Cummings tours, Burton Cummings makes sure to pay tribute to Kurt Winter's contributions: "He was a very good friend, one of my best friends ever in life. He was a major part of The Guess Who legacy. He basically drank himself to death, and he also had an aneurysm. He had it rough the last couple of years, and it was sad. I saw him not long before he passed away. He was a great guy, I do miss him."

43 Let It Die

Feist
Arts & Crafts, 2004

It's like Audrey Hepburn was reincarnated as a really cool indie rock darling with a fist full of talent.

— John Threlfall,
Monday Magazine

Leslie Feist is a new kind of singer: modern and hip, yet rooted in classic vocal performance. She caresses the works like a seasoned jazz interpreter of the past. She has the tenderness of a folkie. She's a chanteuse, still young and cool. She can control a song with the sparest of instrumentation. And she has serious street cred.

Feist started in punk bands and eventually joined By Divine Right as a guitar player. She shared an apartment with the controversial Peaches and appeared on stage and disc with her, as well as with Broken Social Scene. With Peaches, she moved to Berlin and eventually to Paris, a move that significantly broadened her sound. Working with Peaches's mate Gonzales, she pieced together *Let It Die* over 2002 and 2003 in France.

The European influence is immediately evident: light brushes of techno electronics back many of the songs, yet they never overpower the vocals; instead, the modern touches mainly point out this is a new artist. Vocally, Feist takes on the sexy style of Parisienne singers, even covering Françoise Hardy's "L'amour ne dure pas toujours".

There are also nods to Eurodisco, most notably on her smash hit remake of the Bee Gees' "Inside And Out". It's a brilliant production, kicking off with a funk beat more Motown than Gibb. Feist coos the familiar lyrics, and you're caught; the return of a Moog synthesizer, that most dated of seventies' instruments, heightens the joke. By the end, there's no denying the power of the song, the brilliance of the production, and the skill of the singer.

While the cover brought her attention, the originals pointed to an even brighter future. Feist strums the album opener, "Gatekeeper", on the guitar with nothing more than the occasional electric piano chord and harmony from Gonzales. It's a magnificent choice for the first cut, showcasing her vocal abilities and not relegating her to any genre. Next comes "Mushaboom", with its fun Latin bounce. After the simplicity of "Gatekeeper", the big production is stunning and inventive. After that slice of heaven, the slow soul of "Let It Die", which details the end of a relationship, is even more heartrending. Who could do such a thing to this wonderful singer?

With *Let It Die*, Feist managed to court the alternative crowd, mainstream radio, older rock fans, and the dance audience. She did it without compromising in any direction, refusing to be slotted into one genre. She even made the Bee Gees cool again.

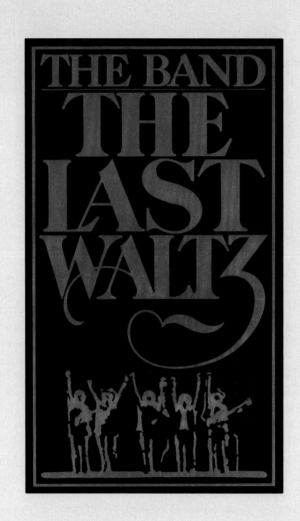

44 The Last Waltz

The Band
Warner, 1978

The Band: Richard Manuel (piano).

Theme From The Last Waltz | Up On Cripple Creek | Who Do You Love (w/Ronnie Hawkins) | Helpless (w/Neil Young) | Stage Fright | Coyote (w/Joni Mitchell) | Dry Your Eyes (w/Neil Diamond) | It Makes No Difference | Such A Night (w/Dr. John) | The Night They Drove Old Dixie Down | Mystery Train (w/Paul Butterfield) | Mannish Boy (w/Muddy Waters) | Further On Up The Road (w/Eric Clapton) | The Shape I'm In | Down South In New Orleans (w/Bobby Charles) | Ophelia | Tura Lur Lural (w/Van Morrison) | Caravan (w/Morrison) | Life Is A Carnival | Baby Let Me Follow You Down (w/Bob Dylan) | I Don't Believe You (w/Dylan) | Forever Young (w/Dylan) | Baby Let Me Follow You Down (reprise) (w/Dylan) | I Shall Be Released (finale) | The Well | Evangeline (w/Emmylou Harris) | Out Of The Blue | The Weight (w/The Staple Singers) | The Last Waltz Refrain | Theme From The Last Waltz

On November 25, 1976, a lineup assembled on the Winterland stage in San Francisco that was the most star studded since Woodstock. There were some influential and legendary characters. And there were The Band.

It was an idea that had spiralled into an event, and the accompanying film is often called the best rock and roll movie ever — it seems so perfect and noble. But Robbie Robertson wanted to get off the road, and the others went along in principle, although, as they took the stage that night, there was no actual agreement that the group was retiring.

Garth Hudson believed there was more to come: "Everybody hoped there would be a different outcome. I know what each individual wanted after *The Last Waltz*. There was no thought of retiring, there was talk about doing more recordings. I wasn't too concerned about it, I was interested in doing something else, but I know

that other members really did want to re-form and do something together again."

Still, The Band were happy to do the show. "Oh, yeah, sure, everybody was up for it," says Hudson. "I thought it was a good idea, whatever the outcome. I just saw professionals that were serious and dedicated and ready to do a good job."

Hudson has something to say to people who consider this a great rock performance: "I think the cookin' live stuff is The Hawks, Levon and The Hawks," referring to the group's days after they left Ronnie Hawkins and before they joined Bob Dylan, in 1964-65. "Some of the tempos are impressive. And you will hear that on a boxed set by Jann Haust and his company Other People's Music, his label. It's incredible, he's an archivist, and he's been working on this project for twelve or fifteen years, gathering from porches and basements and barns.

> He is incredible. He can noodle in every single type of music. There's not a band that he couldn't play with. They could walk off a spaceship and Garth Hudson could jam with them.
>
> — Travis Good, The Sadies

That's when the band was real tight, I was impressed with some of that stuff."

They played so much and so hard that, by the time the rest of the world heard them, they impressed everyone immediately. Forget the guest stars and the sentiment of a last concert — this is simply a great band playing live. And Garth Hudson says he's heard them play much better!

NIGHT TRAIN: THE OSCAR PETERSON TRIO

45 Night Train

The Oscar Peterson Trio
Verve, 1963

C Jam Blues | Night Train | Georgia On My Mind | Bags' Groove | Moten Swing | Easy Does It | Honey Dripper | Things Ain't What They Used To Be | I Got It Bad And That Ain't Good | Band Call | Hymn To Freedom

A confident and mature sounding Peterson caresses the keys as the trio swings solidly, tackling standards, gospel and straight-ahead jazz on an album that keeps the toes tappin' and the fingers snappin'. All aboard!

— James Duplacey, author and historian

It starts off so incredibly simply, any child or tin-eared adult could play it: just find middle C and go CEEE C C C-F, and you have the start of "C Jam Blues". After six bars, it explodes. The piano becomes so soulful and distinct no one else in the world but Oscar Peterson could be playing it. Peterson's crowning triumph, *Night Train,* is the epitome of what a jazz trio could accomplish. The songs are instantly memorable, the interplay instinctive, the soloing both called for and jaw dropping.

The chords of the song "Night Train" are so rich in melody, they seem to be sung. Later, drummer Ed Thigpen's cymbal work fills the background like a layer of clouds. Bassist Ray Brown plays the most melodic and swinging bass solo imaginable. When the trio return, they are so tight, the Canada Council could program the Official Time Signal from them. The first notes of "Georgia

On My Mind" take us down South. The playing is so lyrical that Ray Charles is simply not needed.

At a time when other jazz giants were courting experimental new styles, Peterson chose to revisit the past. These are mainly old songs, steeped in the blues, composed by greats, including four by Duke Ellington. Peterson was a master of melody, coaxing clarity and sweetness out of the piano keys, piling the most ear-pleasing chords next to each other. No matter how fast the tempo, Peterson never lost track of the pretty.

With *Night Train*, Peterson meets the challenge of interpreting already-known songs, paying tribute to them and putting his own stamp on them

at the same time. To end the album, he does something else wonderful. "Hymn To Freedom", his own composition, starts solo with gentle church chords — gospel of a hundred years before. Peterson is talking of freedom, and the band are about to let you know all about it. As he carries the melody with his left hand, his right hand solos independently, making the song that much bigger. He reaches a peak as the song shouts for freedom, bringing both hands together and trilling the chords as fast as possible. He's never one to show off, though, so this lasts only for a verse. He leaves the song with dignity, with total freedom.

That's *Night Train*.

46 Down At The Khyber

The Joel Plaskett Emergency

Brobdingnagian, 2001

Down At The Khyber | There's Love In The Air | Maybe We
Should Just Go Home | Clueless Wonder | This Is A Message |
Unconditional Love | Waiting To Be Discovered | True Patriot Love |
Blinding Light | It's Catchin' On | Cry Together | Light Of The Moon

Down At The Khyber was the
first album that I heard where
I truly connected to the idea of
a Canadian identity that wasn't
bound by cities or provinces.

— Jordy Yack, CFBU

Joel Plaskett was no stranger to
the country's alternative rock scene.
His Halifax band Thrush Hermit had
been one of the favourites through the
nineties, but were now defunct. His
new band were going to be different.

Plaskett was willing to move away
from the alternative scene, at least
musically: "[Thrush Hermit] were
caught up in indie rock, and being
young and wanting to be perceived
as cool. You get so caught up in that,
sometimes, you don't always make
decisions for musical reasons, you
make them for some sort of aesthetic
reason that doesn't necessarily mean
anything to the listener. Having a new
band, we kind of shed a bit of that.
It was, hey, songs — let's figure out
what's the best way to play them,
not worry about what's fashionable
or not."

The Emergency burst out with a set
of riff rockers, a little bit of soul, and
some acoustic-based power ballads.

Lead track "Down At The Khyber"
also announces the band's pride in
their Halifax home, name checking
the city's most cool club and the joys
of floating down to the Musquodoboit
Harbour. These local references set
the band apart from other Canadian
rockers and welcomed listeners into
Plaskett's world. "I like idiosyncrasy,
and I like the idea of it being an
identifiable voice. And it is mine,
I'm writing obviously about certain
things that happened to me or things
I've observed. It's not like I claim
to have lived all the songs. I tend
to write as a narrator, whether it's
'Down At The Khyber' or 'Maybe
We Should Just Go Home'."

If he has any worries about being
labelled an East Coast artist, Plaskett
welcomes the rest of the country to
his sound with something identifiable
for all. "True Patriot Love" quotes
"O Canada" to create Plaskett's own
new anthem. Its image of falling asleep

in front of the TV and waking up at
3 am to the sounds of the anthem sign-
off has been a live-set favourite since
its release. It even seems patriotic, a big
song for a big country. Plaskett admits,
"That's a compliment to me. Aspects of
it were conscious and others weren't.
People often ask me if I feel part of
a big Canadian scene or something.
No, I just feel like part of the Halifax
scene. But just having done so much
touring over the years, it sunk in. I'm
happy to have that be part of Canadian
music, and it fits in there nicely and I'm
pleased by that."

47 Harvest Moon

Neil Young
Reprise, 1992

Unknown Legend | From Hank To Hendrix | You And Me |
Harvest Moon | War Of Man | One Of These Days |
Such A Woman | Old King | Dreamin' Man | Natural Beauty

Harvest Moon was ground-breaking for me in that it was released right after the whole Grunge/Nirvana/Seattle thing started up, and here is this legendary rocker, a Canadian, an activist, who puts out a record at the opposite end of the spectrum, and it really spoke to me.

— Waye Mason,
Halifax Pop Explosion

For years, Neil Young had been hounded to do the acoustic music so many people loved, to recreate the magic of "Heart Of Gold". So he certainly knew what he was doing in 1992 when he made *Harvest Moon*. He might as well have called it *Harvest II*, movie-sequel style. Not only does he stick the H-word in the title, he regroups much of the old gang from '72, The Stray Gators. The invitation even extended to his old pals, James Taylor and Linda Ronstadt, who'd helped in the original.

Harvest Moon wasn't *Harvest*, but it certainly wasn't like the noisy guitar rock the Godfather of Grunge had been making lately, either. It is acoustic, reflective, and personal, yet with a new twist. And most tracks are overwhelmingly positive, charming, and sentimental. *Harvest* had the searching lyrics of "Old Man" and "Heart Of Gold". In contrast, *Harvest Moon* is so upbeat that, at times,

it seems Young has found that heart of gold. "Unknown Legend" refers to a woman the singer admires, at first from a distance, who works in a diner. Later, she's dressing two kids. That's consistent with the story of Neil and Pegi Young.

By then, the couple had passed a decade together, and much of the album is devoted to the nature and length of relationships. Writing about women had always been trouble for Young; some of his harshest criticism had been lobbed at his patriarchal "A Man Needs A Maid". Now, Young offers a glimpse not only of a mature relationship but a loving and successful one. His questions about keeping the home fires burning point to someone looking to make the love continue a lot longer.

The disc is not completely bright. "War Of Man" is not directed at any specific conflict but warns that no one wins. The "Dreamin' Man" carries a

loaded gun and lives in his van. Still, the style is so warm the lyrics can't dampen the mood. When he sings in "One Of These Days" about wanting to get back in touch with all his old friends, even way back in Winnipeg, you know he means it, whether he actually does write that long letter or not.

In 1992, Neil Young was writing about time passing and about trying to keep hold of all the things he values in life. If it were anyone else, you'd think he was feeling his age. That didn't last; within three years, he was recording and touring with Pearl Jam.

48 Cuts Like A Knife

Bryan Adams
A&M, 1983

The Only One | Take Me Back | This Time | Straight From The Heart | Cuts Like A Knife | I'm Ready |
What's It Gonna Be | Don't Leave Me Lonely | Let Him Know | The Best Was Yet To Come

Very prophetic title. Adams and Jim Vallance gave us a track-by-track clinic on songwriting, teen themes, and all the best that pop rock has to offer. A career game-breaker.

— Terry David Mulligan, broadcaster and actor

A chance shopping trip in Vancouver changed the lives of Bryan Adams and songwriter Jim Vallance: "I was twenty-three when I met BryanHe'd just turned eighteen. It was the first week of January, 1978. I was at Long & McQuade with my friend Ali Monroe. Ali knew Bryan, and she introduced us. Bryan said, 'hey, we should get together and do some writing.' A day or two later, Bryan came over to my house, and we spent the next eleven years together, almost every day. He had confidence bordering on arrogance. Just a real sense of 'I'm gonna make it, and nothing's gonna stop me. You couldn't help but be drawn to that."

The two shopped their early efforts around, with no luck. "Our first batch of songs was rejected by every record company in Canada," Vallance remembers. "It just made us want to work harder. We knew we were doing good work, and we were willing to take the blows and put in the hours. As it turns out, it took four years to achieve any kind of recognition."

With *Cuts Like A Knife,* the partnership hit its stride. A mix of ballads, crafty pop, and anthemic rockers, the album had something for every radio format. The song that broke first, however, was the one Vallance didn't co-write, "Straight From The Heart". With a hit single in both Canada and the US, Adams could jump-start his climb to the top. Vallance feels they'd finally done an album with the depth to win over a large audience: "Certainly, the title track seemed to work, and 'This Time' was fairly well crafted. 'I'm Ready' surprised me, because I didn't think it was a very good song. Then, ten years later, Bryan re-recorded it as an 'unplugged' ballad, and he found the song's sweet spot."

Some dismissed Adams's songs as formula pop. But Vallance knows just how hard it is to write a hit: "Simple is always better. Look at Sting's song, 'Every Breath You Take'. It's so simple people tend to think, hey, I could have written that. But they didn't write it. Sting did. As Bryan was fond of saying, 'If it was easy, everybody'd be doing it'."

Adams and Vallance would spend hours a day, for days on end, each coming up with little pieces. *Cuts Like A Knife* proved the more the partners searched, the more hits they'd find. *Reckless* came next, and superstardom.

HARMONIUM

l'heptade

49 L'heptade

Harmonium
CBS, 1976

Prologue | Comme un fou | Sommeil sans rêves | Chanson noire | Le premier ciel | L'exil | Le corridor | Lumières de vie | Comme un sage | Épilogue

Harmonium's three albums all were huge successes. The group's timeless blend of folk, jazz, progressive rock, and classical was unique, exciting, and challenging. Each album was completely different from the others, yet fans accepted them and grew along with the band.

By the time *L'heptade* was released, the group had grown from a trio to a seven-piece, augmented by more singers, composer and pianist Neil Chotem providing orchestral interludes, and members of l'Orchestre symphonique de Montréal. The album, a sprawling two-disc set, was far from the acoustic trio of just two years before.

To this day, leader Serge Fiori can't explain the project: "Yes, it is big. I wasn't thinking. If I would have thought, I would have died. Because of whatever was happening at the time, I just retreated for about nine months, and I got into something spiritual,

blah blah blah. I got to thinking about this epic, Indian stuff, about the seven levels of consciousness. And I went for it."

L'heptade worried everyone involved in the band's career except Fiori: "Myself, I thought it would be accepted. I was pretty much the only one. My manager wanted to kill me. [The record company] was freaking out, they went nuts. So we didn't talk to them. The first time I played the songs, just guitar and voice, [the band] freaked out: 'Oh God, you went nuts'."

Then the record hit the unsuspecting public: "Oh, it was total shock, like, what the hell is that? They put the record on and there's this string intro that's very bizarre. And then it did the same thing! It sold great. You went into [famous record store] Phantasmagoria in Montréal and there was a stack of albums right on the front desk. It was some kind of cult. It was very strange."

Then, without warning or explanation, Harmonium were gone: "I got really sick, very very sick, both mentally and physically. I was totally burned out. I just crashed, and I couldn't get up for about six months. By the time I did, it was gone for me. I didn't want to go back to that. Everybody thought I just disappeared on an island and took acid or something. But no, I couldn't function at all. I wanted to do music, but more background and in a relaxed way. So I chose that. I built a studio, and that's what I've been doing all this time."

Fiori is thrilled that people, including anglophones, still consider his music important and that all three of his Harmonium albums are in this book: "That's so sweet for me; it makes everything worthwhile when you hear people are still aware of you. Oh God, it's so nice."

50 Teenage Head

Teenage Head
IGM, 1979

Top Down | Ain't Got No Sense | Bonerack | Picture
My Face | Lucy Potato | Curtain Jumper | You're
Tearin' Me Apart | Little Boxes | Get Off My Back |
Kissin' The Carpet

Teenage Head (left to right): Nick Stipanitz (drums), Steve Mahon (bass), Frankie Venom
(vocals), Gord Lewis (guitar)

The name came before there was even a band. Fourteen-year-old Gordie Lewis hadn't even picked up a guitar when he was flipping through a rock mag in his hometown of Hamilton: "I still have the magazine, it was *Creem*, the June 1971 issue. On the back of it was, for $3.50, you get a subscription to *Creem* magazine, and you got a choice of albums. One of them was by The Flamin' Groovies, and the album was called *Teenage Head*. I thought, wow, what a great name for a band."

By 1977, something was happening an hour away in Toronto. "It was April," remembers Lewis. "Punk hit downtown Toronto, with The Diodes and the Crash 'n' Burn Club, The Viletones at the Underground Club, all playing original music. As soon as I saw that I said, okay, we gotta play here, there's something going on here, this is where we fit in."

Teenage Head got their chance to record with tiny independent label IGM. The group had no experience in a studio, and were handed over to a much older producer. Says Lewis, "He was a gentleman called Allan Caddy. We didn't know where he came from or anything like that. I found out later he'd performed in a band called The Tornados, who did 'Telstar' — he was the guitar player." Caddy's pedigree would have made other bands drool. Before The Tornados, he'd played with British group Johnny Kidd and The Pirates, who did the original "Shakin' All Over". Caddy died in 2000 at sixty.

Lewis says, "It's really funny, here we are, this punk band from Hamilton with this classically trained musician, and nobody explaining each other to the other person, so there's some friction going on. He was trying to do his best to make us as musical as he possibly could. And he used a lot of elements that I only came to understand later in my career, which helped make that album be what it is: dynamics, harmony, melody lines. But it's only looking back now I see how much he contributed to the overall sound of that recording. I really like it!"

It was an unlikely partnership, but it had the desired result. Teenage Head found an audience of kids searching for something other than the corporate rock and disco playlists of the day. Lewis and the group met them at every show: "It was finally okay to like a Canadian band and be a kid. Believe it or not, that was our goal, because when I was a kid, I was into New York Dolls and Iggy and The Stooges, and I thought, why can't there be this for Canada? And that's what I wanted to be."

Top Eleven Canadian Blues Albums

What can you say about a guy who does a Top Ten, then weeks later insists one more has to go on it? Holger loves the blues so much, he could never stop adding names. As host of CBC Radio's long-running *Saturday Night Blues* program and the owner of Edmonton's Stony Plain Recording Company, he's probably done more to promote blues music in this country than anyone. Forgive Holger if some of his picks come from his own label. He does have excellent taste, after all, and any Stony Plain release is first class. Holger's choices are in no particular order.

Dutch Mason Blues Band
The Blues Ain't Bad
"Dutchy at his best, with a great band and with his guitar-playing abilities intact. The Prime Minister of the Blues was a pioneer who had more character (and jokes) than anyone on the Canadian blues scene. He rightfully received the Order of Canada prior to his death in 2006. This is the album that opened doors for him outside Atlantic Canada."

Downchild Blues Band
Straight Up
"Includes the band's hit version of 'Flip, Flop And Fly' and two originals later covered by The Blues Brothers. Donnie and Hock Walsh paved the way for countless blues bands with this record. Donnie is still fronting the band thirty-five years (and seventy-eight members) later and keeping the Downchild sound alive. This was a toss-up that could have gone to the band's 2007 live album."

King Biscuit Boy aka Richard Newell
Urban Blues Renewell
"His most consistent and straight-ahead blues album. Richard's harp playing is brilliant, his singing always soulful, and choice of material inspiring — including four original songs. The pride of the Hamilton blues scene, Richard worked with Ronnie Hawkins, Crowbar, Duane Allman, The Meters, and Allen Toussaint before passing away in 2003."

Colin James
Colin James & The Little Big Band 3
"Colin's first love is the blues, and he's been making great records of various styles since the mid-eighties. *Big Band 3* gets the nod for its great feel throughout, sense of improvisation and 'on the edge' playing, great production, and strong material. Plus there's Colin's always passionate vocals, his ability to get inside a song, and his amazing guitar playing."

Long John Baldry
Right To Sing The Blues
"This Juno award-winning CD features the transplanted British blues and rock legend backed by great players and singing songs perfectly suited to him. A good variety of jump and Chicago blues, plus acoustic material delivered with his rich, deep voice and sense of humour and theatre. A one-of-a-kind character, Long John Baldry brought out the best in musicians. He passed in 2005."

Jim Byrnes
House Of Refuge
"Recording with the gospel group The Sojourners, Jim and producer Steve Dawson created a Juno award-winning, genre-busting classic. Equally at home as an actor (*Wiseguy*, *Highlander*), Jim Byrnes's fifth album in twenty years showcases his gruff, roadhouse blues voice and soulful delivery. Transplanted from St. Louis as a draft dodger, Jim has expanded blues awareness in Canada."

David Wilcox
Rockin' The Boogie — Best Blues And Boogie
"A compilation of his early hits, including 'That Hypnotizin' Boogie' (1983) through to new material recorded for this project. Canada's Boogie King shows he can adapt deep acoustic blues, write with a sense of humour, and capture some of the best party blues on record. An amazing Telecaster player, whose clean guitar work sets a standard."

Colin Linden
Easin' Back To Tennessee
"Colin has been a musician since the age of eleven when Howlin' Wolf personally encouraged him to follow that path. This CD showcases his fluid guitar style, good 'producer' taste, bandleader instincts, and songwriter chops. Colin puts an official stamp of quality on everything he's involved with."

Various Artists
20 Years Saturday Night Blues
"A double CD of thirty-three Canadian blues artists recorded 'live' or 'off the floor' for CBC Radio One's *Saturday Night Blues* and compiled by producer Dan Cherwoniak. If there is one release that shows the depth of blues talent and the health of the genre in this country, this is it."

Paul Reddick
Revue
"A collection of Paul Reddick's best recordings with The Sidemen, The Rhythm & Truth Brass Band, and his own releases. This songwriting blues poet is an old soul and harmonica

player who pushes the envelope but always stays true to the blues. His singing, with his eyes closed, transports him to another time and place."

Big Dave McLean
Blues From The Middle
"The title refers to his Winnipeg location. As deep, soulful, and authentic as any blues artist from anywhere, Big Dave has been waving the flag for over thirty-five years. He learned directly from friends Muddy Waters and John Hammond."

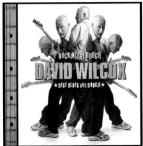

51 High Class In Borrowed Shoes

Max Webster

Anthem, 1977

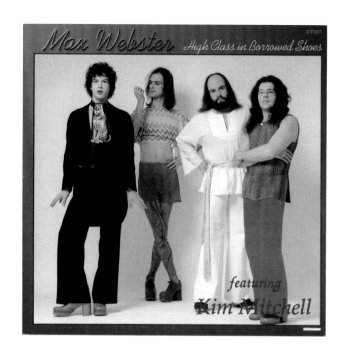

Max Webster (left to right): Mike Tilka (bass), Terry Watkinson (keyboards), Kim Mitchell (guitar, vocals), Paul Kersey (drums)

Like all special groups, Max Webster aren't easy to slot. They have guitar heroics, keyboard ballads, space-age progressive rock, synthesizer solos, and lush productions. They also have a healthy dose of humour; the lyrics are often satirical, including political digs at the US.

High Class In Borrowed Shoes was the flowering of the songwriting partnership of Kim Mitchell and Pye Dubois. Mitchell would first lead this band to success, then grow even bigger in the eighties with his solo career and a string of beloved rockers. But those patio lanterns were still in the distance. Here's where you can find the template. Dubois was the mystery man, the official non-member of the group and main lyric writer. He was in charge of supplying memorable lines. In a putdown of American foreign policy, "Oh War!", his line about saying fuck you instead of thank you certainly stood out in a more conservative time, at least when it comes to swearing.

The best-known track isn't a rocker but a pretty little slice of dreamy pop, "Diamonds Diamonds", with the line, "she takes more whiskey than I wine." There are big Beach Boys' backing vocals and spacey layers of keyboards. It's certainly not the Kim Mitchell of "Rockland Wonderland", but it's undeniably pleasing, and remains one of the best-loved songs of Mitchell's career.

Max Webster became one of the country's biggest bands and live draws. As the seventies closed, Mitchell went solo. He did keep one important Max Webster element, however, Pye Dubois. Together, the team wrote some of the biggest Canadian singles of the eighties, always with the special bit of wit.

52 Hejira

Joni Mitchell

Asylum, 1976

Coyote | Amelia | Furry Sings The Blues | A Strange Boy | Hejira |
Song For Sharon | Black Crow | Blue Motel Room | Refuge of the Roads

In three years, Joni Mitchell recorded three albums — each a major accomplishment — in completely different styles. The leaps from *Court And Spark* to *The Hissing Of Summer Lawns* to *Hejira* are radical and fully realized. On *Hejira*, she focuses on more complete story-songs; musically, she graduates to work with a major collaborator.

Jaco Pastorius was a young and already influential bass player, part of the jazz-fusion group Weather Report. His fluid playing could dominate a song. He wasn't there to keep up the bottom end — Pastorius's bass was a moaning counterpoint to the melody, and working with him meant Mitchell had crossed a line into more advanced modern jazz. His four appearances here began a studio and concert

Hejira continued Mitchell's eschewing of the stardom that knocked on her door so early and is a further exploration of the jazz idioms that had caught her ear.

— Grant Kerr, writer

partnership that completely altered Mitchell's music for the rest of the seventies.

Hejira is a travelling album, its characters restless and on the move. The protagonist of "Black Crow" is even trapped in travel, locked into a cycle of ferry to highway to plane to train, unsure if there's a home and peace to find. "Amelia" makes an icon of that mysterious lost pilot, Amelia Earhart. In this tale, the pilot doesn't crash, she ascends, swallowed by the sky, and the singer dreams of joining

her. Was it a suicidal thought? We are told it was just a false alarm.

For the first time since *Blue*, Mitchell settles into a musical mood for the whole album. Given the lyrics, it's no surprise it's melancholy. Yet each song has power instead of sadness, and the characters have dignity. Coyote, Amelia, the ancient bluesman Furry Lewis, Sharon — they are all heroes, and people on the journey. As much as the singer longs to get home, the trip offers some wonderful stories.

53 The Goldberg Variations

Glenn Gould

Columbia, 1955 and 1982

Image Provided Courtesy of SONY BMG MUSIC (CANADA) INC.

Glenn Gould recorded J.S. Bach's *Goldberg Variations* twice in his career. It was his first album for Columbia, made after his dramatic US debut in Washington, and his last, made just prior to his death in 1982. Our panel couldn't decide which to choose: some preferred the original, some were adamant fans of the latter. Still others could not or would not choose between them. So I threw out the rules, combined the votes, and selected both recordings to occupy the position simultaneously.

Gould himself grew to dislike the original recording, which is part of the reason he re-recorded it. In simple terms, he found it too fast. Indeed, there are drastic differences between the two. The second *Goldberg* is longer and slower — painstakingly slow at some points — and favourite passages are repeated. Some prefer the increased subtlety of the latter, some marvel at the dexterity and exuberance of the former.

Gould himself contributed to the interest that captured the public's imagination. He was simply odd.

He wore sweaters, scarves, gloves, a hat, and a heavy coat right through the summer, insisted on playing on a battered folding chair, and carried around bottles of pills. Annoyingly to many, he sang along to his playing, caught up in the moment. He worked alone in a hotel room and gave up live performances in the 1960s. He preferred recording and made many albums, but it is the *Goldberg Variations* for which he will always be remembered. Glenn Gould died of a stroke in 1982 at the age of fifty, just days after his birthday and the release of his new version of the *Goldberg Variations*. Many hailed him as the greatest classical pianist of his time.

> Though the 1955 version dazzles and reeks of genius, the 1982 version bears the unmistakable mark of a master, a man whose walk through life is coming to a close.
>
> — Sarah Slean, musician

54 Fogarty's Cove

Stan Rogers

Fogarty's Cove Music, 1977

Watching The Apples Grow | Forty-Five Years | Fogarty's Cove |
The Maid On The Shore | Barrett's Privateers | Fisherman's Wharf |
Giant | The Rawdon Hills | Plenty Of Hornpipe | The Wreck Of The
Athens Queen | Make And Break Harbour | Finch's Complaint/
Giant: Reprise

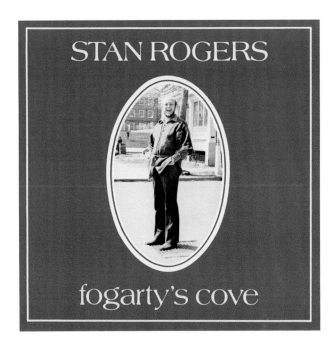

Every folk band in the Maritimes knows "Barrett's Privateers". Of course, no version matches that of Stan Rogers. There's a reason he does the definitive performance of this classic folk song: he wrote it. Most of the people who sing along think it's a vintage seafarers' tale. That it has become part of the national consciousness in just thirty years is a unique tribute to Stan Rogers's vast talents as a songwriter and Maritime patriot.

That's the other irony. For someone who captured both the sound of traditional East Coast music and the spirit of people in the 1970s, Rogers wasn't even born near the seabound coast. He's from Hamilton, Ontario. But both sides of his family were Maritimers, and trips to Nova Scotia cemented his love of the province.

He wrote modern folk anthems, too, which spoke of the changing times in Atlantic Canada. "Make And Break Harbour" tells of the end of the traditional fishery and the people left behind. "Finch's Complaint" is the story of what happens when the plant closes. That the young couple is thereby forced to move to Toronto is delivered like an undeserved damnation to hell.

In a region where, unless you're born there, you're never "from" there, Rogers remains the exception.

Stan Rogers made modern folk music that sounded ancient and made ancient themes come alive for a new generation. In less than a decade of recording, he became, in the opinion of many before his tragic death in an airplane fire in 1983, the greatest twentieth-century Canadian folk musician.

I'm proud to say that I am often the guy that starts things off by singing, loudly "Oh the year was seventeen seventy-eight" in bars (and Trooper shows!) all over the Maritimes.

— Ra McGuire, Trooper

55 Wheatfield Soul

The Guess Who

RCA, 1968

These Eyes | Pink Wine Sparkles In The Glass | I Found Her In A Star |
Friends Of Mine | When You Touch Me | A Wednesday In Your Garden |
Lightfoot | Love And A Yellow Rose | Maple Fudge | We're Coming To Dinner

This was the album that made people start thinking of these guys as more than just that cover band on TV.

— John Wiles, CKBW

The Guess Who had made lots of singles and albums before *Wheatfield Soul*, but in some ways it's their first real album. Burton Cummings remembers: "We had a lot of back-to-back heartbreak before 'These Eyes'. I joined the band in January '66, [and] over the next three years we had about fifteen singles, all of which really kind of bombed."

There was still no true Guess Who style. The trouble was the group could play anything, thanks to two years as the house band for the national CBC-TV show *Let's Go*. Says Randy Bachman, "It was our training ground to try these different mutations of pop music, as we were asked to copy and play the hit parade. The show's producer, Larry Brown, [also] encouraged the songwriting partnership of Bachman-Cummings to write original songs to fit in between the hits on the show." Cummings adds, "One of those we did was 'These Eyes', and [future producer] Jack Richardson was watching that particular day and loved the tune and actually mortgaged his house and got the money to fly us to New York [to record]. It's kind of a Cinderella story."

Even though "These Eyes" attracted all the attention, the group didn't think much of the song. "Oh no, absolutely not," says Cummings. "We fought tooth and nail against [it] as a single, because in '68, '69, everybody wanted to be Led Zeppelin. We absolutely didn't want a ballad." Bachman: "We were rockers from the Prairies. But you take what you can get after five or six years of trying. Everyone was screaming for 'These Eyes', so we rolled with it."

The Guess Who had a smash hit. Then they did something more surprising — they didn't move to the States. The Guess Who proved a Canadian group could join the big international music world. It was the Big Bang moment of the modern Canadian music industry.

56 Si on avait besoin d'une cinquième saison

Harmonium

Polydor, 1974

Vert | Dixie | Depuis l'automne | En pleine face | Histoires sans paroles

These Québécois maestros made Montreal chamber music popular thirty years before its revival. An unbelievable journey with album art to match, leaving you with butterflies in your stomach.

— Tom Thwaits, Trent Radio

The success of the previous year's debut disc *Harmonium* had been a big surprise to the Montreal band. They were barely a band after all, just two guitar players and a bass. The group were being booked into big theatres across the country, and leader Serge Fiori felt they needed to expand their sound, so a new keyboard player and a horn player were hired.

Free to experiment, Fiori and lyric writer Michel Normandeau created pieces based around the four seasons, except the group also imagine a fifth one, the new season that is to come. Instruments include 12-string guitar, mandolin, zither, accordion, dulcimer, flute, piccolo, sax, clarinet, and any sort of string effect the mellotrons and synths can produce. The music crosses back and forth from jazz to folk to progressive rock, usually in the same song. Best known is the summer number, "Dixie", a mesmerizing and incredibly happy piece of music with a light Dixieland theme and playful solos. To this day, most people call the album simply *Cinq saisons*. "I don't know why I put it that long anyway, because I called it *Cinq saisons*, too," Fiori admits. "I guess I was trying to be intellectual."

People who had loved the first, simpler album loved the new, larger sound even more. Harmonium had grown from a Montreal group to a Quebec hit to national stars. All of a sudden, the group were ambassadors for the province, then at the height of the debate over separation. "It was pretty nuts, it was really big. We meant something for the people, the national thing, the French culture. It was fun to see the English audience respond as well. A lot of the people knew the French lyrics."

Fiori had little time to enjoy this success. The move to a bigger band had worked better than he had imagined. For his next project, *L'heptade* (album 49) he would imagine something even more grand.

57 Dancing In The Dragon's Jaw

Bruce Cockburn

True North, 1979

Creation Dream | Hills Of Morning | Badlands Flashback |
Northern Lights | After The Rain | Wondering Where The Lions Are |
Incandescent Blue | No Footprints

Bruce Cockburn considers this album a career peak: "It pretty much sums up what I was doing in the seventies. I would steer people to *Dancing In The Dragon's Jaw*."

The album is full of danger and worry, but Cockburn rises above any doom and gloom, defying the dragons: "There is a lot of darkness around and yet it's folly to ignore it. People are suffering, and their suffering might be alleviated if we pay attention to these things. But in the meantime we have to soldier on and not be destroyed by the knowledge of that darkness or rendered impotent by it."

For the first time in his career, Cockburn found himself in the US with a hit single, "Wondering Where The Lions Are". He did it on *Saturday Night Live*: "I was terrified. I was blind with fear. And nobody helped. The atmosphere in the studio was really tense. It was the last gasp of the original cast, and everybody was out of favour with each other. There was a lot of edginess in the atmosphere, but I got through it.

"They set up these promotional things, and, at one point, I have to go to the Philadelphia Zoo and perform in front of the lion's cage. It's the middle of winter; it's cold. I'm reluctant because it's eight o'clock in the morning, but they tell me I have to go, the cameras are all going to be there. What they didn't tell me was they'd set up bleachers and they had an audience sitting there freezing, along with me, in front of these very bewildered-looking lions.

"Another time they actually rented a lion and took it to a radio station. Scared the bejeebers out of the radio station staff somewhere in the Midwest. They showed up with a frigging lion on a leash. So this is how 'Wondering Where The Lions Are' got to be a hit."

Top Ten Prairie Albums

Jay Semko is one of the great Prairie singer-songwriters. His albums with The Northern Pikes and on his own are both fun and full of images of Saskatchewan. Here are his Prairie picks:

1. Joni Mitchell — *Ladies Of The Canyon*: "Joni Mitchell went to high school with my aunt, the late Elaine McAskill. My aunt Elaine attended a bridal shower Joan attended as well, and my aunt claimed it was one of the first times Ms. Mitchell (Anderson then) performed live with her acoustic guitar for her peers. Aunt Elaine thought she was really good. My mom had a vinyl version of *Ladies* that I listened to, and I recently got the CD. I had forgotten how intense it is. I think it made a pretty big impression on me, without me realizing it. Her voice is so obviously incredible on these tracks — there is no one like Joni Mitchell, as much as people may be influenced by her."

2. The Guess Who — *Share The Land*: "The cover of this album is more poignant than ever. It was the second album I ever bought. It has Prairie all over it. It was pretty cool to me as a kid that a band from Winnipeg was this 'happening,' and believe me, everyone in the Prairies was aware of The Guess Who and how well known they were becoming at the time."

3. Ian & Sylvia — *Lovin' Sound*: "My dad played this eight-track in his car when I lived on the farm as a kid. I always found their voices together fascinating (still do), and every time I hear Ian & Sylvia, I remember watching the fields go by from the back seat."

4. Neil Young — *Prairie Wind* and *Harvest*: "To me these two albums are companion pieces, even though they were recorded many years apart. The combination of Neil's voice and the pedal steel is one of my favourite things. The music always brings autumn in the fields to me, driving in the truck. There's such a great lonely quality to some of these songs — open skies and shedding trees."

5. Bachman-Turner Overdrive — *Not Fragile*: "You can take the boy out of Winnipeg, but you can't take Winnipeg out of the boy. If there's such a thing as a Prairie accent in the voice, Randy's kept his completely. This is a great rock album, period."

6. Crash Test Dummies — *God Shuffled His Feet*: "CTDs opened for The Pikes for the last few dates of our Canadian 'Snow In June' tour. They were pretty unique, and obviously went on to great commercial success, which I think is cool considering they were so different from everything else going on at the time. Great lyrics: 'Mmm Mmm Mmm Mmm' is one of the best singles ever, in my opinion."

7. Corb Lund Band — *Hair In My Eyes Like A Highland Steer*: "Corb Lund writes great songs about the Prairies, and I love his music."

8. Wilf Carter — *A Prairie Legend*: "The original Prairie troubadour. This is a boxed-set collection of much of Wilf's music. It doesn't get more pure than this."

9. Streetheart — *Drugstore Dancer*: "The first time I ever got into a bar (I was fifteen), Streetheart were playing. They were the kings of Prairie rock for a few years, and were the first Saskatchewan-bred band in my youth to make a big impact. This album has a freshness from that era which I love."

10. Jann Arden — *Living Under June*: "Calgary's Jann made this great album in 1994. The songs are superb and her voice can bring on tears. I love it."

Image Provided Courtesy of SONY BMG MUSIC (CANADA) INC.

58 Frantic City

Teenage Head

Attic, 1980

Wild One | Somethin' On My Mind | Total Love | Let's Shake | Infected | Those Things You Do | Somethin' Else | Take It | Brand New Cadillac | Disgusteen

Frankie Venom was and is an original punk. "He's not kidding, he really means it," brags guitar player Gordie Lewis about his band's front man. "He means it to this day at fifty years old, and going on the stage. I've seen things that would have buried me ten times over, I've seen him get up, dust himself off, and move on. He's the real thing, and *THERE'S NOT MANY OF THEM!*"

Venom helped attract attention with his skinny ties, wild eyes, and camp-horror movie antics. With *Frantic City*, Teenage Head became the best-known Canadian alternative band of the time. "We were at our peak," believes Lewis.

Punk was different then, not the hard-core sound. The album features a slick pop song in "Somethin' On My Mind", the sixties'-style dance number "Let's Shake", and, most surprisingly, three fifties' rockabilly covers. "We had a gig at a local place [in Hamilton], but it was a country and western bar. We thought, what in the heck are we going to do?

I remember Slash Booze [band friend Brian Baird] said, 'Here's Eddie Cochran, how about 'Twenty Flight Rock'? 'Somethin' Else'? How about 'Blue Jean Bop'? They're not country, but they're close.' They went over so well we made them part of our repertoire, and we're still playing 'Somethin' Else' to this day."

Lewis is thrilled to have been part of that initial punk wave: "I really appreciate the fact that we were able to experience that. It was kinda like being around when Elvis started, in a way. It wasn't music industry stuff, it wasn't videos thrown at ya, it was so human. If you want to call it punk, that's fine by me, because it identifies a period of time, a very energetic, very creative, very exciting period of time."

I worked at Sunrise Records on Yonge St., Toronto, from 1980 to 1982 and I can tell you that *Frantic City* outsold any other title during those two years. Lead vocalist Frankie Venom was an incredibly cool and charismatic front man.

— Andy Grigg, *Real Blues Magazine*

59 Hymns Of The 49th Parallel

k.d. lang

Nonesuch, 2004

After The Gold Rush | Simple | Helpless | A Case Of You |
The Valley | Hallelujah | One Day I Walk | Fallen | Jericho |
Bird On A Wire | Love Is Everything

Leave it to one of Canada's most accomplished vocalists to record this sublime tribute to our country's songwriters. k.d. lang chooses ten songs, all of them quiet and reflective, and contributes one of her own, co-written with bassist David Piltch, which establishes the mood and theme. "Simple", as the title suggests, is stripped down to its instrumental and emotional core, a hymn to the simplicity of love.

With a singer as enchanting as lang, there's no need to fill up the spaces or embellish the recordings. A gentle touch is used throughout, with Teddy Borowiecki's piano the main instrument. Piltch's acoustic bass and producer Ben Mink's guitar do most of the rest, with a large but hushed string section called in when needed.

Did you see k.d. lang sing "Hallelujah" at the Canadian Songwriters Hall of Fame show? That really was something!

— Leonard Cohen

lang has proven herself to be a marvellous interpreter of Joni Mitchell's work. Here she does two, "A Case Of You" and "Jericho". Both contain superb lyrics, using strong religious imagery to create powerful messages of love. Leonard Cohen's "Hallelujah" is simply one of the greatest songs ever written. Again, the Bible is central, with King David composing the ultimate hymn for God, only to see it wasted in the search for earthly love. Having these three songs together on an album is a joy.

Another Cohen song, "Bird On A Wire", is the highlight of the disc. As charming as Cohen's is, there's simply no argument that, in this case, lang has bettered the original.

Neil Young, Cohen, and Mitchell are the obvious choices here, but it's significant that lang includes songs by Ron Sexsmith, Bruce Cockburn, and Jane Siberry. This disc alone should satisfy anyone's questions about the quality of Canadian songwriting.

60 Hot Shots

Trooper
MCA, 1979

Boys In The Bright White Sports Car | Baby Woncha Please Come Home | General Hand Grenade | Two For The Show | Ready | Santa Maria | We're Here For A Good Time (Not A Long Time) | Oh, Pretty Lady | (It's Been A) Long Time | Round, Round We Go | The Moment That It Takes | Raise A Little Hell

They were what rock and roll was all about. Fun, hooky, riffy, singalong anthems. I felt that if they could get national airplay, they'd become a national fixture, which they have.

— Randy Bachman, Trooper producer

Made up of hits from the Vancouver band's first four albums, *Hot Shots* boasts genuine anthems, songs almost every Canadian knows by heart: "We're Here For A Good Time" and "Raise A Little Hell".

For 1977's *Knock 'Em Dead Kid*, Ra McGuire had a problem: "We still didn't have the ten songs we needed to make a record. We left rehearsals one night and I was starting to panic a little bit. The guy who drove the trucks for us at this time, Smitty, put his arm around me and said, 'hey, Ra,

don't worry, we're here for a good time, not a long time.' The next day, I went down in the morning and sat on a log on the beach, and everything that I wrote was in real time — "A very good friend of mine told me something the other day" — the thing pretty much wrote itself."

The same scenario played out for *Thick As Thieves*, from 1978. "Randy [Bachman] said, 'We just need something to fill this album out." And we said we have this

song that we use to close our set that people seem to like. There was a lot of controversy because Randy wanted to change the name to 'Raise A Little Howl', because he's Mormon.

"Our songs are grad songs, wedding songs, and funeral songs. 'Raise A Little Hell' — it doesn't feel like my song anymore, it feels like I'm playing the anthem. I've disconnected with it on an ownership level — it's their song, not ours."

61 Robbie Robertson

Robbie Robertson

Geffen, 1987

Fallen Angel | Showdown At Big Sky | Broken Arrow | Sweet Fire
Of Love | American Roulette | Somewhere Down The Crazy River |
Hell's Half Acre | Sonny Got Caught In The Moonlight | Testimony

Although the chief writer for The Band, Robbie Robertson had never been a front man. After all, he'd been in perhaps the best performing group in rock and roll, with three brilliant vocalists. There would be a lot to live up to, plus lingering complaints that Robertson had been solely responsible for pulling the plug on The Band. When a solo album appeared, he was bound to face tough criticism and resentment.

Robertson turned to a fellow Canadian, the hottest producer in music. Daniel Lanois had worked with U2 and Peter Gabriel, so some of the world's biggest stars were standing by. With U2, Robertson wrote "Sweet Fire Of Love", Bono taking an equal share of the vocals. Elsewhere, Gabriel provides keyboards, and former Bandmates Rick Danko and Garth Hudson help. Still, all the firepower would be for nothing if the songs weren't good.

All criticisms were washed away when the album arrived. This wasn't Band music. Instead, Robertson had developed a moody and mysterious sound. Before, he had written stories set in the past or with a timeless feel. These were present-day sagas. "Showdown At Big Sky", with its driving beat and thick guitar, isn't about some Western gunslinger but a modern unnamed conflict, this high noon tale involving an arms race. "Hell's Half Acre" finds a soldier in clouds of napalm, not deep in Dixie.

Reviews at the time spoke of "Americana", but perhaps the writers had forgotten Robertson's First Nations' heritage. His mother was Mohawk, and he spent his summers on the Six Nations reserve in Ontario. There are lyrical references throughout, from the broken arrow to the native son going to war in "Hell's Half Acre". Indeed, Robertson spent most of the nineties exploring and creating music for First Nations, and performed a song on that theme at the 2002 Winter Olympics in Salt Lake City.

62 The Trinity Session

Cowboy Junkies
RCA, 1988

Mining For Gold | Misguided Angel | I Don't Get It | I'm So
Lonesome I Could Cry | To Love Is To Bury | 200 More Miles |
Dreaming My Dreams With You | Sweet Jane | Postcard Blues |
Walking After Midnight

Image Provided Courtesy of SONY BMG MUSIC (CANADA) INC.

It sounded almost radical in 1988. It still does. Whether it's
their own sad songs of the words of other musicians, the band
interprets them right in the moment, and perfectly.

— Caitlin Crockard, CBC

Producer Peter Moore suggested a radical setting for Cowboy Junkies' second album: Toronto's Church of the Holy Trinity. The memories still excite Michael Timmins: "It was amazing. Every musician who walked in there and started to play their instrument was a little bit overwhelmed by the sound of this space. 'Omigod it's so much fun to play in here'."

The session is live, direct to two-track, using only one microphone — no overdubs, no doctoring after the fact. Says Timmins, "Musicians playing with other musicians live was unique back then. You didn't hear it, and whether people knew it or not, they were listening to musicians listening to each other, playing off one another. The church gave it that dreamy atmosphere and it was different for the late eighties."

The music itself was new, at least in the mix of styles and subtle, quiet performance. Music fans used to buying by genre now found an album that featured originals, blues numbers, old country favourites, and even a slowed-down, druggy Lou Reed number, "Sweet Jane". Timmins: "I think people looked at the covers and said, what a curious mix. If you were doing covers, you'd do a traditional record or a modern rock song, but you wouldn't mix the two and you wouldn't try to make connections between the two. We listened to different kinds of music from all those genres and decades, so we felt there was no reason why we can't perform them on record as well."

Cowboy Junkies broke down labels and barriers, and predated the alt-country/No Depression era of the nineties. There are now radio formats, magazines, and venues completely devoted to Americana or roots music in the broadest term. It was a Canadian group that spearheaded the style, the sound, and the interest for musicians and fans.

63 Ron Sexsmith

Ron Sexsmith

Interscope, 1995

Secret Heart | There's A Rhythm | Words We Never Use | Summer
Blowin' Town | Lebanon, Tennessee | Speaking With The Angel |
In Place Of You | Heart With No Companion | Several Miles | From
A Few Streets Over | First Chance I Get | Wastin' Time | Galbraith
Street | There's A Rhythm (different version)

For six years, Ron Sexsmith wandered the streets of Toronto. He was a foot-courier and put the time to good use: "A lot of these songs [on his first CD] were written on the job. I still write that way, walking around. I'll get an idea, I'll be singing it or humming it. I think people thought I was crazy when I was a courier, talking to myself, but I was really writing my album."

His writing got him noticed, and US label Interscope signed him. Recording sparsely, he and producer Mitchell Froom created a new kind of pop-folk album. Everyone was thrilled, except the suits: "Pretty much everyone at Interscope hated the record. They wanted it re-recorded." Fellow Canadian Daniel Lanois was a fan, and the duo re-recorded

"There's a Rhythm": "Interscope flipped out, and said it was the best thing I'd done. They wanted the whole album redone. But I was really proud of the work Mitchell and I had done."

> I know him, he's a friend. He's a fine writer.
>
> — Gordon Lightfoot

As a compromise, the Lanois version was included as a bonus track. But record companies don't like to compromise: "There was talk they weren't going to put it out. Everyone was mad at me, they thought I was this difficult guy from Canada,

which I wasn't. When it finally came out, you couldn't find it in stores. There was talk I would be dropped. I was scared."

Froom ran into friend Elvis Costello and gave him Sexsmith's disc. Soon after, Costello appeared, holding the disc, on the cover of *Mojo* magazine's issue on The Best Thing I've Heard All Year. "It was the shot heard 'round the world," says Ron.

Sexsmith's foot-courier's eyes had helped him chronicle the love, longing, and loneliness of normal lives. So if you see Ron Sexsmith out walking, catch his eye — you might end up in his next song.

64 Nothingface

Voivod

MCA, 1989

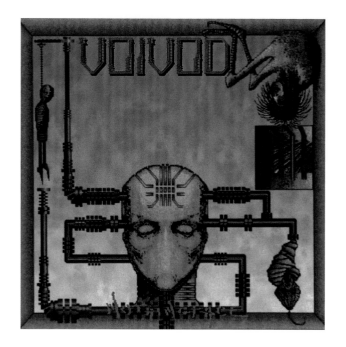

Making them a household name in metal neighbourhoods, their futuristic approach to an often-times closed-minded genre was refreshing, influential, and a listener's delight.

— Danko Jones

Quebec's Voivod was instrumental in changing not only attitudes toward heavy metal but the overall quality of the music as well. They were excellent musicians, capable of blending several styles and creating complex songs full of melody and thoughtful lyric themes, while still providing the thunder. The influential *Nothingface* album has its roots in metal but with full helpings of progressive and psychedelic rock.

Michel "Away" Langevin is the group's drummer, lyricist, and creator of the mythological themes found in the albums: "I think the main reason why the album was so cohesive comes from the fact that we had been very disciplined, rehearsing at least five times a week since the beginning of our career in 1983."

Because the band reached out to other genres, they were open to incorporating anything that would take them to new levels. "The interest we had in other scenes helped a lot," confirms Away. "Mainly in the eighties, when we discovered the Industrial movement. From then on, we stopped trying to be the heaviest or the fastest. It became more of a quest for originality, which turned out to be an even bigger challenge."

Guitarist Denis "Piggy" D'Amour composed much of the music on the disc. Sadly, he passed away from cancer in 2005. By covering Pink Floyd's 1967 track "Astronomy Domine", the band made it cool for metalheads to dig Floyd and vice versa. Says Away, "Syd Barrett's art had a big impact on me. Piggy was a huge fan of David Gilmour's guitar playing. We didn't think of it as being innovative at the time. Nothing was calculated or intentional, it all came out naturally. I was impressed with the gathering of different scenes at our shows, so I guess *Nothingface* created links that were non-existent before. What I'm most proud of is the loyalty of the people listening to Voivod. Thanks to all the Voivodians!"

Ten Influential Canadian Drummers

Neil Peart has won so many international awards for his drumming that everyone's lost count. He's the percussive master and lyricist for a "little Toronto combo", as he calls Rush. Rather than submit a Top Ten list, Neil chose to write a few lines about ten Canadian drummers who have influenced him. A published author, Neil's four books are based around themes of travel, from motorcycle journeys to life on the road with Rush.

"Garry Peterson of The Guess Who came into my life twice early on: first, seeing him play at the Caledonia Fair around the summer of 1965, just before I started playing drums; then again in 1970, when my band, J.R. Flood, played an outdoor festival at Brock University in St. Catharines. The festival was headlined by The Guess Who and Mashmakhan, whose drummer, Jerry Mercer, was also an early influence, especially in soloing. That night I watched from the back of the huge crowd as Jerry played a solo in 'Letter From Zambia', an African-influenced piece, with dark polyrhythms (I also recall Jerry incorporating short blasts on a whistle held in his mouth), and it was one of the most original drum solos I had heard up to that time. Jerry and I crossed paths again in later years, when he was with April Wine, and they played a few shows with Rush. In fact, my present drum tech, Lorne Wheaton, once worked for Jerry, too.

"Other big influences in the late sixties, when I was a teenager, were seeing the amazingly funkadelic Whitey Glan with Mandala at the Lincoln Curling Centre [roller rink] in St. Catharines, and Skip Prokop's beautiful rudimental technique and jaw-dropping solo (featuring three small snare drums high on his right) with Lighthouse at the arena in St. Catharines. Really, there were so many great drummers around southern Ontario in those days that I'm surprised I didn't just give up. Graham Lear is another drummer who came into my musical life twice: first, with George Oliver's Natural Gas at the roller rink; then years later on his fantastic recordings with Gino Vanelli.

"A couple of other Toronto drummers were very influential to me early on: Dave Cairns with Leigh Ashford, and Danny Taylor with Nucleus, both with a powerful, r'n'b-influenced style of rock drumming that is still part of my playing.

"Later on, in the seventies, I was impressed by Martin Deller's fluid technique and resonant touch with FM, the solid timekeeping and dramatic fills of Gary McCracken with Max Webster, and the tasteful economy of Johnny Fay with The Tragically Hip."

JOHNNY FAY

GRAHAM LEAR

65 Come On Over

Shania Twain

Mercury, 1997

Man! I Feel Like A Woman! | I'm Holdin' On To Love (To Save My Life) |
Love Gets Me Every Time | Don't Be Stupid (You Know I Love You) |
From This Moment On | Come On Over | When | Whatever You Do! Don't!
| If You Wanna Touch Her, Ask! | You're Still The One | Honey, I'm Home |
That Don't Impress Me Much | Black Eyes, Blue Tears | I Won't Leave You
Lonely | Rock This Country! | You've Got A Way

I used to be responsible for music at a lot of diverse parties
back in the late nineties, and I could always count on tracks
like "Man! I Feel Like A Woman!"

— Troy Neilson, aka Brockway Biggs
aka Pimp Tea

What's ECMA-winning hip-hop artist Troy Neilson doing voting for Shania Twain in *The Top 100 Canadian Albums*? As the great-grandnephew of Don Messer, he does know about fiddles. But for a hip-hop guy, it's the beats. Those big booms come courtesy of Twain's production mastermind and husband Mutt Lange.

In the CD era, the Canadian Recording Industry Association has handed out just four double-diamond awards recognizing the sales of two million copies of a disc in Canada. Twain has three of them, for *Come On Over*, *The Woman In Me*, and *Up!*. She sold them to country fans and rock fans, teens, adults, and seniors. In some cases, it was the only CD a person would buy all year. People even bought their first CD players just to listen to Shania.

Everything on the album is big, even the song titles with their exclamation points. The synthesized stings and guitar riff that announce "Man! I Feel Like A Woman!" blast out like a huge rock anthem. There aren't just twin fiddles — she has a whole team of them.

Country or not, it doesn't matter; these are amazingly well crafted hits. Like those of Bryan Adams in the eighties, BTO in the seventies, and The Guess Who in the sixties, the tunes are full of hooks. And as Brockway Biggs will tell ya, these are incredible beats.

66 Everything I Long For

Hayden

Hardwood Records, 1995

Bad As They Seem | In September | We Don't Mind | Tragedy |
Stem | Skates | I'm To Blame | Assignment In Space With Rip Foster |
Driveway | Hardly | You Were Loved | When This Is Over | Bunkbed |
I Almost Cried | My Parent's House | Lounging

It's a musician's deepest fear: having your instruments stolen. It's always a heartbreaking disaster. Except for Hayden Desser, who might not be on this list without it: "My friend Noah Mintz [hHead] borrowed my electric guitar that I hadn't played since high school. While touring in Vancouver, it was stolen out of their van. So when he came back, he gave me an old acoustic to replace it. I just began playing it because it was there. I guess I indirectly owe thanks to some Gastown thief."

Hayden started recording at home using the low-fi technique. Many young listeners wanted music from good writers and real, approachable people, not overhyped, overproduced celebrities. Hayden simply said what he had to say:

Not only is Hayden an extraordinary singer/songwriter, he's a compelling storyteller as well. He's sensitive, empathetic, funny, honest, and real, and it is easy to relate to any one of the songs he sings.

— LoriAnn Villani, CJXY

"The songs described things that had happened to me, things that I wanted to happen to me, and things that I didn't want to happen to me."

It was far from polished but emotionally grabbing. Hayden uses his four tracks wisely, often doing two parallel vocal lines. The main one is his low register, gruff and troubled. The higher part is softer, sometimes a whisper, but a sweeter harmony. Its obvious ancestor is the dark, acoustic material from Neil Young albums such as *On The Beach*, with a nod to more current punk in the throatiest vocals.

Some of the added studio tracks include more instruments, but the songs are still spare and the feeling of the original home tracks remains. Hayden feels that's why the album received such a strong reaction: "Perhaps it's simplicity, rawness, and the subject matter of the songs — relatable stories in strong detail, with not much to get in the way."

Please don't take this as an open invitation to steal anyone's guitar.

67 Outskirts

Blue Rodeo

Warner, 1987

Heart Like Mine | Rose-Coloured Glasses | Rebel | Joker's Wild |
Piranha Pool | Outskirts | Underground | 5 Will Get You Six | Try |
Floating

The songwriting and singing partnership of Jim Cuddy and Greg Keelor is one of the longest running in Canadian music history. "Jim and I met at North Toronto Collegiate in 1972," says Keelor. "We eventually became friends. I didn't start playing guitar until I was twenty-one."

Teaming with Cuddy back in the Toronto, the duo formed the punk/New Wave-inspired HiFis in 1977:

"We moved to New York in 1981. Everything in Toronto had shut down. There was nowhere to play if you played original music."

Band life in New York City didn't amount to much success, but it did put the duo on the right track: "It was in New York that a lot of the songs for *Outskirts* were written. By the time we left, we actually had the name Blue Rodeo. Over half the album was written there."

Keelor felt popular eighties' rock in Canada was off course: "You were surrounded by Honeymoon Suite and Loverboy — that was radio at the time. A lot of the people I hung out with liked the sound we were headed toward, the singer-songwriter-with-a-guitar type."

The group's first single was the

title cut, "Outskirts". Not many remember its fate: "It was a bomb. We were taken out by our marketing manager and told this record wasn't going to happen. But then John Martin on MuchMusic played 'Try'. He loved the song, but he hated the video. Still, he kept on playing it and playing it. 'Try' was a hit, so that opened the door for us."

After nearly watching their album die, Blue Rodeo were now the hottest band in the country: "It took about six months to catch on. It sat a long time a bit of a lame duck. Then 'Try' did so well, and that's a very exciting time when a record goes Top Ten. That's a pretty Beatle-esque moment in your career."

68 Joyful Rebellion

k-os

EMI, 2004

Emcee Murdah | Crucial | Man I Used To Be | Crabbuckit | B-Boy Stance | Commandante | The Love Song | Hallelujah | Clap Ur Handz | Neutroniks | Dirty Water | One Blood (Jiggy Homicide) | Papercutz

k-os has had a problem with hip-hop. In the mid-nineties, he started recording singles with some success but quit because he was disenchanted. This, his breakthrough album after returning to recording in 2002, includes many lyrics that criticize the state of the music, with its-guns-and-ho clichés. He is a serious writer, an inventive performer, and takes influences where he can find them, mixing lots of music into the songs. He performs with live instruments, instead of samples, and uses musicians in the studio rather than relying on programming. He's also outspoken about what he perceives as assaults on the higher quality of the art, and has lashed out at musicians and writers, causing lots of controversy.

Joyful Rebellion has scores of musical surprises, including tango guitar, a simple acoustic guitar ballad, and a pulsing track that features rocker Sam Roberts as a co-vocalist — hardly a hip-hop move. It all points to k-os's insistence on stretching outside the rules of the gatekeepers, finding his influences not by culture but by desire.

> Aside from tracks that received commercial success, there are several sons that blend reggae and hip-hop in a way unheard before in the Canadian music landscape.
>
> — Murray Crawford, Trent Radio

It's heady stuff for hip-hop. It helps that there are lots of infectious beats, the most appreciated of which is on "Crabbuckit". With a walking bass line and a Star Trek-theme start, k-os walks on Yonge Street, no time to get down 'cause he's moving up. It grooves with real instruments, including piano, sax, tambourine, and handclaps.

k-os straddles the line between condemning the egos of hip-hop and joining them by extolling his superiority. There are plenty of moments on *Joyful Rebellion* where the music and rhymes are inventive, and you have to take his side. No one's arguing hip-hop doesn't have lots of issues, but k-os leads the way in changing perceptions of the music in Canada.

69 Sit Down Young Stranger/If You Could Read My Mind

Gordon Lightfoot

Reprise, 1970

Minstrel Of The Dawn | Me And Bobby McGee | Approaching Lavender | Saturday Clothes | Cobwebs & Dust | Poor Little Allison | Sit Down Young Stranger | If You Could Read My Mind | Baby It's Allright | Your Love's Return (Song for Stephen Foster) | The Pony Man

A new decade meant a fresh start to Gordon Lightfoot's recording career. He signed with Reprise, a strong US company, with the hope of hits, and delivered an album with a title track that meant a lot to him: "That was put out during the Viet Nam war. That song was supposed to be my contribution to a cause of sorts to try to end the situation over there. I loved the song, and I loved what it said, and that's why I called the album *Sit Down Young Stranger*. It sold 80,000 copies and it stopped.

"They [Reprise] called and said that they'd got a nibble on a single on the album. By this time, it was seven or eight months later. In Seattle, a station was going to program 'If You Could Read My Mind'."

Reprise thought they might be able to capitalize on it: "They said, 'will you change the album title?' And I said no. So they flew me out to California. I said, why do you want to do it, what difference will it make? And one of the guys said, it's the difference between X and 7X. So what he did was, he explained it to me algebraically. I knew he was right; he was telling me we'd probably sell about seven times as many albums. But it took an airplane trip to California and back for a meeting for me to make that decision, that's the really crazy, ridiculous part about it."

By early 1971, the album had a new name and Lightfoot had his first real hit in the US: "The funny thing was, I didn't sing it at all until it got singled off that album. I didn't see the strength in it. I was playing 'Sit Down Young Stranger'."

> When I saw him live at Massey Hall, it clarified what I wanted to do. Here was a guy on stage singing these great songs, not making a big deal about it. He looms so large in my career.
>
> — Ron Sexsmith

70 Love Junk

The Pursuit Of Happiness

Chrysalis, 1988

Hard To Laugh | Ten Fingers | I'm An Adult Now | She's So Young | Consciousness Raising As A Social Tool | Walking In The Woods | Beautiful White | When The Sky Comes Falling Down | Looking For Girls | Man's Best Friend | Tree Of Knowledge | Killed By Love | Down On Him

Here's how Moe Berg and The Pursuit Of Happiness exploded on the Canadian scene with "I'm An Adult Now": "I had a friend who was a filmmaker. He came to me and said, let's make a video, like you'd say, let's play basketball. It was something to do for fun on a Sunday. I had another friend who worked at a video post-production house, so between all our friends we managed to schedule a video shoot. The sound man's son became the famous 'kid in the video'.

"This was back in the days when you could walk into MuchMusic and hand them a video. Days later, I got a call saying not only were they going to play it, they were going to put it into rotation. No one was more shocked than us.

"Was it good luck? That would be a major understatement. The video became huge, and suddenly my answering machine was full of messages from managers, agents, and record companies."

Berg was asked to name someone to produce the album. He said Todd Rundgren: "He was my hero. He was my favourite artist and my favourite producer. Even when we got a record deal, I don't think I realized that I was actually in show business. Real rock stars still seemed like superheroes to me. I didn't think you could meet these people, let alone work with them."

Todd Rundgren often brings up *Love Junk* as one of his favourite productions. Moe Berg made a video with his friends, and his hero thinks he made a great album. How does that make you feel, Moe? "Very gratifying. Whatever people may think of us, Todd's saying he still likes the record is the only validation I need."

71 Jaune

Jean-Pierre Ferland

Barclay, 1970

Prologue | Le petit roi | Quand on aime on a toujours vingt ans |
Sing Sing | God Is An American | Le chat du café des artistes | .... |
Y'a des jours | Ce qu'on dit quand on tient une femme dans ses bras |
Épilogue | It Ain't Fair

By 1970, Jean-Pierre Ferland was already a star in francophone Canada and even in Paris. He was a *chansonnier*, a singer-songwriter of the popular songs of Quebec, a style that dominated after World War II. *Chansonniers* were romantic and mannered, their songs simple, intimate, and expressive. They usually performed solo, with an acoustic guitar. They were people with

something to say, whether personal or observational. The *chansonniers* were an important part of Quebec's Quiet Revolution, inspiring young people toward individuality, helping lead to the expressive blossoming of culture. It sounds a bit like the folk movement, with the chief difference being that the *chansonniers* were trying to identify a culture through individual expression.

By the end of the 1960s, the music was changing, thanks to outside influences, most notably popular music. Young people were searching for a Quebec equivalent; soon, musicians who might have become *chansonniers* were going rock, led by Robert Charlebois and groups such as Harmonium, Beau Dommage, and Les Séguin. Most *chansonniers* stayed the course as their audiences grew older with them. Jean-Pierre Ferland chose to change with the times.

Jaune became the most popular and enduring album of Ferland's career. He'd been a member of a genre based on solo performance. Instead, *Jaune* was a spectacle, with rock, orchestra, studio trickery, inside jokes, synthesizer, and Ferland's usual sharp lyrics. *Jaune* was unlike anything made in Quebec before, a huge leap in production values. It's been called the *Sgt. Pepper* of the province: a concept album by an existing star that revolutionized the recording industry there. Ferland produced many more successes afterward, and enjoyed a thriving career as a TV host as well.

> Un chef-d'œuvre sophistiqué, une symphonie moderne.
>
> — Francis Hébert, *Voir*

Top Ten Quebec Albums

Sophie Durocher broadcaster

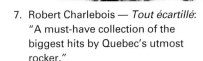

Since September 2004, journalist and author Sophie Durocher has hosted one of the most popular shows on Radio-Canada's new music channel, Espace musique. Called *Les chansons de Sophie*, it is a daily two-and-a-half hour show dedicated entirely to song. The magazine *L'Express* has named Sophie one of Quebec's top one hundred movers and shakers. In November 2005, to mark the thirty-fifth anniversary of Jean-Pierre Ferland's cult hit album *Jaune*, she published her first biography, the best-seller *Ferland, hey boule de gomme, s'rais-tu dev'nu un homme?* Here are Sophie's picks for the best from *la belle province*.

1. Jean-Pierre Ferland — *Jaune*: "With this album, Quebec left the world of *chansonniers* to enter the world of modern music."

2. Jean-Pierre Ferland — *Écoute pas ça*: "The unplugged masterpiece of an aging and vulnerable songwriter."

3. Leonard Cohen — *Songs Of Leonard Cohen*: "The coolest album by Montreal's most famous poet."

4. Harmonium — *L'heptade*: "Take a deep breath. Inhale. This is Quebec's best progressive rock album."

5. Beau Dommage — *Beau Dommage*: "The birth of a group, the birth of a legend, the birth of a generation of urban songwriters."

6. Daniel Bélanger — *Rêver mieux*: "Innovative hitmaker Bélanger's successful mix of electro and classical *chansons*. Jacques Brel meets Coldplay."

7. Robert Charlebois — *Tout écartillé*: "A must-have collection of the biggest hits by Quebec's utmost rocker."

8. Pierre Lapointe — *La forêt des mal-aimés*: "The most original album by the most gifted young Quebec artist."

9. Richard Desjardins — *Tu m'aimes-tu*: "Is he a poet? Is he a songwriter? No, he is Richard Desjardins."

10. Jean Leloup — *L'amour est sans pitié*: "The perfect introduction to the crazy world of John the wolf, the illegitimate son of Jacques Dutronc and Serge Gainsbourg."

72 Somewhere Outside

The Ugly Ducklings

Yorktown, 1966

Nothin' | Do What You Want | She Ain't No Use To Me | Just In
Case You Wonder | Not For Long | Ain't Gonna Eat My Heart |
Hey Mama | 10:30 Train | That's Just A Thought I Had In My Mind |
Postman's Fancy | Windy City (Noise At The North End)

Somewhere Outside is a smoker, every ounce as vital and vicious as The Stones and The Pretty Things, easily the best Canadian rock record of the 1960s.

— John Westhaver, Birdman Sound

The Ugly Ducklings burst out of the Yorkville Village scene with a great bit of timing. They simultaneously released their single "Nothin'" and grabbed a gig opening for The Rolling Stones at Maple Leaf Gardens on June 29, 1966. Singer Dave Bingham remembers: "In those days, because of union rules, you had to have somebody [on the bill] from the town you were in. When The Stones were coming in from the airport by limousine, they put on CHUM and they heard "Nothin'" on *The Battle Of The New Sounds*. We won that night, and we won for thirteen nights in a row. So Mick Jagger heard it on the way in, and consequently that's why, when he was asked later what his favourite Canadian band was, he said Ugly Ducklings, because we were the only Canadian band they had heard!"

The group had enough savvy and guts to insist that the record properly capture their brand of aggressive rock: "When we went in the studio, we said the hell with the VU meters. We just did it our way and forgot about the stupid VU meters. They were always telling us to turn down and we just told them to f-off."

"Nothin'", the first song Bingham had ever written, was a hit in many markets of the country. A single the following year, "Gaslight", actually made it to number one in some cities, but, by 1968, the band were no more. Collectors rediscovered the disc in the 1980s, and *Somewhere Outside* is now considered a classic, a Canadian album on par with the legends of 1966.

73 Electric Jewels

April Wine

Aquarius, 1973

Weeping Widow | Just Like That | Electric Jewels | You Opened Up
My Eyes | Come On Along | Lady Run, Lady Hide | I Can Hear You
Callin' | Cat's Claw | The Band Has Just Begun

In 1973, I saw my first rock show: April Wine's *Electric Jewels* tour. It was also their first rock show for dozens of people I've met, and probably for thousands of others across Canada. This wasn't an accident. April Wine were the first big rock band to play many smaller Canadian communities.

Leader Myles Goodwin felt the group could be big, but they needed a stronger sound: "We'd been making just a collection of two-and-a-half minute pop songs for radio. We convinced the record company and the producer that we wanted to do a little more than that. We just wanted to make it a little heavier, get away from the Top Forty."

New members joined, drummer Jerry Mercer and guitarist Gary Moffet, and the difference was immediate, says Goodwin: "Jerry's more meat and potatoes, straight ahead, more powerful. That alone would make a huge difference in any band. Some of the best guitar work that April Wine ever did was Gary Moffett's. He was incredible, a real craftsman on the guitar, really underrated in this country, I believe."

No longer a pop-oriented band, April Wine were able to tap into a brand-new audience of harder-rock fans keen on guitar and looking for a group to cheer. "We realized that people wanted to hear the bands live that were out on the radio, but bands weren't coming. So we're gonna go down there, we're gonna see what happens, and it worked out well. The venues kept becoming bigger, playing hockey rinks and arenas, and it was great because it was just a whole other level. So it was a real concentrated effort."

A hard-rock sound, with on-stage pyrotechnics and light shows, April Wine brought modern rock to much of Canada. For tens of thousands of seventies' kids, *Electric Jewels* holds a well of memories.

74 Sundown

Gordon Lightfoot

Reprise, 1973

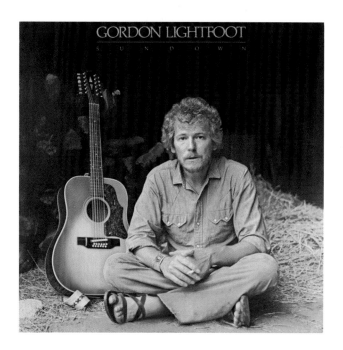

The album contains ten of the most gritty, yet beautiful original Lightfoot songs to be found. And unlike many artistic triumphs, this album resonated with the public worldwide.

— Wayne Francis, www.lightfoot.ca

Gordon Lightfoot hadn't hit the Top Forty since "If You Could Read My Mind" in 1970. For this album, a change was in the works. Lightfoot got to reunite his core sixties' players — musicians he trusted and with whom he loved playing: "I got my old bass player [John Stockfish] back for that, and I got Red Shea [on guitar] back, too."

With his other guitar player, Terry Clements, there as well, the basic tracks for the album were recorded in Toronto. Producer Lenny Waronker had a few tricks to add, though: string parts, some keyboards, and drums, something Lightfoot still didn't use in concert.

The album was just that little bit more modern, a little more produced. Lightfoot says the hit "Sundown" put his career back on track: "We really needed [a hit], and that was the perfect place to get one. It set me up to continue on for another five or six years after that."

"Carefree Highway" came next. Lightfoot attributes his affinity for songs about travelling to an early favourite singer: "Hank Snow: I've been everywhere, man. Definitely the country music influence. I wrote that in Arizona, I was driving one night from Flagstaff to Phoenix, and I saw a road sign that said 'Carefree Highway,' and I said, here's a song. Just very perfunctorily I had the whole thing done in fifteen minutes in my head."

Travelling is a good metaphor for Gordon Lightfoot's career. It's not about the destination, it's about the journey. "When it's done, it's done, you might as well keep moving," he says. Apart from illness, he's never stopped touring or recording. Or, as Hank Snow put it, "I'm Movin' On".

75 Left And Leaving

The Weakerthans

G7 Welcoming Committee, 2000

Everything Must Go! | Aside | Watermark | Pamphleteer |
This Is A Fire Door Never Leave Open | Without Mythologies |
Left And Leaving | Elegy For Elsabet | History To The Defeated |
Exiles Among You | My Favourite Chords | Slips And Tangles

Left And Leaving is a cathartic listening experience for its fans. It's not a place that its writer, John Samson likes to go, though: "I'm not sure what it is that people like about *Left And Leaving*. It feels a bit strange talking about it, as I haven't actually heard the record since it came out. It's not that I don't like it — there's just something overwhelming about it for me. But I appreciate it when someone tells me it moved them."

A common description of the album is that it is filled with sadness. That doesn't surprise Samson: "I do think that *Left And Leaving* is a particularly sad record, and the product of a very specific place and time. I don't think I could write the same way again, and am very thankful I don't have to. It wasn't a good time

for me. Nothing dramatic or anything, just difficult."

The characters in the songs seem trapped, in rooms, cities, homes. Around them is decay — cracked plates, broken glass, rusted parts.

> To make such songs, they're just so heartfelt . . . so moving.
>
> — Ra McGuire, Trooper

Says Samson of his lyrics, "I often come back to concepts of confinement and decay. Partly because the city of Winnipeg is a main character in the songs, and confinement and decay are a real part of living here. And partly

I was trying to link the struggle of the soul under capitalism to concrete objects and locations and use them to reach the subject in an indirect way, a way that would show how everything is connected. Which is, I guess, a pretty unclear way of saying that every form of expression is political."

Left And Leaving shows you don't have to be happy to strike a chord.

76 Clumsy

Our Lady Peace

Sony, 1997

Superman's Dead | Automatic Flowers | Carnival | Big Dumb
Rocket | 4am | Shaking | Clumsy | Hello Oskar | Let You Down |
The Story Of 100 Aisles | Car Crash

Image Provided Courtesy of SONY BMG MUSIC (CANADA) INC.

One great thing about having a hit album is you get to see a lot of new places. For the members of Our Lady Peace, their first tour turned into a huge, two-year trek. Lead singer Raine Maida recalls: "It was the first time we'd really left Canada. All of a sudden you get exposed to a lot of different music. Playing all these different festivals and seeing all the different bands, it was very enlightening. So when we came back for *Clumsy*, we bought this huge Kurzweil keyboard and just started opening up the curves to what the sound of Our Lady Peace was."

Maida also had a lot more things to write in his journal: "I had "Carnival" for probably a year. [Then] we were in Chicago and saw this crazy sign, 'Yoga For Cats And Dogs.' You gotta be kidding me, is that for real? Nowadays, everything goes, but you gotta figure that was in '95. I think the music, a cacophony of weirdness, ran parallel with the feeling that I got when I saw that sign. We're heading down a crazy road in this life right now."

Those observer lyrics continued on the hit "Superman's Dead": "Seeing these kids at all these festivals all through the US and Canada and getting a sense of what's going on culturally, the whole Grunge movement. It just seemed to me if you weren't engaged at that point in life, you must be in a coma. There was a lot of anger, and the music that was going on was angry. There was something interesting about that,

and I took it to mean if you weren't passionate or feeling some sort of anger at that point, you're missing what life's about right now. That's what spawned the lyric, everyone feeling nothing's good enough today."

It's a simple formula: start a band, see the world, and remember to take lots of notes.

77 Harmonium

Harmonium

Polydor, 1974

Harmonium | Si doucement | Aujourd'hui, je dis bonjour à la vie |
Vieilles courroies | 100,000 raisons | Attends-moi | Pour un instant |
De la chambre au salon | Un musicien parmi t'ant d'autres

The first French-language album I ever owned. The only Quebec music I had ever heard before this was bad covers of US Top Forty, sung in French. It opened up my eyes to a vibrant musical culture in *la belle province.*

— Paul Bisson, CBC Ottawa

In 1973, Serge Fiori got a call to help at Université de Montréal. "The manager for some shows needed a bass player and a guitar player. Louis [Valois] and I were there to accompany some singer, so we just played the gig and it really clicked. Michel Normandeau, who was the manager, was interested in what we did, too, so we met a month after that just for fun."

The trio began finding their sound. Says Fiore, "Michel wasn't a musician, so I taught him all the chords so he could play rhythm guitar and give support when I do solos. Day in, day out, we were literally living together. We co-wrote some lyrics together in the same way we would play — we would sit around the table and improvise the lyrics until the sun

was in our eyes in the morning. We started playing small clubs just for fun and to see if there was something to it. It caught on real fast."

Harmonium invented a sound that was a mix of many styles in Montreal at the time. The city had always been a hotbed of support for European progressive rock bands such as Pink Floyd and Genesis. Harmonium took a bit of that, a bit of folk music, some jazz, and stuffed it all into their lineup of two acoustic guitars and bass. This was a major move because francophone Montreal

was looking for its own rock scene: "We needed something, because the music then was only *les chansonniers,* so you felt the young kids, they wanted something more."

The group touched a nerve in Quebec: "It was a complete acknowledgement. Everybody — critics, papers, television, fans — everybody was unanimous. Everybody played the total album on radio shows, which was amazing — they didn't play only cuts, they played the album. In about two months, we had a hundred and fifty thousand records sold."

78 Share The Land

The Guess Who

RCA, 1970

Hand Me Down World | Bus Rider | Do You Miss Me Darlin' |
Moan For You Joe | Share The Land | Hang On To Your Life |
Coming Down Off The Money Bag | Song Of The Dog | Three
More Days

The Guess Who had just scored the biggest hit of their career with "American Woman". It should have been a tremendous ride. Instead, the band were suddenly without leader Randy Bachman. "We had to scramble

Cummings, Garry Peterson, and Jim Kale knew there was an untapped well of talent in their hometown. "We were all in rival bands," says Cummings of the Winnipeg sixties' scene. "Kurt was in a trio called Before, and they were

Proved the pop hitmakers could rock the FM counterculture crowd and carry on without Mr. Bachman and redefine themselves.

— John Einarson, writer

to find other guys," recalls Burton Cummings. "So we got Kurt [Winter] and Greg [Leskiw] from Winnipeg. We came back and picked guys from Winnipeg because we thought that was the right thing to do."

phenomenal. That's where 'Hand Me Down World' came from, that's where 'Bus Rider' came from. I'd known him for years and he seemed to be the logical choice. It was sure big news in Winnipeg, I'll tell you that."

Winter's song catalogue was a godsend for Cummings: "We needed a follow-up to 'American Woman'. We were really scrambling not to lose the momentum we had. The lyrics to 'Hand Me Down World' were in the same vein as 'American Woman' — it was a 'hey, wake up world' song. That single was forced out immediately when 'American Woman' started coming down the charts."

Just months before, Burton Cummings had been thought of as the new kid in the band. Now he was in charge of the group's future: "At that point, I inherited the leader's seat, even though when I had first joined the band, I was a young eighteen-year-old kid scared out of my mind. All of a sudden, four years later, I was the leader. And it was fine by me."

Top Ten Manitoba Albums

John Einarson writer

John Einarson is a prolific and influential music writer, and a historian specializing in the rich Manitoba music community. His books include in-depth biographies of Randy Bachman, Neil Young, and John Kay and Steppenwolf.

1. The Guess Who — *Wheatfield Soul*: "The album that put the province on the international music map and gave us our sound."

2. Neil Young — *After The Gold Rush*: "Hey, Toronto, he got his musical start right here in Manitoba, just ask him!"

3. The Weakerthans — *Reconstruction Site*: "World-class indie rockers' best so far, including the singalong anthem 'I Hate Winnipeg'."

4. Crash Test Dummies — *God Shuffled His Feet*: "Million-selling eclectic fare from frog-throated singer and his hippie band."

5. Loreena McKennitt — *The Visit*: "Breakthrough album from Morden, MB's very own Celtic Queen in gumboots."

6. Burton Cummings — *Burton Cummings*: "Big Bad Burt's solo debut boasted the million-selling hit single 'Stand Tall' (his one and only)."

7. Harlequin — *Love Crimes*: "Heirs to The Guess Who throne rock out with CanCon classics 'Innocence' and 'Thinking Of You'."

8. The Wailin' Jennys — *40 Days*: "Award-winning acoustic roots folk from three Prairie princesses."

9. The Pumps — *Gotta Move*: "Winnipeg's finest New Wave rockers, who could have been contenders."

10. Mood Jga Jga — *Mood Jga Jga*: "Ex-Guess Who man Greg Leskiw's quirky jazz-rock debut."

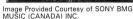

Image Provided Courtesy of SONY BMG MUSIC (CANADA) INC.

79 Greatest Hits!

Ian & Sylvia

Vanguard, 1970

Early Morning Rain | Tomorrow Is A Long Time | Little Beggarman |
The Mighty Quinn | Nancy Whiskey | Catfish Blues | Come In Stranger |
The French Girl | The Renegade | Mary Anne | You Were On My Mind |
Four Strong Winds | Short Grass | Southern Comfort | Some Day Soon |
Ella Speed | Circle Game | 90° x 90° | Cutty Wren | Un Canadien errant |
Lonely Girls | Spanish Is A Loving Tongue | This Wheel's On Fire

Ian Tyson started performing in Vancouver in 1955 while attending art school, "singing rockabilly, radio stuff," he recalls. After graduating, he hitch-hiked to Toronto, where the jobs were for commercial artists. Not long after, Tyson met Sylvia Fricker, and the two jumped headfirst into the mushrooming folk club scene: "We were the big dogs on the block at that time. We had a sound that was pretty unique, and we went to New York and we got a contract, it was that simple."

Ian Tyson is simplifying one of the great careers in folk music, one that produced enduring anthems and helped introduce the world to Canadian songwriting: "We were just at the right place at the right time. It got very big until the British Invasion put a stop to that nonsense, the Folk Scare, as it's commonly known," he deadpans.

Tyson began writing songs after meeting another folkie in New York: "It was directly influenced by Bob Dylan. For a period of time there, I knew him quite well. He sang us some songs in a bar that we used to frequent, in the Kettle Of Fish, I think it was, and I said, yeah, I can do that. So I started exploring it, and shortly after that I wrote 'Four Strong Winds'. It was a twenty-minute thing. That's not an uncommon phenomenon in this business. The first songs, you've got all that unused material to draw from."

Sylvia, too, could write — "You Were On My Mind" is hers. That didn't surprise Tyson, either: "I knew she was a talented girl and had that very exciting and electric vibe that was going on. It would follow that a bright talent like her would write. It was the thing to do, we all started doing it."

80 Steppenwolf

Steppenwolf

RCA, 1968

Sookie Sookie | Everybody's Next One | Berry Rides Again |
Hootchie Kootchie Man | Born To Be Wild | Your Wall's Too High |
Desperation | The Pusher | A Girl I Knew | Take What You Need |
The Ostrich

German immigrant John Kay had been born at the end of World War II, his father killed in action. Moving to Toronto in 1958, he started playing folk in clubs in the States and Canada, eventually joining The Sparrows, an established Yorkville band. The band became just The Sparrow, and followed record contracts to California. It never worked out, but just a couple of months later, a restructured version of the group was reborn as Steppenwolf.

You could still hear the Yorkville r'n'b all over their debut album. "Berry Rides Again" is straight bar-band stuff that could have come from any of Ronnie Hawkins's backing groups. It's filled with barrelhouse piano, and pretty much every Chuck Berry cliché.

Nothing sounded like "Born To Be Wild", though. It is in many ways a radical song, and is a deserving, lasting anthem. Though the song is regarded as hard rock, it's actually Goldy McJohnson's organ that dominates. Distorted, and recorded at the same level as Kay's vocals, its chords rip through like electric jolts. The organ effectively takes the job of the lead guitar, getting all the solos and doubling the lead vocals. It's such a radical rethinking of the instrument's role, and such a heavy one, that no one thinks of this as a keyboard song. The song was already a huge hit by the time it appeared in the film *Easy Rider*, which only cemented its status as a symbolic hit of the era.

"Born To Be Wild" wasn't an original composition of the band but credited to a mysterious Mars Bonfire. That turned out to be a pseudonym for Dennis Edmonton from Ontario, the brother of band drummer Jerry, and the former Sparrow leader. It's considered an American classic, but both the song and the album course with Canadian blood.

81 Ladies Of The Canyon

Joni Mitchell

Reprise, 1970

Morning Morgantown | For Free | Conversation | Ladies Of
The Canyon | Willy | The Arrangement | Rainy Night House |
The Priest | Blue Boy | Big Yellow Taxi | Woodstock |
The Circle Game

Ladies Of The Canyon is the last blush of Joni Mitchell's pure, revealing folk period. The following album, *Blue*, would take her in new directions and moods, but here you'll find the songs that best chronicle the still-hopeful last days of the sixties.

Most of the album is Mitchell alone, with guitar or piano. Her radical open guitar tunings give that instrument a rich ring, which complements her sweet singing. The piano piece "For Free" is a precursor to *Blue*'s "River", with a similar tune and wonderful moments. A lone cello sneaks in for one line, underscoring the reflective mood; at the culmination of the lyrics, Mitchell soars into one of her quavering octave leaps on the words "for free," as a clarinet takes over the note and solos to the end of the song.

The album ends with three important Mitchell songs. "Big Yellow Taxi" is one of the smartest hits of the era. It's a fun, danceable tune, with a message so simple and powerful it's still quoted: every time a new piece of construction goes up on a former green space, someone will say "they paved paradise and put up a parking lot." "Woodstock", here an electric piano dirge, was probably handled better by the rock and roll boys in CSNY, but its lyrics remain an impressive summation of the counterculture's big moment.

Smartly, though, Mitchell doesn't end the album, or the sixties, on that dubious triumph. Instead, possibly sensing the folk and hippie days were passing, she went back into her songbook for the three-year-old "The Circle Game". With its bittersweet advice that we can't return but can only look back, Mitchell bids adieu to those idealistic times. When next we meet her, the music would be called singer-songwriter, with Joni Mitchell its brightest star.

82 Bud The Spud And Other Favourites

Stompin' Tom Connors

Dominion, 1969

Bud The Spud | The Ketchup Song | Ben, In The Pen | My Brother Paul | Rubberhead | Luke's Guitar (Twang, Twang) | The Old Atlantic Shore | My Little Eskimo | Reversing Falls Darling | She Don't Speak English | The Canadian Lumberjack | Sudbury Saturday Night | TTC Skidaddler | (I'll Be) Gone With The Wind

Connors is our greatest folk artist, comparable to Woody Guthrie, with one major difference: I can't listen to Guthrie (he's boring, see), but I can listen to Tom.

— Bruce Mowat, music writer

Stompin' Tom's songs aren't complicated, they have funny lyrics, and his singing voice is as gruff as his exterior. Yet every Canadian knows them. Tom's secret, he says, is writing about what the country's really like. "Most of the songs I write are taken from real-life experiences. That resonates with people because they've done those things. There's people who have primed tobacco in Ontario and there's people who have had, if not a Sudbury Saturday night, a good old Fredericton Saturday night or whatever it might be. I didn't pull any punches, you know. You have a fight sometimes in a bar, so I threw that into 'Sudbury Saturday Night' and all this other stuff. What the hell do the boys do when the girls are out to bingo on a Saturday night? Well,

they're frequenting the bars, and they have a hoopla."

Connors says he has always set out to teach with his writing. "That's what I do. I think ahead. I don't write a song for the song's sake. I say, how will this affect not only kids, but everybody in the country? I got one song especially that I get an awful lot of teachers writing me letters on, and that's a song called 'Name The Capitals.' It's almost impossible to teach kids the names of the provinces and the names of the capitals. I call out a province and I ask kids in the song to name the capital. And little do they know it. Then, when somebody asks them, OK, what's the

capital of Saskatchewan, right off the bat — Regina. And the teachers tell me it's magic."

"I was over in London, England," he remembers. "They said, 'We've never seen the like of you. You get on there for an hour, and you sing these songs about Canada. We learn more about Canada than in all the books. Now we think we know, we wanna go there and see all this stuff.' Well, thank you very much. That's my job. That's what I do."

Along with Anne of Green Gables, he's the most famous P.E. Islander ever. "The only difference there is Anne was fictitious. This is the real thing here."

83 Shine A Light

Constantines

threegutrecords, 2003

National Hum | Shine A Light | Nighttime/ Anytime (It's Alright) |
Insectivora | Young Lions | Goodbye Baby & Amen | On To You |
Poison | Scoundrel Babes | Tiger & Crane | Tank Commander (Hung
Up In A Warehouse Town) | Sub-Domestic

This album is the reason that the world looked to Canada and discovered Arcade Fire. Arcade Fire may be driving the bus, but the Cons built the engine.

— Paul Loewenberg,
Northern Lights Festival

Beginning with a blast of full-bore punk rock called "National Hum", Constantines pick up where they had left off with 2001's self-titled debut album. Things get different, however, by track two. They're still rough at the edges and Bryan Webb's vocals are still gruff, but "Shine A Light" ushers in a new melodic sense and songwriting style. "Shine A Light" is a neat song," says Webb. "It's about family. It's one of the first songs I wrote directly for specific people. That's become something that I try to do more often now."

At one point in the song, there's simply a quiet, one-note organ solo, courtesy of brand-new keyboard player Will Kidman. The group knew Kidman from the punk scene around Guelph, Kitchener-Waterloo, and London, and asked him along for a road trip. "They were doing an Ontario tour," remembers Kidman. "I was like, alright, I'll come learn some songs.

"I remember walking through a lineup in Ottawa getting into the club for a show," says Kidman. "I heard this conversation about how we used to be a punk rock band before we got a piano player. All of us grew up playing in punk bands, but we kinda just realized we were a rock and roll band and that's just the way it was gonna be."

For Bryan Webb, the album is all about friendship and his new, personal songwriting. "A friend of mine wrote me this really nice letter a couple of years ago," he says. "He was working at a hospital, volunteering, and had some really hard times. He was listening to the record a lot, and he said it helped ease his time a bit. That meant a hell of a lot to me. I tend to get really excited when friends of ours like what we do."

84 Shakespeare My Butt

The Lowest of the Low

A&M, 1991

4 O'Clock Stop | So Long Bernie | Just About "The Only" Blues | Salesmen, Cheats And Liars | Rosy And Grey | Kinda' The Lonely One | Eternal Fatalist | For The Hand Of Magdelena | Subversives | Bleed A Little While Tonight | Bloodline | St. Brendan's Way | Letter From Bilbao | Under The Carlaw Bridge | The Taming Of Carolyn | Gossip Talkin' Blues | Henry Needs A New Pair Of Shoes

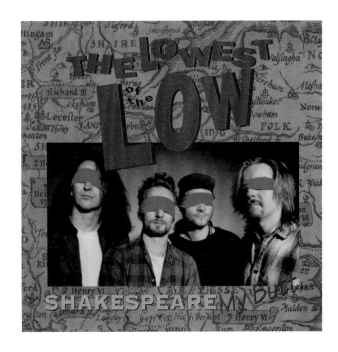

Unlike many of the trend-conscious Toronto acts of the day, The Lowest of the Low had a guitar-strumming, singalong sound influenced by a blend of folk, Celtic, and punk rock. "We wanted to bring [music] back to the people and make it much more about community and making connections," confirms singer-songwriter Ron Hawkins. "I think a lot of people liked that about us, and a lot of people mock us and think we're too working class."

Their demos were only meant to be shopped around to attract a company, but independent label LSD thought they were good enough as they were, and distributor A&M agreed. Toronto radio powerhouse CFNY championed the band, making hits out of the raw recordings. "It goes

to show that the honesty and charm it has shone through the lack of production," Hawkins figures.

How does success affect a somewhat political, socially aware band of the people? "The band broke up in '94, basically an implosion," says Hawkins. "It got really tense and became a huge pressure. The deeper we got into the music industry, the farther we were getting away from what we thought we were good at: playing the smaller places. It just seemed like we were out there selling shoes. Everybody was very hostile

with each other. When the band broke up, we didn't speak for a long time."

Hatchets eventually were buried, however, and with the new millennium came reunion gigs and, in 2004, a new studio album, *Sordid Fiction*. Hawkins appreciates "the fact we did that reunion thing and got a chance to be friends again. We got a chance to break up properly, not hating each other."

> "Salesmen, Cheats and Liars" stands as one of the finest and overlooked rock anthems in Canadian history.
>
> — Peter Anawati, CBC Radio

85 Clayton Park

Thrush Hermit

Sonic Unyon, 1999

From The Back Of The Film | (Oh Man!) What To Do? | Violent
Dreams | The Day We Hit The Coast | Headin' South | Western
Dreamz | Songs For The Gang | Uneventful | Oh My Soul! |
We Are Being Reduced | Before You Leave

With their high energy and smart lyrics, you could tell they
were having a lot of fun, and they had you hooked from
the first track.

— Wendy Salsman, Goddess

Thrush Hermit's singer and guitarist Joel Plaskett grew up near Sloan's Chris Murphy in the Halifax suburb of Clayton Park: "I saw Sloan's second show. Chris was at one of our earliest shows and befriended us. He was really instrumental in helping us get gigs. The great thing about Sloan was they had an extended family, and tried to share the attention that was coming to them."

US heavyweight Elektra signed the new band. That meant touring across Canada and the States: "We started so young, and we had this collective travel experience. We all went on tour for the first time, went to New York for the first time together. We'd go on a five-week American tour, and we'd go to the South sleeping in a school bus, bunked up, five guys sleeping in a half-size school bus. We crossed the Prairies, the Rocky Mountains, we did all this stuff for the first time."

The group separated from Elektra, but by then they'd worked themselves into a top-flight touring act. Plaskett had also developed a writing style that often mentioned place names and stories from the band's travels. "Headin' South", "Western Dreamz", and "The Day We Hit The Coast" all told road stories. Rivers, rocks, mountains, oceans — it all became part of a travelogue style of writing, landscape paintings of sweet melodic songs on a canvas of loud guitar rock. Says Plaskett, "I'm really proud of that record, I think we all are. That was when we really defined ourselves more thoroughly. I think it was all the travelling, all about being twenty-three years old, finding our feet as a band."

Clayton Park proved to be Thrush Hermit's swan song. But it also marked the start of a bigger career for Joel Plaskett.

Top Ten
Cape Breton Albums

Jimmy Rankin has made hit records both with his family in The Rankins and as a solo artist. He's called the Songdog, always on the hunt for a great story wherever he travels. Growing up in a Cape Breton home full of music, he witnessed first-hand the popular revival of the Celtic music tradition of the East Coast, and got to see some of the amazing and largely unheralded greats performing in small halls and, yes, even at kitchen parties. Here are Jimmy's picks, his favourite Cape Breton albums.

1. Winston Scotty Fitzgerald — *Canada's Oustanding Scottish Fiddler*: "Winston revolutionized Cape Breton fiddle music. There's something higher ground about his playing, it's simply joyful to listen to. He only recorded a few albums (all great); this one stands out for me."

2. Donald Angus Beaton — *A Musical Legacy*: "This is a selection of kitchen recordings released on cassette. Donald Angus for me is like the Muddy Waters of CB fiddle music. I don't think anyone has ever come close to capturing this kind of natural spirit on a Cape Breton fiddle studio recording."

3. Howie MacDonald — *Howie MacDonald And His Cape Breton Fiddle*: "Howie played in the Rankin band for years, he is one of my favourite living Cape Breton fiddlers. He's also one of the craziest guys I know."

4. Dave MacIsaac — *From The Archives*: "Dave was born and raised in Halifax, but he is really a Cape Bretoner. He's got one of the best collections of CB fiddle music around."

5. Buddy MacMaster — *Mabou Firehall 1983 (With John Morris Rankin)*: "Although this is not an officially released recording, it should be. It's Buddy, relaxed and great."

6. Ashley MacIsaac — *Hi How Are You Today?*: "Brilliant. Diabolical. The darker side of CB fiddle."

7. John Allan Cameron — *Weddings, Wakes And Other Things*: "He was playing and singing CB music when it wasn't cool. A real troubadour."

8. Matt Minglewood — *The Matt Minglewood Band*: "Matt was the first Cape Breton rock star. I wore out several copies of this album."

9. Rita MacNeil — *Part Of The Mystery*: "Rita wrote all of her own songs about things close to her heart. She was a great inspiration for a budding songwriter."

10. Gordie Sampson — *Sunburn*: "He's a natural. This is a breakthrough album on all fronts for Gordie."

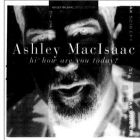

86 Smeared

Sloan

Geffen, 1992

Underwhelmed | Raspberry | I Am The Cancer | Median Strip | Take It In | 500 Up | Marcus Said | Sugartune | Left Of Centre | Lemonzinger | Two Seater | What's There To Decide?

Sloan (left to right): Chris Murphy, Jay Ferguson, Andrew Scott, Patrick Pentland

Halifax's Sloan was signed by US company Geffen Records, which liked the group's similarities to Nirvana. "This was just as Grunge was going in Seattle," says Sloan's Chris Murphy. "We were all affected by punk and hard core and British pop groups and had a similar sort of timeline to the Nirvana story."

For a brief few shining weeks, Halifax became known as the New Seattle. "There was a lot going on before us, we were the ones who got lucky," reflects Murphy. Geffen took Sloan's already-recorded album *Smeared*. For a few thousand dollars, they did a professional remix of the tracks; other than that, it's the Halifax sound of Sloan. "Underwhelmed" became the immediate hit, a sneering slice of raw guitar rock that perfectly captured the blasé attitude of current punk. "Left Of Centre," a Lou Reed pastiche, showed the band had deeper, cool roots as well. "We're all kind of like musicologists," says Murphy. "That can be dangerous, to be just a whole bunch of nerds in a band. That's kind of what we are in a way."

At first, the group were happy with the success, but then they realized they were going to have to live past the New Seattle tag. "We had some degree of popularity in our hometown. But after that, we became international. We were signed to an LA record label. We felt we had to make our own thing. We felt there was a whole lot of imposter bands that were being signed or getting considered cool that we really wanted to separate ourselves from. We just thought the floodgates were open in the cool club, let's get out of here."

Of course, that just made them all the more cool. Many punk and Grunge fans find the group's debut album one of the best of the time.

87 Living Under June

Jann Arden
A&M, 1994

Could I Be Your Girl | Demolition Love | Looking For It (Finding Heaven) |
Insensitive | Gasoline | Wonderdrug | Living Under June | Unloved |
Good Mother | Looks Like Rain

There was a June, and Jann Arden was living under her, renting her tiny basement apartment while writing the songs for her second, breakthrough album. "June didn't like me very much, and she was threatening to kick me out. I could never pay my rent," Arden remembers. So much for her star status. Even though she'd earned a gold record for her debut, *Time For Mercy*, two 1993 Juno awards, and had a smash radio and video hit with "I Would Die For You", Jann Arden was struggling and searching, and no superstar.

"I was kind of blissfully miserable at that time. I still hadn't made a dollar. I had this really sick cat that I'd adopted. So the sick cat and I were down in the basement apartment, and I didn't have any money to go

Just when I begin to happily wallow in a sad, syrupy sweet song like "Demolition Love", "Good Mother" pops up and hints that maybe, just maybe, I have something in common with a superstar like Jann Arden.

— Rebecca Black, CFCY

anywhere. And that was after *Time For Mercy*. People think that you make all these millions of dollars, but they don't understand that you owe the record company three hundred thousand."

A&M was about to get its money back. Arden tapped into a sadness and loneliness to which many could relate, a desire for unconditional love that could make the hurt go away. She longed for the warmth and security of her beloved parents and the safety of her rec room where she'd grown up

singing songs by The Carpenters and ABBA. Instead, she was writing songs at the kitchen table in a basement apartment. So she just put all her fears and emotions into the songs.

Arden recognizes it as the definitive time of her career: "My whole life just changed. I'm glad I didn't know what I was doing at the time. It was a scary record for me and a joyful record." Her ability to write and sing simply and honestly about both pain and joy created a tremendous bond between Jann Arden and her audience.

88 The Hissing Of Summer Lawns

Joni Mitchell

Asylum, 1975

In France They Kiss On Main Street | The Jungle Line | Edith And
The Kingpin | Don't Interrupt The Sorrow | Shades Of Scarlett
Conquering | The Hissing Of Summer Lawns | The Boho Dance |
Harry's House/Centerpiece | Sweet Bird | Shadows And Light

How blindingly gorgeous this "folk" album is, with its field
recordings, free jazz, and wild studio experimentation —
I mean, forget Canadian; this is my favorite album ever.

— Mark Abraham, cokemachineglow

Joni Mitchell's audience was little prepared for *The Hissing Of Summer Lawns*. Fans aching for another *Court And Spark* were shocked, and each successive song brought different and challenging material. For better or for worse, Mitchell's days as a Top Forty star were over.

As with all works of fine art, time and distance reveal true beauty. Listeners returning to the album discover rich lyric themes, inventive compositions, and songs that bravely enter new musical territories. Long before World Beat, Mitchell records

rich, pounding Burundi drummers on "The Jungle Line". The lyrics follow the painter Rousseau as the line snakes its way to Europe and North America, Mitchell singing a hypnotic, complex melody without any other instruments. Jazz players join her for rich chords and unusual changes on "The Boho Dance" and "Edith And The Kingpin", Mitchell soaring and weaving her vocals throughout.

"In France They Kiss On Main Street" should have been a hit, but it's too smart for its own good. Mitchell gives us a picture of the late fifties, as

kids exploded with the liberation of rock and roll, fighting their own war of independence. The characters are as colourful as Springsteen's: there's Chickie and Lead Foot Melvin with the cars, Gail and Louise with their push-up brassieres, and everybody wanted to dance.

A dancer, a poet, a singer, a player — it was getting a little too complicated for quick pop consumption. The last cut helps to explain that this is an artistic statement. "Shadows And Light" uses the painter's secret, darkness to heighten the colors, as a metaphor for wrong and right, God and the devil, the sinner and the saint in us all. People were just going to have to get used to the fact that Joni Mitchell was, above all, a painter, and her albums were going to be canvasses from now on.

89 Bad Manors

Crowbar

Daffodil, 1971

Frenchman's Filler 1 | Too True Mama | Let The Four Winds Blow | House Of Blue Lights | The Frenchman's Cherokee Boogie Incident | Train Keep Rolling | Baby Let's Play House | Oh What A Feeling | Frenchman's Filler 2 | Frenchman's Filler 3 | Murder In The First Degree | In The Dancing Hold | Mountain Fire | Prince Of Peace | Frenchman's Filler 1

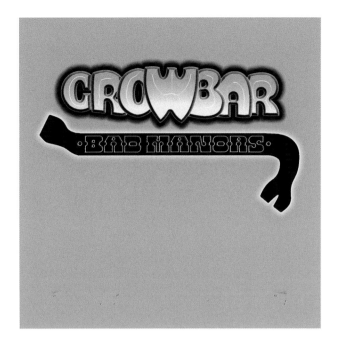

The group that became Crowbar had been serving the master of Canadian music, Ronnie Hawkins. Says piano player Kelly Jay, "If Ronnie got stuck on something, he'd call us in. We could go and play a dinner club as well as play a rock and roll show. We played the Fillmore East with Ronnie for five days, opening up for [Joe Cocker's] Mad Dogs & Englishmen, with Robbie [Robertson], Levon [Helm], and all the boys sitting in the third row. And Dylan! They wanted to see how the new band would do."

Hawkins was not the easiest boss: "Ronnie had given us more hassle and more hassle. We were saying, what the hell, this is not going anywhere, we quit." (Other versions have Hawkins firing them.) As a parting gift, Hawkins provided the band's new name. "They're a nice bunch of guys but they could fuck up a crowbar in ten seconds," laughs Jay.

The album that resulted was a *tour de force* of roots-rock rhythm and blues. And it had a smash hit: "Oh What A Feeling". Says Jay, "We used to come out at the beginning of the evening and go right into it, and the crowd would go wild. My God, they're opening with 'Oh What A Feeling'. Then we'd stop and go into something else. But boy,

by the time we did it at the end of the set, we knew we had them right between the eyes. That always felt good, that you could shoot them with a .22 until they were really wounded, then you had a Panzer tank with this huge cannon and you could just blow them out of the water."

Kelly Jay has a million great Crowbar stories, and one other thing left from this classic album: "I still owe $1,138.27 for the making of *Bad Manors*, my share."

Joyful energy, rootsy rock and roll, and an apprenticeship with Rompin' Ronnie Hawkins (just like The Band). Why shouldn't the critics be floored?

— Andy Grigg, *Real Blues Magazine*

90 Official Music

King Biscuit Boy With Crowbar

Daffodil, 1970

Highway 61 | Don't Go No Further | Unseen Eye | I'm Just A Lonely Guy | Key To The Highway | Corrina | Biscuit's Boogie | Hoy Hoy Hoy | Badly Bent | Cookin' Little Baby | Shout Bama Lama

Richard Newell, aka King Biscuit Boy, came out of Hamilton, Ontario, with a head full of blues and an encyclopedic knowledge of its history. At the end of the sixties, his best friend, fellow musician Kelly Jay, needed a gig and talked to Ronnie Hawkins, who needed a new group. "He said, do you know anybody? and I said, yeah, and got a hold of Richard."

Eventually, Jay and Newell and others parted with Hawkins and, with the new name Crowbar, headed to the bandhouse, Bad Manors. Meanwhile, Hawkins and Toronto journalist Ritchie Yorke travelled to London, England, where they met record man Frank Davies and told him about these talented players. Says Davies, "I came to Canada in February 1970 on an exploratory trip. I went to hear the group recording some demos — and was blown away by their energy, raw power, and their hell-bent-for-leather, tight, frantic musicianship. Before I knew it, I found myself thrown in the deep end producing an album of these songs, moving to Canada, and forming the label [Daffodil]."

> The guy never made anything but genius records. He truly was my best friend.
>
> — Kelly Jay, Crowbar

Newell on record was a revelation, a harmonica virtuoso who brought fire and joy to the classics, and wrote great new songs as well. Andy Grigg, who became Newell's manager in the 1980s, discovered boxes of clippings: "I was astounded by the massive volume of totally rabid reviews from publications all over the world. Every critic with a rep was blown away by it. *Creem*, *Melody Maker*, *New Musical Express*, *Playboy*, *Rolling Stone*, *Crawdaddy*, and dozens of others all gave King Biscuit Boy their highest ratings."

Richard Newell made albums off and on for years, always to great praise. Davies recalls, "As a person he was funny, real, and badly bent — a beautiful original who lived, sang, and played the blues better than any white guy I ever heard". Richard Newell died in 2003 at the age of fifty-eight.

91 Lightfoot!

Gordon Lightfoot

United Artists, 1966

Rich Man's Spiritual | Long River | The Way I Feel | For Lovin' Me |
The First Time | Changes | Early Morning Rain | Steel Rail Blues |
Sixteen Miles | I'm Not Sayin' | Pride Of Man | Ribbon Of Darkness |
Oh, Linda | Peaceful Waters

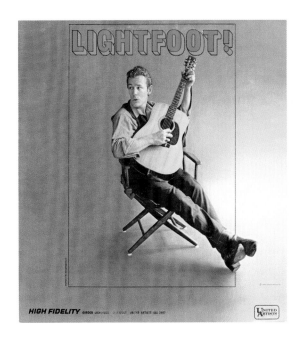

Gordon Lightfoot started out in folk music during the revival of the early 1960s. At first, he played the usual covers, but by 1964, new singers were being encouraged to write their own songs. "By that point, I was hearing Ian & Sylvia and Bob Dylan and people like that. Around about the time I wrote 'Early Morning Rain'."

Lightfoot added another element, some Hank Snow-inspired country, to give his act a bit more edge for the types of places he was playing: "I had one place where I used to have to work in around the hockey game. It was Steele's Tavern, Saturday night. I would always let the hockey game go because I knew people wanted to see it."

At least in 1964 the Leafs were winning, and Toronto was a happening music town: "I had a good place in the pecking order there. I had a bit of a reputation as a songwriter, which was what drew Ian & Sylvia in to see me at Steele's Tavern. Which is how the song ['For Lovin' Me'] got from Ian & Sylvia to Peter, Paul and Mary. One thing just led to another."

Lightfoot had those country chops, too: "Marty Robbins took that song 'Ribbon Of Darkness' and turned it into a hit. Before we knew it, we had a whole list of cover recordings. Of course, the importance of all that sunk in later. Through that I got a good contract with United Artists, so I had pretty good distribution with that *Lightfoot!* album. When it sold a hundred thousand copies, I was actually quite shocked, I never believed that would be possible."

Having been influenced and supported by the leading folk and country performers of the day, Lightfoot was now writing hit songs and selling albums just like them: "I did feel that I had gotten into that particular club, yes."

92 Mad Mad World

Tom Cochrane

Capitol, 1991

Life Is A Highway | Mad Mad World | No Regrets | Sinking Like A
Sunset | Washed Away | Everything Comes Around | The Secret Is
To Know When To Stop | Brave And Crazy | Bigger Man | Friendly
Advice | Get Back Up | Emotional Truth | All The King's Men

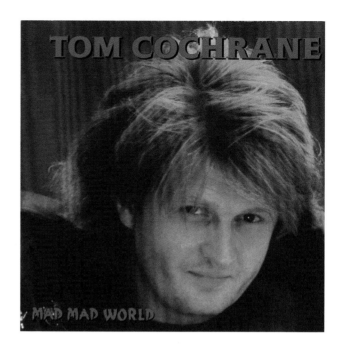

Take "Life Is A Highway" off this album and you'd still have one heck of a record. There's "No Regrets", "Sinking Like A Sunset", "Washed Away" — all choice songs filled with great hooks. Tom Cochrane had come to the recording with a mission: "I really wanted to make a record that cut to the chase. I always tried to have a positive resolve to my records. *Mad Mad World* has a sense of fun, and a sense of urgency."

The urgency came from a trip to Africa, sponsored by World Vision: "That trip was overwhelming. You go into a war zone like Mozambique — we got shot at. You come home and try to digest it. It left some scars on my psyche, and I needed something to pull me out of this funk, something cathartic."

The song that came from the trip was "Life Is A Highway". Instead of reacting with rage or sadness, Cochrane returned to a tune he'd had for his old band: "Nothing is more positive or uplifting a song than 'Life Is A Highway'. It was a sketch at first, but we'd always go thumbs down on it. We thought it was too commercial for Red Rider."

It certainly was commercial: a Top Ten single in both the US and Canada. Cochrane had concocted a tonic for troubled times: "You have to remember that 'Life Is A Highway' came out when there was a lot of dark, heavy music, Grunge. It was so uplifting for people. Kids could play it around campfires."

Cochrane has had a long career of hits with Red Rider and solo, but he'll forever be linked to this massive one. He has no regrets: "I probably wouldn't be doing what I'm doing without *Mad Mad World*."

Bubbles's Top Ten Canadian Albums

Bubbles is the secret hero of Canadian rock music. He's an inspiration to famous musicians the world over, who seek him out for the chance to jam. He's performed with Rush and Axl Rose, and even tender Ron Sexsmith begged him to share a microphone. Bubbles knows music like he knows kitties. Here are his picks, from his many friends in Canadian music.

1. Rush — *A Farewell to Kings*: "'Closer To The Heart' is on there, for fuck's sake!"

2. The Tragically Hip — *Road Apples*: "I love The Hip, even though Gord Downie never gave me the macaroni salad he promised me when we stole that engine for him."

3. Neil Young — *Harvest*: "My kitties like it when I sing 'Old Man' to them."

4. Stompin' Tom Connors — *Bud the Spud*: "My fuck, I love potatoes."

5. The Band — *Music From Big Pink*: "I have kitties named Big Orange and Big Grey!"

6. The Mamas And The Papas — *If You Can Believe Your Eyes And Ears*: "I think this one should count, seeing how Denny was from Nova Scotia. Holy sweet fuck, he could sing, God love him."

7. Skid Row — *Skid Row*: "Trains."

8. Helix — *Walkin' The Razor's Edge*: "Ricky made me promise to put this on here. I'm not giving them a fucking 'R' though."

9. Mike O'Neill — *What Happens Now?*: "This is one of the guys with the camera crew that follows us around in Sunnyvale. Ricky stole his CDs out his car."

10. The Guess Who — *American Woman*: "A great cart-working-on record!"

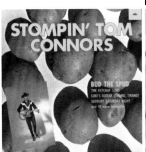

93 Rufus Wainwright

Rufus Wainwright

Dreamworks, 1998

Foolish Love | Danny Boy | April Fools | In My Arms | Millbrook | Baby | Beauty Mark | Barcelona | Matinee Idol | Damned Ladies | Sally Ann | Imaginary Love

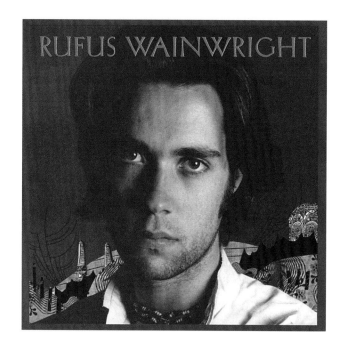

It's an album made from powerfully ambivalent emotions: melancholy and longing and world-weary hope. It's a lot of good sex with bad lovers.

— David Berry, *Vue Weekly*

The eldest of the two children of Loudon Wainwright III and Kate McGarrigle, Rufus Wainwright grew up surrounded by music. "How lovely and fortunate I was to have such an artistic upbringing without it being forced upon us," he marvels. "It was very laid-back in true Canadian style. I think one of the reasons my mom, when her marriage ended, brought Martha and me back up to Canada was that she really wanted us to live lives and experience childhoods that were somewhat idyllic and slow paced and also be able to do music for music's sake."

It's no surprise he was writing and performing in his early teens in Montreal. "My father, who had my demo, was really worried about me as a person. I was being quite lascivious at the time and was pretty active in the bar scene at a very young age — I started at fifteen. He was quite troubled by my situation, and yet I was writing all these songs. I was ferried out of St-Laurent Boulevard to Hollywood."

Wainwright arrived as a unique artist, mixing Quebec chansons, opera, pop, and anything else he fancied with confidence and direction. The lyrics, he says, are pure hometown: "My first album is definitely steeped in Montreal lore, whether it's 'Sally Ann,' which is the Salvation Army, or 'Foolish Love,'

where I'm talking about Park Avenue in Montreal, not Park Avenue in New York — a pretty big difference there. It's an encapsulation of my formative years as a young artist living in that city."

Wainwright remains proud of his debut. "What's fabulous about it is I would bet that it might be one of the last sort of old-fashioned albums ever made. It was all done on tape. It was done at Ocean Way studios, which is this sort of grand, old-fashioned recording studios. It was also done at Capitol Records, in the same room that Frank Sinatra recorded a lot of his records. It took three years to do, it was very, very expensive. I'm still in massive debt from it. But it was done with such care and such respect. It's great to have that in my roster."

94 Face To The Gale

Ron Hynes

EMI, 1997

Constance | Leaving On The Evening Tide | Sonny's Dream | Killer Cab | Common Man | Gone To Canada | Godspeed | St. John's Waltz | The Final Breath | Primitive Thunder | Lighthouse | Away

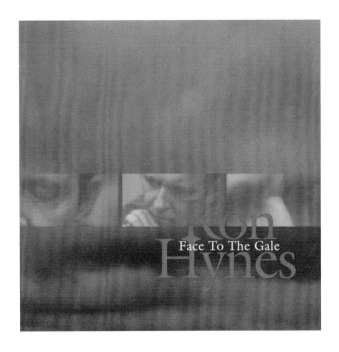

"Sonny's Dream", Ron Hynes's best-known song, has been recorded dozens of times, including by Emmylou Harris. Yet Hynes agrees it's not even the best song on this album. That honour goes to "Godspeed", his moving tribute to songwriter Gene MacLellan, who wrote such hits as "Snowbird". It came after MacLellan's suicide: "I was to co-write with him in about two days down the road. The phone rang, it was my wife Connie, and she said, 'It looks like you'll never get to write with Gene MacLellan.'

"I was really mourning over it, I was heartsick. I had to go to a Songwriters' Association of Canada conference and I wanted to say something about him. I knew what I wanted to say, but when I stood up, I blanked. All I could say was 'Godspeed'. I sat down and I felt awful that I couldn't remember the words that I'd come up with on the plane. I just wrote the one word down, Godspeed, and then the song just started itself. Godspeed went to God bless, went to Goddamn. I excused myself from the meeting and I went up to the room and I picked up my guitar and I sat at the edge of the bed and just sang it, just like that, like the way that great songs should come. Full blown, ten minutes, music and lyrics altogether, and nothing has ever changed from that point. I've never changed a melody or a lyric. I always felt that [Gene] was kinda sitting there on my shoulder. That was our co-write."

Every time Ron Hynes picks up a guitar, he tells a story. Each song is a musical sleight of hand that can transport you, in the blink of an eye, from the deck of a St. John's trawler to the heart of a young man trying to make it in the big city.

— Stuart Mclean, CBC Radio

95 Hobo's Taunt

Willie P. Bennett

Woodshed, 1977

Come On Train | Lace And Pretty Flowers | Storm Clouds | Hobo's
Taunt | Stealin' Away | A Woman Never Knows | Lonely One Car
Funerals | If You Have To Choose | You | Faces

This collection of songs is as honest in emotion as it comes.
No second-hand stories here — all first person experience,
strong lyric poetry delivered from the heart.

— Robin MacIntyre, Mac's Music

Willie P. Bennett once learned a trick that helped him throughout his career: "I realized quite early that it wasn't a good idea to compare or critique my own songwriting, just try to make sure that when I looked at it, it would be something that I would want to listen to, and that the lyric would stand up not just by listening to it but by reading it — that the stories were there. I think that's perhaps why this record has lasted as long as it has."

Bennett never earned the record sales that should go with the quality of his songwriting. That didn't bother him a whole lot: "I'm not one of those people that's interested in having a successful career, by other people's standards. I want to go out and explore what I need to explore, and I want to play what makes me feel happy, because that's the only reason to play music, because it makes you feel good."

One of Canada's top bands exists only because of Bennett. The trio of Colin Linden, Tom Wilson, and Stephen Fearing admired his songs so much, they formed Blackie & The Rodeo Kings (named after another Bennett album) to do a tribute disc, and they still feature Bennett's songs on disc and on stage. "It was the first time I'd ever heard a body of my work sung by other people. I went, this really isn't bad — wish I hadn't been such a knucklehead. Because I know most of the time I thought I was fighting the music business, but what I was really fighting was myself. It was a great show of respect and love and it made me feel really happy." As Willie often said, feeling happy playing music is the best reward.

96 Cowboyography

Ian Tyson
Stony Plain, 1986

Springtime | Navajo Rug | Summer Wages | Fifty Years Ago |
Rockies Turn Rose | Claude Dallas | Own Heart's Delight | The Gift |
Cowboy Pride | Old Cheyenne | The Coyote & The Cowboy

When Ian Tyson wrote "Four Strong Winds" in 1963, he included the line, "think I'll go out to Alberta." He had no idea that's exactly what he'd do. "Yeah, kinda strange," is his response today.

"I was involved with ranching horses primarily, and cowboying. I was in Nashville for a while, and then I was in Texas off and on. I had border difficulties. I chose Alberta as being the best alternative and came out here. I left the music biz pretty much for a couple, three years, and was just riding, training horses, and working on the ranch. That was in '76, and I've been here ever since.

"There was this renaissance, and there were scattered guys all over the West, way out at the end of gravel roads, doin' stuff, whether it was making beautiful saddles or writing poetry or painting or doing music in my case. We were just doing it for ourselves, but it was too big, there was too much creativity at that time for just the grass level, and it spread.

"I invented the music, the new music. I'm not just blowing my own horn, I brought up a new form. That's why *Cowboyography* is the album that it is. It was renaissance music for contemporary cowboys. That was a great big deal, and I was the one that made the new music about that lifestyle. It wasn't made for urban people at all, but it was nice that it crossed over. Who the hell knows how that happens? I was very surprised that the album sold a hundred and twenty thousand copies."

"The Gift" celebrates the landscaping painting of artist Charlie Russell: "I think that's probably the most important song on the album and the one that will probably last the longest. This is Russell country here and, of course, Montana. His paintings were a huge, huge influence on me and all of us really. He's the iconic figure to Northern cowboys, I would say."

Cowboyography is the iconic album.

97 Favourite Colours

The Sadies
Outside, 2004

Northumberland West | Translucent Sparrow | 100 Cities Falling (Part 1) | Song Of The Chief Musician (Part 2) | The Curdled Journey | Why Be So Curious (Part 3) | The Iceberg | A Good Flying Day | Only You And Your Eyes | As Much As Such | A Burning Snowman | Coming Back | Why Would Anybody Live Here?

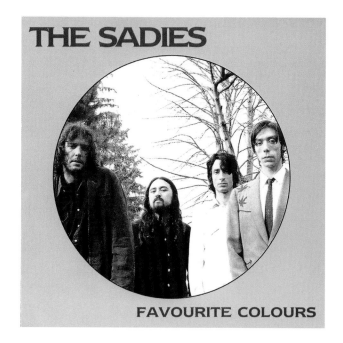

Travis Good joined the family business in 1986, when he was eighteen: "There was an opening in my Dad's band [The Good Brothers] and I took it. I knew I wanted to play guitar."

While Travis was earning his stripes with The Goods, brother Dallas was doing instrumental rock music in other bands. When the two brothers finally teamed up for The Sadies, all the pieces were in place for a country-rock-bluegrass-surf powerhouse. Except a singer. "When we started out, I was of the mind that it was brave and crazy to sing," says Travis. "That's what took the stones. Anybody can play the guitar, but to actually sing and play guitar, I thought that was the real trick. I really had no interest in singing for the longest time."

On *Favourite Colours*, the group hit their signature blend of instrumentals and vocal tracks: "That was around the time we started touring a lot with Blue Rodeo. When we got out of clubs and started singing in theatres and really hearing ourselves, that's when we thought we gotta nail these harmonies."

The Sadies take music very seriously. It all goes back to the fact that they are Good sons. Says Travis, "I think people are brought up to work hard by their parents. We were brought up to work hard as musicians because our parents are musicians. We saw that you can make a living in Canada by playing music, but you gotta work fuckin' hard to do it. That was instilled in us from a very early age."

> I want to take a picture of their audience because all the girls are dancing, and a lot of the guys are just standing there with their jaws open. Any guitar player in the crowd is humbled.
>
> — Rick White, musician

Top Ten Newfoundland and Labrador Albums

As a member of Great Big Sea, Alan Doyle performs for sold-out crowds across the country and in the US and Europe as well. Each night, he says, he feels as if he's an ambassador for his home province, spreading the traditional songs and culture. He also knows a thing or two about the modern music of the province.

"I cannot, with any degree of humility, include my own work on this list. There are those that would argue that one or a number of Great Big Sea releases should be included. But St. John's is a small town, and I will never be able to walk down Water Street again if I publicly brag about myself in any way. So check out Great Big Sea's catalogue, where you'll hear me bashing and yelling frequently, as well as Barry Canning's 'Last Man Standing', The Punters' 'Songs For Sunday Morning', Michelle Doyle's self-titled CD, and The Irish Descendants' 'Southern Shore', all of which I produced and are well worth a listen, but will not be considered below."

1. Various — *All The Best Folk Music of St. John's, Newfoundland*: "Not just being politically correct here; this contains several gems, including 'St. John's Waltz' by Ron Hynes and 'The Portuguese Waltz' by Art Stoyles."

2. Figgy Duff — *Figgy Duff*: "This is the first release from the band that showed the world Noel Dinn's genius in bringing traditional material into the modern era."

3. Ron Hynes — *Cryer's Paradise*: "It's tough to pick a favourite album from Ron, the best songwriter from the Rock."

4. Wonderful Grand Band — *Living In A Fog*: "The most popular Newfoundland TV show led to this collection featuring varied treatments of traditional and original songs, as well as a bit of comedy thrown in for good measure."

5. Émile Benoit — *Vive la rose*: "Tunes, songs, and stories from the Godfather of the Port-au-Port fiddle. More genius from Figgy Duff's Noel Dinn, as he wraps Émile Benoit's sparse and honest voice and fiddle in worldly instruments and sounds."

6. Plankerdown Band — *The Jig Is Up*: "This is one of the most influential instrumental albums in the province. The marriage of Maestro Kelly Russell and producer-guitarist Don Walsh was sadly short-lived, as this, their only collection of music, is amazing.

7. Various — *11:11*: "This is a collection of Newfoundland and Labrador ladies singing songs by Ron and Connie Hynes. Check out 'Mary's Got A Baby' or 'Picture To Hollywood'."

8. Colleen Power — *Lucky You Are*: "'Happy Girlfriend' should have been a national hit, but 'No Greater Queen' and 'Dick-All' are my favourites."

9. The Thomas Trio and The Red Albino — *Jam It On Ya*: "By far the best live rock and roll band from the province, this rock-funk gem might be the best indie Canadian record you've never heard."

10. Duane Andrews — *Duane Andrews*: "This list would not be complete without including Duane's fusion of traditional music and jazz, played by one of the most unique and gifted guitarists in the world."

98 The Way I Feel

Gordon Lightfoot

United Artists, 1967

Walls | If You Got It | Softly | Crossroads | A Minor Ballad | Go-Go Round | Rosanna | Home From The Forest | I'll Be Alright | Song For A Winter's Night | Canadian Railroad Trilogy | The Way I Feel

When the time came to release his second album, Gordon Lightfoot had already had a hit from it, at least in Canada. "Canadian Railroad Trilogy" had captured the nation's spirit of patriotism in its Centennial year, on TV: "Bob Jarvis called me up from CBC one day and said they were doing a New Year's Day special. There's a railroad segment, could you write a song for it? And I said, about how long? As long as you want to make it. I said it should be fairly long. Then he sent me to read a book about Sir William Cornelius Van Horne, who was in charge of the building of the railway. And I took it from there. Three days later I had the song and I was singing it for him at his desk."

One song directly inspired by

"Go-Go Round" — I'll tell you who did that one great. Blue Rodeo did a wonderful job on that tribute album. They sang the balls off it, I'll tell ya, it was great.

— Gordon Lightfoot

Lightfoot's Toronto folksinger days was "Go-Go Round": "You know how I got the idea for that song? I got it from hanging out with Ronnie Hawkins. And I don't really think I have to say anything more. It was just from that atmosphere of watching Ronnie on the strip, and they would, in turn, come up and see me up in [Yorkville] Village. It was really quite

an interesting time. Our families interacted, and it was quite fun there for a number of years."

There were many triumphs in 1967, including a month-long stay at the Riverboat, the first of the now-traditional yearly sold-out shows at Massey Hall, a week outdoors at Expo '67, and this landmark album. It was also the year of "Canadian Railroad Trilogy", the best six minutes and ten seconds of history class Canadian kids have spent ever since.

99 A Farewell To Kings

Rush

Anthem, 1977

A Farewell To Kings | Xanadu | Closer To The Heart |
Cinderella Man | Madrigal | Cygnus X-1

What an amazing recording. You just put on the headphones and disappear into your happy place. Beautiful.

— Marc Perry, EMI

Despite the surprising success of their previous album, *2112*, Rush were not content to copy the formula. Drummer-lyricist Neil Peart explains that, as musicians, the group collectively felt the need to grow: "We did the guitar-bass-drums trio, established ourselves that way with *2112*, and then became a little bit frustrated with that limitation. We talked about adding a fourth member, a keyboard player at the time, and decided, no, we'll expand on our own. So the other guys got into acoustic guitars, 12-string guitars, double neck, and bass pedals. I was getting into keyboard percussion, from glockenspiel to tubular bells and temple blocks and anything you could hit with a stick, basically. Musical technique, too — we were learning a greater level of complexity and different time signatures and all of that. Let's do a song in 13/8 — okay, yeh. And let's put some mini-moog and tubular bells on it. Yeh! It was that kind of excitement and enthusiasm."

Two years before, the record company had demanded a radio-ready single. Rush had refused, instead coming up with long, complicated pieces. This time, however, they did provide a radio hit, though completely by accident. Of "Closer To The Heart", Peart says, "It's unconventional with no verse and chorus. A friend of mine's grandmother had an etching of a blacksmith pounding on a ploughshare, and the caption under it was 'moulded closer to the heart.' We never considered it a single. It was the only short one, it was by default."

Rush did everything the opposite way. When a hit single was needed, they wrote twenty-minute cuts. When epics were working, they had a hit single. When they became rock stars, they ignored the rock-star life, staying away from drug and alcohol addiction. "We walked a little different line," Peart says. "It's not like we didn't go to all those places, we just didn't stay there. As Winston Churchill said, when you're going through hell, keep going."

100 We Were Born In A Flame

Sam Roberts

Universal, 2003

Hard Road | Where Have All The Good People Gone? | Brother Down | Higher Learning | Dead End | Taj Mahal | Every Part Of Me | The Canadian Dream | Rarefied | On The Run | Don't Walk Away Eileen | No Sleep | This Wreck Of A Life | Paranoia

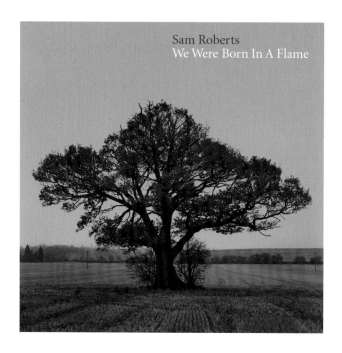

When Sam Roberts burst onto the scene in 2002, it seemed like a masterstroke of modern marketing. A little mini-album called *The Inhuman Condition* announced the arrival, with the big hit "Brother Down", followed by instant classics "Don't Walk Away Eileen" and "Where Have All The Good People Gone?". The following year, fans were lined up to make a bestseller out of the debut full-length album *We Were Born In A Flame*.

Who was behind this savvy lesson on how to break a band? No one, Sam Roberts laughs: "I wish there was that much strategy put into planning out my career, because that would mean I could duplicate it. Unfortunately, that's not the way it worked at all. I recorded that EP independently for the sum total of about fifty dollars, thanks to my friend Jordan Zadorozny. He had this great little studio in his parents' basement. Then one of our friends who was hanging out at the sessions sent that EP to a radio station, The Bear, in Ottawa. They started playing 'Brother Down' and playing it a lot. People out there responded, they kept calling and they said, 'I want to hear that again.' There was no meddling, influence, or heavy-handed prompting to propel the record forward."

Sam Roberts is a likeable, humble guy. He never forgets that Sam Roberts are a band: "I'm terrible at names. Our first band broke up, and it was widely assumed that it achieved no success because we never came up with a proper name. All the good ones were taken: Velvet Underground, The Rolling Stones." Roberts was worried a bad name could kill a band's career before they even got a chance to be heard: "Then I said, hey guys, why don't we call the band Sam Roberts?"

TOP 100 CANADIAN ALBUMS CHECK LIST

001 ❑ Harvest
002 ❑ Blue
003 ❑ After The Gold Rush
004 ❑ Music From Big Pink
005 ❑ Fully Completely
006 ❑ Jagged Little Pill
007 ❑ The Band
008 ❑ Funeral
009 ❑ Moving Pictures
010 ❑ American Woman
011 ❑ Songs Of Leonard Cohen
012 ❑ Reckless
013 ❑ Five Days In July
014 ❑ Twice Removed
015 ❑ Up To Here
016 ❑ Everybody Knows This Is Nowhere
017 ❑ 2112
018 ❑ Court And Spark
019 ❑ Whale Music
020 ❑ Acadie
021 ❑ Day For Night
022 ❑ Rust Never Sleeps
023 ❑ Gord's Gold
024 ❑ You Were Here
025 ❑ Fumbling Towards Ecstasy
026 ❑ Road Apples
027 ❑ Gordon
028 ❑ You Forgot It In People
029 ❑ I'm Your Man
030 ❑ Tonight's The Night
031 ❑ Decade
032 ❑ Miss America
033 ❑ Surfacing
034 ❑ One Chord To Another
035 ❑ Songs Of Love And Hate

036 ❑ Cyborgs Revisited
037 ❑ Ingénue
038 ❑ Melville
039 ❑ Love Tara
040 ❑ On The Beach
041 ❑ Not Fragile
042 ❑ The Best Of The Guess Who
043 ❑ Let It Die
044 ❑ The Last Waltz
045 ❑ Night Train
046 ❑ Down At The Khyber
047 ❑ Harvest Moon
048 ❑ Cuts Like A Knife
049 ❑ L'heptade
050 ❑ Teenage Head
051 ❑ High Class In Borrowed Shoes
052 ❑ Hejira
053 ❑ The Goldberg Variations
054 ❑ Fogarty's Cove
055 ❑ Wheatfield Soul
056 ❑ Si on avait besoin d'une cinquième saison
057 ❑ Dancing In The Dragon's Jaw
058 ❑ Frantic City
059 ❑ Hymns Of The 49th Parallel
060 ❑ Hot Shots
061 ❑ Robbie Robertson
062 ❑ The Trinity Sessions
063 ❑ Ron Sexsmith
064 ❑ Nothingface
065 ❑ Come On Over
066 ❑ Everything I Long For
067 ❑ Outskirts
068 ❑ Joyful Rebellion

069 ❑ Sit Down Young Stranger/If You Could Read My Mind
070 ❑ Love Junk
071 ❑ Jaune
072 ❑ Somewhere Outside
073 ❑ Electric Jewels
074 ❑ Sundown
075 ❑ Left And Leaving
076 ❑ Clumsy
077 ❑ Harmonium
078 ❑ Share The Land
079 ❑ Ian & Sylvia's Greatest Hits!
080 ❑ Steppenwolf
081 ❑ Ladies Of The Canyon
082 ❑ Bud The Spud and Other Favourites
083 ❑ Shine A Light
084 ❑ Shakespeare My Butt
085 ❑ Clayton Park
086 ❑ Smeared
087 ❑ Living Under June
088 ❑ The Hissing Of Summer Lawns
089 ❑ Bad Manors
090 ❑ Official Music
091 ❑ Lightfoot!
092 ❑ Mad Mad World
093 ❑ Rufus Wainwright
094 ❑ Face To The Gale
095 ❑ Hobo's Taunt
096 ❑ Cowboyography
097 ❑ Favourite Colours
098 ❑ The Way I Feel
099 ❑ A Farewell To Kings
100 ❑ We Were Born In A Flame

The Jurors

Mark Abraham, Cokemachineglow, Toronto
Julie Adam, CHFI, Toronto
Steve Adams, Hot 103, Winnipeg
Jim Agnew, Warner Music, Toronto
Del Aitchison, collector, Huntsville, ON
Scott Alan, 99.3 The Fox, Vancouver
André Alexis, CBC Radio, Toronto
Ralph Alfonso, Bongo Beat Records, Vancouver
Chris Allen, CKUA, Edmonton
Peter Anawati, CBC Radio, Fredericton
Jonathan Anderson, Musician, Langley, BC
Terry Arsenault, Sam the Record Man, Halifax, (R.I.P.)
Trinette Atkinson, KICX, Midland, ON
Beth Auerbach, Collector, Falls Church, VA
Ray Auffrey, Spin-It Records, Moncton, NB
Alan Auld, Rock 94, Thunder Bay, ON
Ryan Awram, 100.3 The Q, Victoria

Don Bailey, CKUW, Winnipeg
Ed Bain, 100.3 The Q, Victoria
Sophie Barbe, Universal Music, Montreal
Jill Barber, Musician, Halifax
Dulce Barbosa, dB Promotions, Toronto
Greg Barratt, Universal Music, Toronto
Brian Bartlett, Professor, St. Mary's University, Halifax

Mark Bartlett, Head Librarian, New York Society Library, New York
Jeff Bateman, Writer, Sooke, BC
Ken Beattie, Killbeat Music, Vancouver
Martin Beaucage, Radio Energie, Drummondville, QC
David Beckingham, Hey Ocean, Vancouver
Tom Bedell, Q104, Halifax
Jaymz Bee, Jazz FM, Toronto
Adrien Begrand, PopMatters.com, Saskatoon, SK
Jean-Francois Benoit, Rock Détente, Sherbrooke, QC
Geoff Berner, Musician, Vancouver
Don Berns, former Program Director, CFNY, Toronto
David Berry, *Vue Weekly*, Edmonton
Dave Bidini, Rheostatics
John Biggs, CKOC, Hamilton
Ted Bird, CHOM FM, Montreal
Bryan Birtles, *Vue Weekly*, Edmonton
Paul Bisson, CBC TV, Ottawa
Fiona Black, Capilano College, North Vancouver
Rebecca Black, CFCY, Charlottetown
Karen Bliss, Music Writer, Toronto
Dean Blundell, 102.1 The Edge, Toronto
Eric Bollman, CHEZ 106, Ottawa

Steve Bolton, Media Professor, Loyalist College, Belleville, ON
Jonas Bonnetta, Musician, Peterborough, ON
Paul Borchert, *Mote Magazine*, Edmonton
Genevieve Borne, TV & radio host, Montreal
Janesta Boudreau, Sonic Entertainment, Halifax
Catherine Bourderon, Espace Musique, Montreal
Andre Bourgeois, Instinct Artist Management, Halifax
Glen Bourgouis, Musician, Cheticamp, NS
Steven Bowers, Musician, Halifax
Rob Bowman, Music writer, Toronto
Sam Boyd, Boyd Management, Brampton, ON
Charles Breton, Archambault, Montreal
Christian Breton, Outside Music, Montreal
Robin Brock, Musician, Vancouver
David Brown, Sam The Record Man, Toronto (RIP)
Keith Brown, Aquarius Records, Montreal
Mark Browning, Ox
Jon Bruhm, *The Coast*, Halifax
Sean Buchanan, Music Buyer, Winnipeg
Melissa Buote, CKDU, Halifax
Michael Burke, Cordova Bay, Victoria

Ace Burpee, Hot 103, Winnipeg
Michelle Butterly, CHFI, Toronto
Brian Byrne, Musician, Steady Brook, NL

Doug Caldwell, EMI, Toronto
Harry Callaghan, CHUM, Toronto
Mike Campbell, Artist Manager, Halifax
Roddy Campbell, *Penguin Eggs Magazine*, Edmonton
Darrin Cappe, Tempus Fugit, Toronto
Keith Carman, Freelance Writer, Toronto
Cam Carpenter, XM Satellite Radio, Toronto
Lorraine Carpenter, *Montreal Mirror*, Montreal
Joel Carriere, Bedlam Music Management, Toronto
Cub Carson, 106.9 The Bear, Ottawa
Vicki Charal, Trent Radio, Peterborough, ON
Patrick Henry Charles, Q92, Montreal
Brady Chamberlain, Frank's Music, Moncton, NB
Matt Charlton, Sonic Entertainment, Halifax
Scott Chasty, Rock 94, Thunder Bay, ON
Dan Cherwoniak, Producer, Saturday Night Blues, Edmonton
Amelia Chester, Sam the Record Man, Halifax, (R.I.P.)
Marc Chouinard, Capitol Theatre, Moncton, NB
Jenna Chow, CBC Radio & TV, Vancouver
Stephen Claire, Music Writer, Halifax
Darin Clark, Z99, Red Deer, AB
Caroline Clarke, Five For Silver
John Clarke, Slideguy
Jennifer Claveau, Speak Music, Toronto
Scott Clements, Magic 104, Moncton
Eric Cohen, Global TV, Montreal
Holly Cole, Musician, Toronto
Tammy Cole, CHFI, Toronto
Dianne Collins, CBC Radio, Toronto
Steve Colwill, CHEZ 106, Ottawa
Shawn Conner, Writer, Vancouver
Andrew Connors, Yukon Film Society, Whitehorse, NWT
Jose Contreras, By Divine Right

Nathalie Cook, S.L. Feldman & Associates, Toronto
Stephen Cooke, *Halifax Herald*, Halifax
Tom Cooke, Standard Radio, Toronto
Judith Coombe, Starfish Entertainment, Toronto
Sylvain Cormier, *Le Devoir*, Montreal
Todd Cornish, Collector, Fredericton
Geneviève Côté, Frilance Musique, Montreal
Catherine Couture, CHYZ, Quebec City
Doug Cox, Musician-Producer, Vancouver Island
Steve Cranwell, Universal Music, Toronto
Murray Crawford, Trent Radio, Peterborough, ON
Jim Creeggan, Barenaked Ladies
Marc Crevier, Universal Music, Toronto
Caitlin Crockard, CBC Radio, Ottawa
Alan Cross, Program Director, 102.1 The Edge, Toronto
Krista Culp, FACTOR, Toronto
Andy Curran, Musician, Toronto
Jen Cymek, Listen Harder Music/Publicity, Toronto

Lori D'Agostino, S.L. Feldman & Associates, Toronto
Diane d'Almeida, CHUO, Ottawa
Frank Davies, Daffodil Records, Toronto
Shauna de Cartier, Six Shooter Records, Toronto
Gourmet Delice, Bonsound, Montreal
Phil Dellio, Writer, Toronto
Geneviève Dempsey, Rythme FM, Montreal, QC
Roch Denis, 105.7 Rythme FM, Montreal
Dominic Denny, Canadian Songwriters Hall Of Fame, Toronto
Mitch DePalma, Warner Music, Montreal
Phillipe Descheneau, Bonsound, Montreal
Robert Dickson, somerekords.blogspot.com, Winnipeg
Curtis Donat, Corus Radio, Guelph, ON
Denise Donlan, Music and Broadcasting Executive, Toronto
Matt Dotzenroth, Trent Radio, Peterborough, ON

Luke Doucet, Musician
JC Douglas, Newcap Radio, Halifax
Alan Doyle, Great Big Sea
Lloyd Doyle, Sandbar Music, Charlottetown
Lyle Drake, Avondale Music, St. John's
Brad Dryden, 106.9 The Bear, Ottawa
Darren Dumas, The Salads, Toronto
Andrea Dunn, CFPL, London, ON
James Duplacey, Author & Historian, Calgary
Sophie Durocher, Espace Musique, Montreal

Fred Eaglesmith, Musician, Port Dover, ON
Steven Ehrlick, Orange Record Label, Toronto
John Einarson, Writer, Winnipeg
Michael Elves, CJUM, Winnipeg
Russ Empey, CJAY 92, Calgary
Sarah Etherden, Planet 3 Communications, Toronto

Rob Farina, CHUM, Toronto
Bob Farrow, Wave 94.7, Hamilton, ON
Richie Favalaro, CHUM FM, Toronto
Bonnie Fedrau, SoStarStruck! Management, Toronto
Shaun Ferguson, Musician, Caraquet, NB
Cristina Fernandes, Listen Harder Music/Publicity, Toronto
Daniel Field, University of British Columbia, Vancouver
Bernie Finkelstein, True North Records, Toronto
Hank Fisher, Washboard Hank
Richard Flohil, Richard Flohil & Associates, Toronto
Roy Forbes, AKA Bim, Musician, North Vancouver
Gérard Forest, Radio-Canada, Moncton, NB
Yuani Fragata, CBC Radio 3, Montreal
Brian Francis, Film Producer, Elsipogtog First Nation
Wayne Francis, lightfoot.ca, Charlottetown
Ian Fraser, Deejay, Toronto
Dave Freeman, Club Bass, Toronto

Andy Frost, Q107, Toronto
Lily Frost, Musician, Toronto
Chris Fudge, Collector, Saint John, NB

Doug Gallant, *The Guardian*, Charlottetown
Lennie Gallant, Musician, Rustico, PEI
Rachelle Gallant, Warner Music, Toronto
Bill Garrett, Borealis Records, Toronto
Jodi Gaskell, CJXY, Hamilton, ON
Randy Gatley, Collector, Vancouver
Mark Gaudet, Eric's Trip
David Gawdunyk, Megatunes, Edmonton
Lana Gay, CFOX, Vancouver
Randy Gelling, CFUV, Victoria
Jian Ghomeshi, Host, *Q*, CBC Radio, Toronto
Rebecca Gilbert, Rock Détente
Ian Gilchrist, Rounder Records, Toronto
Ron Gillespie, Ocean 100, Charlottetown
Wendy Gilmour, Gilmour Productions, Halifax
Martine Girard, À L'infini Communications, Trois-Rivières, QC
Richard Godson, Alsek Music Festival, Haines Junction, YT
Gary "Pig" Gold, Musician, Producer, Fanzine Pioneer, etc., Toronto
Josh Goodbaum, DMD Entertainment, Toronto
Terry Gorman, Moncton, NB
Jeff Graham, KISS FM, Ottawa
Mike Greatorex, Sonic Entertainment, Halifax
Peter Greenall, Trent Radio, Peterborough, ON
Andy Grigg, *Real Blues Magazine*, Victoria
Fish Griwkowsky, Writer, Edmonton
RJ Guha, Kindling Music, Toronto

James Hale, Jazz Journalists Assoc., Ottawa
Doc Halen, CHEZ 106, Ottawa
John Hall, Outside Music, Toronto
Bob Hallett, Great Big Sea
Ivar Hamilton, Universal Music, Toronto
Chris Hand, Zeke's Gallery, Montreal
Jay Hannley, CJSR, Edmonton
Chad Hansen, 100.3 The Bear, Edmonton

Chris Harding, BX 93, London, ON
Mavis Harris, Maple Music, Toronto
Tom Harrison, *The Province*, Vancouver
Liz Harvey-Foulds, By The Bay Productions, Red Rock, ON
Bill Hayes, Q107, Toronto
Reg Hayes, HATband
Leitha Haysom, CKBW, Bridgewater, NS
Francis Hebert, *Voir*, Montreal
Paul Henderson, Sappy Records, Sackville, NB
Donna Henry, Mix 106, Owen Sound, ON
Marc Henwood, 103.5 The Pirate, Saint John, NB
Brian Hetherman, Curve Music, Toronto
Brad Hilgers, CJSD Thunder Bay, ON
Julie Hill, Toronto Blues Society, Toronto
Mike Hill, Artistic Director, Mariposa Folk Festival, Orillia, ON
Kevin Hilliard, Writer, Halifax
Noyan Hilmi, S.L. Feldman & Associates, Toronto
David Hilson, NXNE Publicity, Toronto
Steve Himmelfarb, Paquin Entertainment, Toronto
Rick Hodge, CHUM FM, Toronto
Natalie Holdway, Orange Record Label, Toronto
Lynn Horne, Lynn Horne Marketing, Halifax
Brian Howe, Pitchforkmedia.com, Chapel Hill, NC
Kevin Howes, Producer-Writer, Toronto
Boris Hrybinsky, *Winnipeg Free Press*, Winnipeg
Jennifer Hyland, ole
Sharon Hyland, CHOM FM, Montreal
Ted Hyland, Newcap Radio, Halifax
Ron Hynes, Musician, St. John's

Tish Iceton, CHFI, Toronto
J. Lawrence Ingles, Musician, Toronto
Dave Ingrouville, DEP Distribution, Montreal
John Iverson, CKUW, Winnipeg

Krysta J, K 94.5 FM, Moncton, NB
Gord James, CHUM FM, Toronto

Reid Jamieson, Musician, Victoria
Diane Jaroway, Rock 94, Thunder Bay, ON
Peter Jaycock, K-Lite FM, Hamilton, ON
Billy Jaye, FREQ 107, Winnipeg
Codi Jeffreys, CHUM Ottawa
Paul Jessop, Universal Music, Toronto
Brian Johnson, The String Guy, Toronto
Gordie Johnson, Musician
Jamie Johnston, 98.5 The Jewel, Ottawa
Jason Johnston, Revolution Audio, Mississauga, ON
Denis Jolicoeur, Collector, Winnipeg
Cathy Jones, *This Hour Has 22 Minutes*, CBC TV, Halifax
Danko Jones, Musician, Toronto
Danny Jones, Scratch Records, Vancouver
Marc Jordan, Musician, Toronto
Sass Jordan, Musician, Montreal
RC Joseph, Musician, Vancouver
Karl Josephs, CKSL, London, ON
Al Joynes, Q107, Toronto
Kim Juneja, Indoor Recess

Michael Kaeshammer, Musician, Toronto
Kevin Kelly, Magic 106.1, Guelph, ON
Kevin Kelly, *Newfoundland Herald*, St. John's
Sarah Kelly, FM 96, London, ON
John Kendle, *Uptown Magazine*, Winnipeg
Barry Kent, Music Consultant, Dartmouth, NS
Grant Kerr, *Telegraph-Journal*, Saint John, NB
Vish Khanna, CFRU, Guelph, ON
Moon-Hee Kim, Bonsound, Montreal
Cory Kimm, CHUM FM, Toronto
Danny Kingsbury, 105.3 KISS FM Ottawa
Al Kirkcaldy, *Peterborough Examiner*, Peterborough, ON
Olga Kirgidis, CFMU, Hamilton, ON
Heather Kitching, Publicist, Vancouver
Carsten Knox, Music Writer, Halifax
Bob Kohl, Jr., Cornwall, ON
Kevin Komoda, Bongo Beat, Montreal
Ron Korb, Musician, Toronto
Nancy Koubsky, Acoustic Edge Concert Series, Belleville ON

Mitch Lafon, Majic 100.3, Ottawa
Kirk Lahey, Universal Music, Halifax
Krista Lamb, Anya Wilson Publicity, Toronto
Wilfred Langmaid, *Daily Gleaner*, Fredericton
Justin Lanoue, CFUV, Victoria
Jennifer Larkin, Nettwerk Management, Vancouver
Grit Laskin, Borealis Records, Toronto
Judith Laskin, Canadian Folk Music Awards, Toronto
Janet LeBeau, Collector, Hamilton, ON
Larry LeBlanc, Music Writer, Toronto
Remi LeClair, The Comic Hunter, Moncton, NB
Alain Lefebvre, CFOU, Trois-Rivières, QC
Marie Lefebvre, Rock Détente, Sherbrooke, QC
Randy Lennox, President, Universal Music, Toronto
Bruce Leperre, CKDM, Dauphin, MB
Martin Levin, *Globe and Mail*, Toronto
Lenny Levine, Last Gang Records, Montreal
Mary Levitan, Macklin/Feldman Management, Vancouver
Eric Lewis, *Times & Transcript*, Moncton, NB
Gord Lewis, Teenage Head
Jason Lewis, Music Writer, Calgary
Pat Leyland, Taylor Mitsopulos Burshtein Entertainment Lawyers, Toronto
Donna Lidster, Universal Music, Toronto
Colin Linden, Blackie & The Rodeo Kings
Cam Lindsay, *Exclaim! Magazine*, Toronto
Paul Loewenberg, Northern Lights Festival, Sudbury, ON
Mark Logan, Busted Flat Records, Kitchener, ON
Andrew Lord, CHOM FM, Montreal
Noah Love, Chart Magazine, Toronto
Corb Lund, Musician, Edmonton, AB

Ellen Mably, Lyricist, Calgary
Ian MacArthur, CHFI, Toronto
Brad MacDonald, Musician, Toronto

Craig MacInnis, Music Writer, Toronto
Robin MacIntyre, Mac's Music, Goulais River, ON
Jason MacIsaac, The Heavy Blinkers
Rob MacIsaac, Musician, Saint-Lazare, QC
James MacLean, S.L. Feldman & Associates, Toronto
Scott MacLean, spiritofradio.ca, Toronto
Tara MacLean, Shaye
Michael MacLeod, The Acoustic Guitar, Calgary
David MacMillan, Eagle Rock Entertainment, Toronto
Wade MacNeil, Alexisonfire
Mike Magee, Union Label Group, Montreal
Cam Malcolm, Hamilton, ON
soraya mangal, Linus Entertainment, Toronto
Francois Marchand, *SEE Magazine*, Edmonton
Pete Marier, CHOM FM, Montreal
Jon Gonzo Mark, 97.7 HTZ-FM, St. Catharines, ON
Nancy Marley, Fusion 3, Montreal
Antonio Marsillo, In2Music, Hamilton, ON
Craig Martin, Creator, Classic Albums Live, Toronto
Amanda Martinez, Jazz FM, Toronto
Waye Mason, Halifax Pop Explosion Association, Halifax
Matt Mays, Musician, Dartmouth, NS
Sue McCallum, True North Records, Toronto
Angie McConnell, CFCW, Edmonton
Glenn McFarlane, Brampton Folk Festival, Brampton, ON
Arthur McGregor, Ottawa Folklore Centre, Ottawa
Ra McGuire, Trooper
Aubrey McInnis, CJSW, Calgary
Chris McKee, Agent, Oakville, ON
Stuart McLean, *Vinyl Café*, CBC Radio
Josh McLellan, K 94.5 FM, Moncton, NB
Trent McMartin, *Mote Magazine*, Edmonton
Carolynn McNally, CKUM, Moncton, NB

Holly McNarland, Musician, Winnipeg
Josh McNorton, S.L. Feldman & Associates, Vancouver
Terry McRae, Shantero Productions, Toronto
Luke Meat, CITR, Vancouver
Briand Melanson, Grand Dérangement
Ray Michaels, CKOC, Hamilton, ON
Victor Mijares, Warner Music, Toronto
Greg Mikolas, Webmaster, Canadian Classic Rock, Regina
Carolyn Mill, Manager, Victoria
Adam Miller, *Being There Magazine*, Toronto
Lisa Miller, Bullseye Records, Toronto
Suzy Miller, Manager, Port Dover, ON
Sarah Miller, CHUM FM, Toronto
Ruth Minnikin, Musician, Halifax
Don Mitchell, CFNY, Toronto
JD Moffat, Bayshore Broadcasting, Owen Sound, ON
James Monaco, Monaco Publicity, Toronto
Hilary Montbourquette, Newcap Radio, Moncton, NB
Sam Moon, Musician, Halifax
Nigel Moore, 100.7 Hank FM, Winnipeg
Jeffrey Morgan, Canadian Editor, *Creem Magazine*, Detroit, MI
Scott Morin, Universal Music, Toronto
Paul Morris, 97.7 HTZ-FM, St. Catharines, ON
Marc Morrissette, Kids These Days
Richard Moule, Writer, London, ON
Bruce Mowat, Writer-Manager, Hamilton
Christine Mulkins, Boost PR, Toronto
Jenny Mulkins, Collector, Toronto
Terry David Mulligan, City-TV, Vancouver
Eden Munro, *Vue Weekly*, Edmonton
Bill Munson, Collector, Toronto
Spencer Mussellam, DEP Entertainment, Toronto

Troy Neilson, Brockway Entertainment, Brockway, NB
Allen Nolan, Collector, Ottawa
Sarah Norris, Universal Music, Toronto
Craig Northey, Musician, Toronto

Matt O'Blenis, Spin-It Records, Moncton, NB

Bryndis Ogmundson, Meow Records, Prince George, BC

Kathleen O'Grady, QUOI Media Group, Montreal

Mary Christa O'Keefe, Writer, Edmonton

Ronan O'Leary, Collector, Markham, ON

Mike O'Neill, Musician, Halifax

Terry O'Reilly, Pirate Radio, Toronto

Heather Ostertag, President & CEO, FACTOR, Toronto

Blair Packham, Musician, Toronto

Tracey Page, Dog My Cat Records, Vancouver

Brant Palko, Amigos

Carla Palmer, Maple Music, Toronto

Ken Palmer, Collector, London, ON

Sean Palmerston, Sonic Unyon Records, Hamilton, ON

Laurel Paluck, Trent Radio, Peterborough, ON

Sofi Papamarko, *Exclaim! Magazine*, Toronto

Julien Paquin, Paquin Entertainment

Patrick Parise, Spin-It Records, Moncton, NB

Kelly Parker, 99.9 BOB-FM, Winnipeg

Mike Parker, Musician, Dieppe, NB

Ryan Parker, Q107, Toronto

Keith Parry, Owner, Scratch Recordings, Vancouver

Nate Patrin, Writer, St. Paul, MN

Helen Patriquin, Collector, Halifax

Dominic Patten, *Vancouver Sun*, Vancouver

Andrew Patton, Universal Music, Toronto

Amber Payie, CHUM, Toronto

Ryan Peake, Nickelback

Ben Pearlman, Halifax Pop Explosion Association, Halifax

Arthur Pearson, Arbor Records, Winnipeg

Neil Peart, Rush

David Perri, *BW&BK Magazine*, Montreal

Marc Perry, EMI, Halifax

Holger Petersen, Stony Plain Records, Edmonton

George Pettit, Alexisonfire

Darrin Pfeiffer, 102.1 The Edge, Toronto

Ford Pier, Musician, Vancouver

Carole Pigeon, Manager, Verchères, Quebec

Craig Pinhey, Pop Culture Writer, Rothesay, NB

Paul Pittman, Young & Sexy

Sandra Plagakis, 105.3 KISS FM, Ottawa

John Poirier, Warner Music, Halifax

Silas Polkinghome, Writer, Saskatoon, SK

Steve Pratt, CBC Radio 3, Vancouver

Blake Prendergast, Collector, PEI

Blair Purda, Endearing Records, Vancouver

Jake Quinlan, Trent Radio, Peterborough, ON

Al Rankin, Live Wire Music Series, Kingston, ON

Dave Rave, Musician-Producer, Hamilton, ON

Mark Raymond, Sonic Unyon Records, Hamilton, ON

Allan Reid, Universal Music, Toronto

Pat Reid, Warner Music, Toronto

Randy Renaud, CHOM FM, Montreal

Jim Reyno, *Halifax Daily News*, Halifax

Mike Reynolds, Writer-Broadcaster, Peterborough, ON

Mark Rheaume, CBC Radio, Toronto

David Adams Richards, Writer, Toronto & Miramichi, NB

Mike Richards, CKBW, Bridgewater, NS

Peter Richards, *The Buzz*, Charlottetown

Norman Richmond, CKLN, Toronto

Clemence Risler, *Voir*, Montreal

Maxime Roberge, Rock Détente, 96.9, Saguenay, QC

Mark Roberts, East Coast Music Show, Fredericton

Ed Robertson, Barenaked Ladies

Charles Robicheau, Grand Dérangement

Andrew Robinson, CHSR, Fredericton

Red Robinson, Deejay, Vancouver

Andrew Rose, Fusion 3

Kim Rossi, CHOM FM, Montreal

Peter Rowan, Kindling Music, Toronto

John Rutherford, Epcor Centre, Calgary

Kristen Rutherford, CFCR, Saskatoon

Jeremy Sachedina, Orange Record Label, Toronto

Catherine St. Germain, Musician, Vancouver

Julie St-Pierre, RadioÉnergie, Montreal

Wendy Salsman, Goddess

Jane Samis, S.L. Feldman & Associates, Vancouver

Eric Samuels, Z95.3 CISL, Vancouver

Steven Sandor, 24 Hours, Toronto

Guillaume Savard, Energie 98.7, Rimouski, QC

Dave Schneider, KICX, Waterloo, ON

Tonia Schroepfer, Collector, Calgary

Aaron Schubert, Paquin Entertainment, Toronto

Franz Schuller, Grimskunk

Ingrid Schumacher, CHUM FM, Toronto

Jody Scotchmer, Canadian Songwriters Hall Of Fame, Toronto

Ian Scott, Writer, Calgary

Jay Semko, Northern Pikes

Rocky Serkowney, CIUT, Toronto

Tony Servello, Fontana North, Toronto

Ron Sexsmith, Musician, Toronto

Kendall Shields, Editor, theratio.org, Halifax

Peter Sisk, The Good Brothers

Colin Skrapek, Sir, Handsome Records, Saskatoon

Amy Sky, Musician, Toronto

Lorie Slater, Universal Music, Toronto

Sarah Slean, Musician, Toronto

Tara Slone, Musician, Toronto

Adam Smith, CHMA, Sackville, NB

Graham Smith, 827 Dorchester, Winnipeg

Nat Smith, Collector, Winnipeg

Devon Soltendieck, MuchMusic, Toronto

Elizabeth Spear, ole, Toronto

Sandra Sperounes, Music Writer, *Edmonton Journal*, Edmonton

Brent Staeben, Harvest Jazz & Blues Festival, Fredericton

Eric Stafford, 106.9 The Bear, Ottawa

Jill Staveley, Trent Radio, Peterborough, ON

John Steele, VOCM, St. John's

Mark Steinmetz, Director of Radio Music, CBC Radio, Toronto

Tyler Stewart, Barenaked Ladies

Kim Stockwood, Musician, Bona Vista, NL

Stu Strang, Collector, Halifax

Michael Stroh, District Six Music, Toronto

Stafford Swain, Collector, Winnipeg

Paul Symes, The Blacksheep Inn, Wakefield, QC

Troy Tait, C103, Moncton, NB

Joe Tangari, Pitchforkmedia.com, Chapel Hill, NC

Tony Tarleton, EMI, Toronto

Gord Taylor, 106.9 The Bear, Ottawa

Jowi Taylor, Host, *Global Village*, CBC Radio, Toronto

Julian Taylor, Staggered Crossing

Ric Taylor, *View Magazine*, Hamilton, ON

Chuck Teed, Writer, Halifax

William "Skinny" Tenn, Artist Manager, Toronto

James Tennant, CFMU, Hamilton, ON

Kath Thompson, 106.9 The Bear, Ottawa

Steve Thompson, 99.9 BOB-FM, Winnipeg

Holly Thorne, Q 92, Sudbury, ON

Tara Thorne, *The Coast*, Halifax

John Threlfall, *Monday Magazine*, Victoria, BC

Tom Thwaits, Trent Radio, Peterborough, ON

Martin Tielli, Rheostatics

Elly Tose, Elster Productions, Thunder Bay, ON

Georges Tremblay, DEP Distribution, Montreal

Brad Trew, Cyclone Records, Aurora, ON

Eric Trudel, Writer, Montreal

Meg Tucker, CHUM FM, Toronto

Scott Tucker, FM 96, London, ON

Sarah Turner, DMD Entertainment, Toronto

Jenny Usher, 105.3 KISS FM, Ottawa

Mathieu Valiquette, Archambault, Montreal

Jim Vallance, Songwriter, Vancouver

Vickie Van Dyke, WAVE 94.7 Hamilton, ON

Caitlin Veitch, Six Shooter Records, Toronto

Jaimie Vernon, President, Bullseye Records, Toronto

Daniel Victor, Neverending White Lights

Jeff Vidler, Solutions Research Group, Toronto

LoriAnn Villani, CJXY, Hamilton, ON

Gui Violette, NBDot, Fredericton

Kim Wagner, Kool FM, Kitchener, ON

Vit Wagner, *Toronto Star*, Toronto

Carey Walker, 101.5 The Wolf, Peterborough, ON

Park Warden, 100.3 The Bear, Edmonton

Betty Watson, Collector, Ottawa

Jeff Weaver, CBC Radio, Victoria

Shannon Webb-Campbell, Writer, Halifax

Cory Weeds, Cellar Jazz Club, Vancouver

Darryl Weeks, Stagefreight Publicity, Barrie, ON

Frank Weipert, Teamworks Management, Vancouver

Matt Wells, MuchMoreMusic, Toronto

Adam West, Hot 103, Winnipeg

Jim West, Owner, Fusion 3, Montreal

John Westhaver, Birdman Sound, Ottawa

Dave Wheeler, Power 97, Winnipeg

Tim White, Collector, Montreal

Lindsay Whitfield, *Soul Shine Magazine*, Toronto

Allan Wigney, *Ottawa Sun*, Ottawa

John Wiles, CKBW, Bridgewater, NS

Nathan Wiley, Musician, Summerside, PEI

Andy Wilson, CBC TV, Fredericton

Anya Wilson, Anya Wilson Publicity, Toronto

Tom Wilson, Blackie & The Rodeo Kings

Chris Wodskou, CBC Radio, Toronto

Jeff Woods, 107, Toronto

Ed Woodsworth, Producer-Musician, Albert Bridge, NS

David Worthington, Labwork Music, Toronto

Melissa Wright, K-Rock, Edmonton

Michael Wrycraft, A Man Called Wrycraft

Jordy Yack, CFBU, St. Catherines, ON

Ted Yates, CKOC, Hamilton, ON

Tim Yerxa, The Playhouse, Fredericton

Ritchie Yorke, Writer, Australia

Anna Zee, Q104, Halifax

Acknowledgements

My name's on the cover, but the key to this book is the work of the jury — the 580 people who searched their collections and their souls, and submitted their personal Top Ten lists. I thank them deeply for their time and for making the tough choices.

I have had the honour to work with many fine people in the music industry over the years. Devoted fans and ardent supporters of Canadian music, many have become personal friends and were central not only to this book but also to my ongoing work as a reviewer of music and interviewer of artists. Among them: Wendy Salsman, John Poirier, Pat Reid, Kirk Lahey, Nicole Asaff, Marc Perry, Daniel Robichaud, Nancy Marley, Sue McCallum, Kerry Goulding, Kim Juneja, Joanne Setterington, Eric Alper, Ken Beattie, Anya Wilson, Krista Lamb, Stephanie Hardman, Darryl Weeks, Sean Palmerston, Theresa Micallef, Heather Kitching, Lynn Horne, and Keith Maurik.

Many others helped to arrange interviews or acquire rights and permissions for artwork and photographs: Holger Petersen, John Einerson, J.C. Douglas, Barry Harvey, Sarah Norris, Ed Sanders, Maud Hudson, Caitlin Vetch, Suzanne Little, Lorne Saifer, Mike Campbell, Andy Curran, Jaime Vernon, Kathryn Blythe, James Maclean, Holly Cybulski, Jude Coombe, Margaret Marissen, Heather Uhi, Gary "Pig" Gold, Christine Peters, William Tenn, Shauna de Cartier, Catherine Jones, Keith Brown, Suzy Miller, Dave Spencer, Andy Grigg, Janesta Boudreau, Mike Nelson, Marie-Claire Sauvé, Bruce Mowat, Wendy Phillips, Mike Greatorex, and Louis Thomas.

The people at Goose Lane Editions were completely enthusiastic and incredibly talented throughout. Thanks to Susanne Alexander and Julie Scriver, who wanted one music book but got another — your confidence from the start is this project's greatest reward. Editor Barry Norris gently took a sloppy television writer's script and turned it into a manuscript. Kent Fackenthall insisted on high quality — the visual excellence of the book is his. Angela Williams somehow kept her patience and humour throughout the countless hours of the confusing chase for artwork and permissions. Great thanks to Kathleen Doucette, Viola Spencer, Lisa Alward, and Colleen Kitts, whose professionalism made this a wonderful experience for a first-time author.

I owe a lifetime of thanks to the many friends who have shared with me their love of music, particularly Todd Cornish, J.J. Duplacey, Mark Bartlett, Terry Gorman, and Rob Gilmore. I dedicate the book itself to my family, who encouraged and supported me at the price of a sometimes tired and cranky father and husband: my sons Evan, Aidan, and Ben, and my incredible wife, Colleen — fool if you think it's over.

And now to all of those who granted permission to us to reproduce photos and album covers, our deepest gratitude. Here they are:

Top 100: Album Covers
1. Under license from Reprise Records. 2. Under license from Reprise Records. 3. Under license from Reprise Records. 4. Courtesy of EMI Music Canada. 5. Courtesy of Universal Music Canada Inc. 6. Courtesy of Maverick Recording Company. 7. Courtesy of EMI Music Canada. 8. Album art c/o Merge Records. Artist: Tracy

Maurice. 9. Copyright © 1981 Anthem / All Rights Reserved. Used by permission. 10. Courtesy of SonyBMG Music Entertainment. 11. Courtesy of Sony BMG Music (Canada) Inc. 12. Courtesy of A&M Records. 13. Courtesy of Warner Music Canada. 14. Courtesy of Michael Nelson at Two Minutes for Music. 15. Courtesy of Universal Music Canada Inc. 16. Under license from Reprise Records. 17. Copyright © 1976 Anthem / All Rights Reserved. Used by permission. 18. Under license from Asylum Records. 19. Original art and design by Martin Tielli. 20. Album photo: Bob Lanois. 21. Courtesy of Universal Music Canada Inc.. 22. Under license from Reprise Records. 23. Under license from Reprise Records. 24. Courtesy of Cold Snap Records. 25. Used by permission of Nettwerk Productions. 26. Courtesy of Universal Music Canada Inc. 27. Under license from Reprise Records. 28. Copyright © 2002 Arts & Crafts Productions Inc. Courtesy of Arts & Crafts and EMI Music Canada. 29. Courtesy of Sony BMG Music (Canada) Inc. 30. Under license from Reprise Records. 31. Under license from Reprise Records. 32. Courtesy of Mary Margaret O'Hara. 33. Used by permission of Nettwerk Productions. 34. Courtesy of Michael Nelson at Two Minutes for Music. 35. Courtesy of Sony BMG Music (Canada) Inc. 36. Sonic Unyon Records. Photo: Rick Bissell. Restoration: Janice Peshke. 37. Under license from Sire Records. 38. Original art and design by Martin Tielli. 39. Cover photo by Rick White. 40. Under license from Reprise Records. 41. Courtesy of Mercury Records. 42. Courtesy of Sony BMG Music (Canada) Inc. 43. Copyright © 2004 Polydor under exclusive license to Arts & Crafts Productions Inc. Courtesy of Arts & Crafts and EMI Music Canada. 44. Under license from Warner Bros. Records. Inc. 45. Courtesy of The Verve Music Group. 46. Courtesy of Joel Plaskett at Songs for the Gang. 47. Under license from Reprise Records. 48. Courtesy of A&M Records. 49. Courtesy of Sony BMG Music (Canada) Inc. 50. Courtesy of Sonic Unyon Records. 51. Copyright © 1977 Anthem / All Rights Reserved. Used by permission. 52. Under license from Asylum Records. 53. Courtesy of Sony BMG Music (Canada) Inc. 54. Stan Rogers copyright © 1977. Used by permission. 55. Courtesy of SonyBMG Music Entertainment. 56. Courtesy of Universal Music Canada Inc. & PolyGram Records. 57. Courtesy of True North Records. 58. Courtesy of Unidisc Music Inc. 59. Under license from Nonesuch Records. 60. Courtesy of Universal Music Canada Inc. 61. Courtesy of Geffen Records. 62. Courtesy of Sony BMG Music (Canada) Inc. 63. Courtesy of Interscope Records. 64. 1989 MCA ART©AWAY. 65. Courtesy of Mercury Records. 66. Courtesy of Sonic Unyon Records. 67. Courtesy of Warner Music Canada. 68. Courtesy of EMI Music Canada. 69. Under license from Reprise Records. 70. Courtesy of Chrysalis Records and EMI Music Canada. 71. Avec l'aimable autorisation de GSI Musique. 72. Courtesy of Unidisc Music Inc. 73. Courtesy of Aquarius Records and EMI Music Canada. 74. Under license from Reprise Records. 75. Courtesy of G7 Welcoming Committee Records. 76. Courtesy of Sony BMG Music (Canada) Inc. 77. Courtesy of Universal Music Canada Inc. & PolyGram Records. 78. Courtesy of SonyBMG Music Entertainment. 79. Courtesy of Vanguard Records, A Welk Music Group Company. 80. Courtesy of Geffen Records & ABC Dunhill Records. 81. Under license from Reprise Records. 82. Courtesy of EMI Music Canada. 83. Artwork by Dallas James Wehrle. 84. Courtesy of Universal Music Canada Inc. & Page Publications. 85. Courtesy of Sonic Unyon Records. 86. Courtesy of Michael Nelson at Two Minutes for Music. 87. Courtesy of A&M Records. 88. Under license from Asylum Records. 89. Courtesy of Unidisc Music Ltd. 90. Courtesy of Unidisc Music Inc. 91. Courtesy of EMI Music Canada. 92. Courtesy of EMI Music Canada. 93. Courtesy of Geffen Records & Dream Works Records. 94. Courtesy of EMI Music Canada. 95. Photo: Kim Yuhasz. 96. Courtesy of Stony Plain Records. 97. Courtesy of The Sadies. 98. Courtesy of EMI Music Canada. 99. Copyright © 1977 Anthem / All Rights Reserved. Used by permission. 100. Courtesy of Universal Music Canada Inc.

Top 100: Artist Photos
1. Courtesy of Warner Music Canada. Courtesy of Warner Music Canada. 2. Courtesy of Warner Music Canada. 3. Courtesy of Warner Music Canada. Courtesy of Warner Music Canada. 5. Courtesy of Universal Music Canada Inc. 6. Copyright © Clay Butler. www.picslive.com. 7. Photo by David Gans. www.dgans.com. 8. Courtesy of Merge Records. 9. Courtesy of Anthem Entertainment. All Rights Reserved. 10. Guess Who publicity photo. 11. Photo: Lorca Cohen. 13. Blue Rodeo (1993). 14. Studio Photo from Smeared Booklet: Alison Dyer. 19. Photo: Regina Garcia. 20. Photo: Jennifer Tipoulow. 21. Courtesy of Universal Music Canada Inc. 22. Courtesy of Warner Music Canada. 23. Photo: Denise Grant. Used by permission. 27. Photo: Chris Woods. Courtesy of Nettwerk Management / Desperation Records. 28. Courtesy of Arts & Crafts Productions. 34. Studio photo from *One Chord To Another* booklet: Catherine Stockhausen. 35. Photo: Lorca Cohen. 36. Courtesy of Sonic Unyon Records. 39. Courtesy of Sub Pop Records. 1995 band photo by Tara White. 41. Courtesy of Universal Music Canada Inc. 43. Courtesy of Arts & Crafts Productions. 44. Photo by David Gans. www.dgans.com. 45. Photo: Tom Marcello. 46. Photo: Ingram Barss. 50. Photo: Arthur (Art) Usherson. www.teenagehead.ca. 51. Courtesy of Anthem Entertainment. All Rights Reserved. 50. Photo: Arthur (Art) Usherson. www.teenagehead.ca. 81. Courtesy of Warner Music Canada. 86. Studio Photo from *Smeared* booklet: Alison Dyer. 91. Photo: Denise Grant. Used by permission.

Top Ten Lists

Page 23: Author photo: Scott Gardner. www.teenagehead.ca. Album covers (L to R): *Crush*: Courtesy of A&M Records. *Talk's Cheap*: Original Artwork by Lyndon Andrews. Copyright © 1979 Ready Records. All Rights Reserved. Used by permission. *Picture of Health*: Courtesy of Universal Music Canada Inc. Page 27: Author photo: Mark Maryanovich. Performer photos (L to R): Jeff Healey: Courtesy of Jeff Healey. Colin James: Andrew MacNaughton. Brian Smith: Claire Rance, crance@telus.net (604) 532-7885. Liona Boyd: Deborah de Turbeville. Alex Lifeson: Courtesy of Anthem Entertainment. All Rights Reserved. Page 35: Author photo: Courtesy of Ra McGuire. Performer photos (L to R): Kim Mitchell: Andrew MacNaughton. Bachman-Turner Overdrive: Courtesy of Universal Music Canada Inc. The Tragically Hip: Courtesy of Universal Music Canada Inc. Page 43: Author photo: Courtesy of Anthem Entertainment. All Rights Reserved. Album covers (L to R): *2112*: Copyright © 1976 Anthem / All Rights Reserved. Used by permission. *Who Cares?* Copyright © 1978 Greg Godovitz. Courtesy of Bullseye. *Hello Master*: Courtesy of Priestess & Indica Records. Illustration by Arik Roper. Page 51: Author photo: Russ Harrington. Album cover: *Home in Halifax*: Stan Rogers © 1993. Used by permission. Pages 78-79: Author photo: Courtesy of True North Records. Album covers (L to R): *Music from Big Pink*: Courtesy of EMI Music Canada. *After the Gold Rush*: Under license from Reprise Records. *Nothing But a Burning Light*: Courtesy of True North Records. *Acadie*: Album photo: Bob Lanois. *Hobo's Taunt*: Photograph by Kim Yuhasz. *Five Days in July*: Courtesy of Warner Music Canada. (Page 106) Album covers (Top row: L to R): *36c*: Courtesy of ♡ (originally released 1994). *More of Our Stupid Noise*: Courtesy of Nettwerk Productions. *Does This Look Infected*: Courtesy of Aquarius Records. (Bottom row: L to R): *He Poos Clouds*: Courtesy of Co-operative Blocks Recording Club. *Take Penicillin Now*: Packaging designed by Brent Corey, inspired by domestic terrorism. *Clown Heaven and Hell*: Illustration by Mel Melymick. Graphic design by Barry Tremaine. Art direction by John Jordan. Page 107: Author photo: Courtesy of Terry O'Reilly, Host, "O'Reilly and the Age of Persuasion," CBC Radio One. Album covers (L to R): *Cowboyography*: Courtesy of Stony Plain Records. *Absolute Torch and Twang*: Under license from Sire Records. *Music from Big Pink*: Courtesy of EMI Music Canada. Page 137: Author photo: Kees Snyders. Album covers (L to R): *Urban Blues Renewell*: Courtesy of Stony Plain Records. *Rockin' the Boogie*: Courtesy of Stony Plain Records. Page 145: Author photo: Kevin Hogarth. Album covers (L to R): *A Prairie Legend*: Layout: Sylke Lohmeyer & Gerd Weiser. Bear Family Records, www.bear-family.de. *God Shuffled His Feet*: Courtesy of Sony BMG Music (Canada) Inc. Page 153: Author photo: Courtesy of Anthem Entertainment. All Rights Reserved. Performer photos (L to R): Martin Deller:

Joe del Tufo, Studio M Live. Johnny Fay: Courtesy of Universal Music Canada. Graham Lear: Courtesy of Graham Lear. Page 161: Author photo: Copyright © Michel Cloutier.com. Album covers (L to R): *Écoute pas ca*: Avec l'aimable autorisation de GSI Musique. *Tu m'aimes-tu?* Copyright © Productions Foukinic. Illustration: Yves Paquin. Graphisme: Marie Chicoime. *L'heptade*: Courtesy of Sony BMG Music (Canada) Inc. *L'amour est sans pitié*: Copyright © 1990 Audiogram. *Rêver Mieux*: Copyright © 2001 Les Disques Audiogramme Inc. *La Forêt des mal-aimés*: Copyright © 2006 Les Disques Audiogramme Inc.. Page 169: Author photo: Courtesy of music historian and author John Einarson. Album covers (L to R): *Wheatfield Soul*: Courtesy of SonyBMG Music Entertainment. *After the Gold Rush*: Courtesy of Reprise Records. *Reconstruction Site*: Cover art by Marcel Dzama. Courtesy of Epitaph and the Weakerthans. *God Shuffled His Feet*: Courtesy of Sony BMG Music (Canada) Inc. *The Visit*: Copyright © 1992 Quinlan Road Limited www.quinlanroad.com. *40 Days*: Courtesy of Jericho Beach Music. www.wailinjennys.com. www.jerichobeach.com. *Gotta Move*: Thanks to Arun Chaturvedi for providing album jacket. Page 177: Author photo: Courtesy of Margaret Malandruccolo. Album covers (L to R): *From the Archives*: Courtesy of Dave MacIsaac. Recorded @ Solar Audio 1999. *Howie MacDonald and His Cape Breton Fiddle*: Courtesy of Howie MacDonald. Produced by Howie MacDonald, John Morris Rankin, & Dave MacIsaac. Recorded at Solar Audio, Halifax, November 1984. *Hi How Are You Today?* Courtesy of Ashley MacIsaac and Linus Entertainment. Page 185: Author photo: Courtesy of Mike Smith (Bubbles). Album covers (L to R): *A Farewell to Kings*: Copyright © 1977 Anthem / All Rights Reserved. Used by permission. *Road Apples*: Courtesy of Universal Music Canada Inc. *Harvest*: Courtesy of Reprise Records. *Bud the Spud and Other Favourites*: Courtesy of EMI Music Canada. *If You Can Believe Your Eyes And Ears*: Courtesy of Geffen Records & Dunhill Records. *What Happens Now?* Courtesy of 2000 Perimeter Records. Cover illustrations: Mike O'Neill. Design: Chris Mueller. Available at zunior.com. *American Woman*: Courtesy of SonyBMG Music Entertainment. Page 191: Author photo: Andrew MacNaughton. Album covers (L to R): *All the Best Folk Music of St. John's, Newfoundland*: Courtesy of Pigeon Inlet Productions. *Figgy Duff*: Copyright © Amber Music.

Index